Offshoring and the Internationalization of Employment

A challenge for a fair globalization?

Peter Auer, Geneviève Besse
and Dominique Méda (eds.)

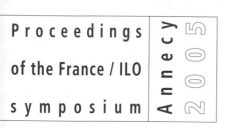

Proceedings of the France / ILO symposium

Annecy 2005

International Labour Organization
International Institute for Labour Studies

Ministère de l'emploi, de la cohésion sociale
et du logement

Published by the International Institute for Labour Studies

The *International Institute for Labour Studies* (IILS) was established in 1960 as an autonomous facility of the International Labour Organization (ILO) to further policy research, public debate and the sharing of knowledge on emerging labour and social issues of concern to the ILO and its constituents — labour, business and government.

ISBN (Print) 92-9014-783-0
ISBN (Web PDF) 92-9014-784-9

First published 2006

Copies can be ordered from: ILO Publications, International Labour Office, CH-1211 Geneva 22, Switzerland. For on-line orders, see www.ilo.org/publns

Photocomposed in Switzerland
Printed in France

BRI
SAD

TABLE OF CONTENTS

PREFACE

The World Commission on the Social Dimension of Globalization called for decent work to become a global goal, and for employment objectives to be embedded much more firmly in international economic policies. Because of the growing interdependence of national economies, employment policies and goals increasingly need to be seen in an international context. This theme of the internationalization of employment was addressed in a conference, bringing together French and international researchers and organized jointly by the International Institute for Labour Studies, the Employment Sector of the ILO and the French Ministry of Labour, Employment and Social Cohesion in Annecy, France, on 11-12 April 2005. The conference was the third in a series of France-ILO debates on important current policy issues, which began in 2001. The conference had also a political follow-up, in that its theme and conclusions served as background for an informal meeting of the European Labour and Social Affairs Ministers during the ILO' s International Labour Conference in June 2005.

The papers presented and the opinions expressed at the conference, do not necessarily reflect the views of the ILO or the French Government, but rather those of the researchers and analysts participating in the meeting in their individual capacity. While the conference mainly discussed the impact of globalization on the labour markets of developed countries, a global perspective was pursued and participants from the new EU member countries and from developing countries also participated in the conference and commented on the issues raised.

The conference debated three related issues. A first objective was to shed light on some of the facts of the employment impacts of trade and investments abroad, including such highly controversial themes as off-shoring of the production of goods and services. The growing interlinkages in global production systems in both industry and increasingly services make a quantitative assessment in terms of winners and losers difficult. Delocalization of production still concerns only a minor portion of lay-offs and on the global level one might anticipate at worst a zero sum game between the gains and losses in employment. Among the causes of employment problems, globalization is only one of many factors. However, for popular perception what counts is not the global outcome over the long term, but the short-term experience of downsizing, plant closings, and pressures on working conditions and wages, which have serious consequences for many workers and their families. Decision-makers have to respond to the short and medium term national and local problems, even if they are created globally.

A second objective was to debate the options for coping with the short term and medium term problems related to the internationalization of employment. Here a historical perspective showed that from the beginning trade liberalization was -in the developed world- accompanied by flanking socio-economic measures. There now seems to be a trend towards the development of a process and a legal frame, and the slow emergence of an adjustment management system both on the national as well as on the international (regional) level, as can be seen by the recent initiative of the European Union to introduce a growth adjustment fund. This adjustment system comes into play when redundancies occur but it requires policies that go far beyond it, because an answer to the increased uncertainty and volatility of labour markets under globalization requires that women and men's the management of careers be considered over the lifecycle. These developments indicate a lifelong need for adjustment measures and protected transitions at critical moments in the life cycle. Being made redundant is one of these critical moments.

A third objective was to discuss the importance of international instruments that could help to introduce a level playing field in trade and promote development. ILO labour standards are one of these instruments, and different ways of promoting them were discussed, such as international framework agreements between trade unions and multinationals. It was found that labour standards are particularly important in developing countries, as increasing south-south competition might lead – in the absence of a social floor – to a downgrading of working conditions. However, labour standards do not merely provide a level playing field; they are also key elements in growth and development independent from trade considerations. As indicated in the report of the World Commission on the Social Dimension of Globalization the conference reiterated the need for more policy coherence in the multilateral system. A common view on how to manage the short term effects of globalization and their local impact would help those negatively affected and install the conditions for long-term success.

The essence of the conclusions is the urgent need to cope with the short and medium term effects of globalization and the internationalization of employment through adequate labour market policies, including permanent institutions to manage adjustment and support job transitions with security at the local, national and international levels. Notwithstanding the importance to find a direct political response to the consequences of off-shoring and trade displacement, these institutions should be regarded as public goods and be open to all those displaced, whether by globalization or other causes. In the future, worker's adaptation to structural change should be seen as a right, to which corresponds the duty for equipping oneself with the elements of employability required to survive increased turbulence in the labour market. Such policies are important for decent work as a dynamic concept, as decency requires that protection and security go beyond a single job and extends to the transitions between jobs.

However, such supply-oriented policies must be backed by employment-supporting macro-economic and industrial policies.

Gerry Rodgers
Director, International Institute of Labour Studies
ILO

Annie Fouquet
Inspectrice Générale
Director of DARES* during the symposium.

The articles of this book, with the exception of the annexes have already been published in a French version at the end of last year. See: Auer, P., Besse, G., Meda, D. Delocalisations, normes du travail et politique d'emploi. Editions La Découverte, Paris, 2005.

---

* Direction of the animation of research, studies and statistics of the French Ministry of employment, social cohesion and housing.

OFFSHORING AND THE INTERNATIONALIZATION OF EMPLOYMENT

A CHALLENGE FOR A FAIR GLOBALIZATION?

PETER AUER, GENEVIÈVE BESSE, DOMINIQUE MÉDA*

1. INTRODUCTION

Does globalization threaten employment? When asked this question in a public opinion poll in May 2005, a representative sample of French people answered 'yes' in a very large majority. A total of 73 per cent of those questioned stated that they perceived globalization as a threat to jobs in France and 75 per cent of those polled said that they feared the consequences of globalization.[1] During the referendum campaign on the European constitution, the issue of offshoring also played an important part in the debate. It seems that almost everywhere in the industrialized countries, globalization is seen as a threat to employment and not as an opportunity.

And yet, according to recent studies in France as elsewhere in Europe, offshoring – which is often considered to be the most obvious consequence of globalization – represents only a very small percentage of job losses. A recent study revealed that in France, throughout the period 1995-2001, "offshoring-outsourcing concerns at most an estimated 2,4 per cent of the industrial workforce",[2] i.e. some 13,500 jobs a year, which seems very little.

How then to explain the extraordinary difference between, on the one hand, the groundswell of disquiet caused by globalization and offshoring and, on the other, the relative insignificance of the figures? Are we faced by an under-estimate of the scope of the phenomenon as a result of inadequate measurement, and if so are we not in the initial phase of a phenomenon that will develop and even begin to affect service industries? Or, on the contrary, are we in the presence of a limited phenomenon, spectacularly blown out of proportion by the media because of the dramatic consequences for those affected by it? In order to

---

* The opinions expressed in this paper are not necessarily those of DARES or the ILO.

[1] Data from a public opinion poll on the French and globalization carried out by Sofres in February 2005.

[2] P. Aubert, P. Sillard (2005): *Délocalisations et réductions d'effectifs dans l'industrie française*, Document de travail de l'INSEE, G 2005/03, April.

properly understand the precise meaning of all this, should we not also take account of a whole series of factors weighing on the internationalization of employment, such as the positive and negative effects of trade and global investments?

The papers that follow attempt to answer these questions and were presented by international experts at a conference in Annecy, on 11-12 April 2005, at the invitation of the French Government and the ILO. The debates that took place were primarily intended to take stock of the situation regarding the internationalization of employment at the global level in terms of job losses and jobs created, of the effects on working conditions, on the inequality of incomes and on the development of poverty in different countries. The mechanisms put into operation to accompany offshoring and restructuring in the leading industrialized countries are described and followed by proposals aimed at better managing the impact on employment of globalization and to demonstrate, mainly through the promotion of international labour standards as well as active accompaniment measures, that the negative effects of globalization can be attenuated.

2. HOW FAR HAS THE INTERNATIONALIZATION OF EMPLOYMENT PROGRESSED?

As opposed to the 'old-style' globalization, where long-haul trade led to exchange of goods between dissimilar countries, world trade currently consists largely of ordinary products exchanged by neighbouring countries whose consumers have similar tastes. Daniel Cohen points this out in his paper '*Globalization and employment*'. But the manufacturing process has undergone 'vertical disintegration', as perfectly illustrated by the example of the Barbie doll, whose raw materials come from Taiwan and Japan, whose assembly takes place in the Philippines, Indonesia and China, but whose design and final coat of paint come from the United States. Using this example and others, Cohen provides evidence that the different links in the value chain that come into play during the globalized production process do not have the same weight. The design and marketing of products, which still represent most of their value, remain with the industrialized countries, while manufacture – the least valuable aspect – is left to low-income countries. This is why he considers that the entire production process stands little chance of being relocated to low-income countries, as a number of American studies have predicted. Cohen concludes that, based on the most recent studies, not only is the employment deficit that is generated by international trade low for developed countries but also that the relocation of jobs in the services sector remains marginal (some two per cent of service jobs). Offshoring – like trade and international investments – could even have a positive effect on developed countries, by stimulating productivity gains and increasing market share.

In *Service jobs on the move – offshore outsourcing of business related services*, Barbara Gerstenberger and R. Alexander Roehrl confirm this analysis with some reservations. Referring to the Forrester Research 2002 study which forecast that by 2015, 3.3 million US jobs would be transferred 'abroad' to countries with low-cost labour such as India, they show that, based on 2,533 cases of restructuring in the European Union, the percentage of offshoring remained low. *"More than 80% of announced job losses (almost 1,080,000 jobs) were due to internal restructuring, stemming from the need to adapt to technological change, from changes in consumer demand and from changes in work organization. In comparison, less than 5% of job losses (around 63,000) were clearly attributable to the company's decision to relocate its production activities. In other words, of the 50,000 jobs lost on average each month, due to restructuring activities in the 18 countries monitored, less than 3,000 were lost due to relocation."* According to the two authors, no acceleration in the number of jobs lost due to offshoring has been noted in recent years. On the other hand, more and more relocated jobs are of the type requiring high skill levels. They also note spectacular growth in offshoring to East European countries. *"It is quite clear that many previously secure jobs have come under greater threat, due to the possibility of offshore outsourcing. Also, the organizational change is likely to have an impact on skill requirements (language and communication skills, for example) thus creating a risk of exclusion among those who lack up-to-date skills."* But good business practices are also developing at the same time.

In his article on *Globalization and it impact on jobs and wages*, Michel Fouquin analyses the effects of globalization in terms of jobs as well as of salaries and revenues. The good news is that globalization has seen a reduction in poverty across the world: 40 per cent of the world's population lived with less than a dollar a day in 1981, against 20 per cent today. But inequalities have grown too and the gap between successful and unsuccessful countries is widening. The poorest countries are getting poorer. The idea that economic opening-up will automatically resolve their problems must be discarded. Lack of infrastructure and problems of access to the European market are still major obstacles for many countries. For those that have been winners in globalization it is clear that the key to success is productivity gains. Some countries have made massive leaps in this respect. China has a huge reserve of manpower and has become the workshop of the world, but its development is uneven across its regions. Is mass underemployment compatible with wage progression? Yes, according to the author: *"On the one hand, we can see that there are certain controls on worker mobility, even if they are being relaxed in order to allow workers from the poorer provinces to go and work in those that are wealthier. But on the other, we know that farmers do not become manual workers, much less skilled manual workers, overnight, which reduces the supply of labour for the modern sector."*

The issue of China is also at the heart of Thomas Palley's article *Trade, employment and outsourcing: some observations on US – China economic relations*. The economist recalls that economic relations between the United States and China are currently dominated by the enormous US trade deficit with China, which is responsible for nearly one-third of the worsening of the overall trade deficit. Viewed from this perspective, the deficit in advanced technology products is particularly important. In the author's opinion, the trade deficit is responsible for a significant part of the United States' domestic labour market problems. One recent study calculated the lost job opportunities in the United States due to the trade deficit with China in 2004 (US$162 billion) at 1,808,055. One of the reasons behind the trade deficit is flagrant under-valuation of the Chinese yuan, which should be re-valued at all costs, otherwise the Forrester study forecasts on mass offshoring in services could become a reality. Some studies point to the fact that offshoring in the services industry have developed significantly over the last three years and that the trend is also progressing in highly-skilled services due to fantastic progress in training and education levels in emerging countries, mainly China and India. Three major risks are highlighted by Thomas Palley: the risk of 'undermining the engines' of productivity and the standard of living in the United States; the risk of deepening wage pressures; the risk – already witnessed – of seeing enterprises brandishing the threat of offshoring and thereby reducing the ability of trade unions to defend American workers, wages and the distribution of income.

The balance sheet of the effects of globalization on employment is therefore, as can be seen, uneven. While most studies in Europe and the United States highlight the small number of employees affected by offshoring, three points nevertheless deserve attention.

Firstly, the phenomenon has not yet been completely measured. Statistics often only take into account major companies and fail to capture data for services and SMEs, where it seems that the trend to offshoring has accelerated of late. In addition, the concept of "potential non-created jobs" revealed by a trade deficit, is dubious since engaging in import substitution policies requires a whole range of unwanted policies, probably including low wages and minimal labour standards or a straightforward return to protectionist policies in order to bring about domestic job creation rather than job creation outside the country. Uncertainty therefore reigns as to measuring the effects on employment, mainly because, at a global level, these effects can translate into a zero sum or positive sum game between winner and loser countries. The vertical disintegration of goods and services production adds a new dimension to globalization, making it even more difficult to assess the impact on employment. An increasing number of intermediate inputs in the production (and service) process are carried out abroad, while the products themselves are being marketed both domestically and internationally – often by multinationals which have their headquarters and main workforce in developed countries.

Secondly, the phenomenon of relocation is not the only one that requires being taken into account when looking at the evolution of employment in different countries. The internationalization of employment includes the impact of trade and international investment, a sphere in which the developed countries continue to dominate, which plays in favour of stabilizing and even of providing growth in national employment via increased productivity, increased market share and new partnerships. Moreover, restructuring activities which cause major workforce shifts are only partly due to offshoring, but they help to increase the sense of insecurity felt by people.

Finally, some analysts stress the lack of certainty surrounding developments in countries such as China and India. What happens to these countries' national currencies, salaries, rural exodus, and development of education and training will significantly affect relations with the industrialized countries.

3. WHAT KIND OF RESTRUCTURING ACTIVITIES?

Structural changes are underway that are destroying jobs in some places, sectors and for certain categories of workers, while creating them in other places, in other sectors and among other groups of workers, making adjustment to these changes difficult and painful. The internationalization of employment adds a new dimension to this phenomenon: a job lost in one country can resurface in another. Taken at global level, this can translate into a zero sum or positive sum outcome, with winners taking what the losers have had to give up. But this type of argument does not help national political decision makers, who have to resolve the tensions between job gains and job losses. These job transfers affect people who often lose their job suddenly, who most often have the greatest difficulty in finding a new one, and who often live in the most badly affected regions.

Bernard Gazier, in his report on *Using active and passive employment policies to accompany globalization-related restructuring* reminds us of "*the dramatic nature of what is at stake, particularly for the least-skilled workers who often find themselves in long-term unemployment or suffer major loss of income...*" before analysing the tools available to manage crises in different countries. He explains that there are three factors that will trigger a collective reaction: major corporations carrying out mass lay-offs; the impossibility of spreading out over time job losses that appear massive and sudden; and job cuts in a single geographic area. Yet the phenomenon is not new: the manner in which the European Coal and Steel Community (ECSC) managed the coal crisis in the 1950s was a good example of accompaniment of restructuring activities by use of various public policies.

Between the 1950s and the 1970s, it was a mix of subsidies to maintain activities and employment, the use of the possibilities offered by natural attrition of the workforce and the use of early retirement that featured widely in the management of restructuring in the industrialized countries. Gazier believes that there are three major options: laissez-faire; prevention; and active reallocation policies. Laissez-faire merely involves providing unemployment insurance. The preventive option starts with protectionist measures and goes on with temporary or permanent subsidies to maintain production, and can go as far as nationalization. Active reallocation policies aim to link mobility of capital and mobility of labour by redirecting them to dynamic sectors through the application of employment policies. Since the 1980s, employment policies have also been heavily relied on, from training assistance to re-integration, job search, public assistance in geographic mobility, subsidies for start-up of a small enterprise, re-employment premiums, and wage compensation mechanisms. The trend to group different measures for a single purpose is not unique to Europe; it is also the case of Australia, and the United States with Trade Adjustment Assistance, created in 1962 by the Trade Expansion Act, which marked the start of multi-lateral tariff reductions in the framework of GATT. This programme provided income guarantees and reclassification services to workers directly affected by trade liberalization. Eligibility criteria were initially very strict, but the programme became more successful once they were relaxed. In 1993, when the North American Free Trade Agreement (NAFTA) was signed, it was extended to workers in supplier or subcontractor companies and to those whose companies had relocated to Canada or Mexico. The programme has benefited two million workers since its inception.

The approach to adjustment to globalization is becoming increasingly "Schumpeterian", according to Gazier, i.e. there is no point in delaying job losses resulting from this process, nor should this be done to protect workers under threat. On the other hand, it is justifiable to compensate for the consequences and to organize the offloading of workers rejected by certain sectors or businesses onto other sectors that are taking workers on. This permanent requirement for flexibility results in two main changes: collectivization of restructuring, and proceduralization and active approaches.

Continued restructuring activities make recourse to the law a central issue. In the United States, it is the anti-discrimination aspect that comes to the fore in any mass redundancy procedure. In Europe, the social plan includes substantive and procedural requirements to be complied with by major companies (the 1975 European directive, amended in 1992). Among European countries, however, 'hard' and 'soft' versions of the law can be noted. These instruments are often used to protect long-serving older workers who are weak in skills and therefore unlikely to be mobile and who will be difficult to train.

Typical tools of active labour market policies have gained in importance over the last 20 years: the trend to activation has seen early retirement schemes coming under fire, perhaps due to the fact that typically 50 per cent of the workforce made redundant is affected by them. National changes of policy in favour of active ageing are more the brainchild of governments than of the social partners. The trend to activation partly gets round this resistance by making the benefits less advantageous.

This leads us to the issue of the efficiency of policies aiming at reclassification of workers who are victims of restructuring activities: these rarely exceed 50 per cent of those involved in job search. The effectiveness of training also seems to be limited unless it is carried out professionally.

In *Social accompaniment measures for globalization: sop or silver lining?* Raymond Torres confirms that globalization can be a creative destruction process that can improve the well-being of countries involved because of the benefits of having the comparative advantage, the resulting economies of scale, and the greater choice offered to consumers. "*We can see in particular that the countries that are most open to the outside have a higher growth rate over the long term than countries that are less open, which would explain why most countries – including the developing countries – do not want globalization to pass them by.*" But, Torres stresses, the benefits of globalization are not automatic and entail adjustment costs. "*Public measures are therefore needed if the benefits of globalization are to be felt in practice.*" According to a recent OECD study, workers who are victims of restructuring due to trade do not have a different profile from workers who are victims of restructuring due to other reasons. International competition affects specific types of workers less than it does jobs in specific sectors. The rates of return to employment are weaker in Europe than in the United States, in the same way as loss of salary in the case where a new job is found. On both continents, half of the workers who lose their job in the manufacturing industry find a new job in the same sector.

In her paper *The internationalization of employment and the debate about offshoring in France: a legal perspectives*, Marie-Ange Moreau returns to the initial paradox. "*...the debate about offshoring in France, as reported in the media particularly since September 2004, (shows) that, for political reasons, the consequences of the internationalization of employment are seen only in terms of restructuring and its impact in the form of redundancy programmes and net job losses at local and national levels. The problem of offshoring is thus addressed solely as a matter of job losses in France, ignoring its European and international dimensions and without any attempt to understand the offshoring in question as part of a movement towards the internationalisation of employment beyond French borders. The only aspect highlighted has been the negative impact on employment. The questions that have been asked reflect national and corporatist thinking – justified by the need to explain at national level the loss of jobs and the lack of a satisfactory political response – and fail to take proper account of the European dimension in issues concerning companies' freedom of movement in Europe.*" She claims that legal instruments are no longer in phase with the new requirements of labour organization and can no longer be limited to national territory.

4. THE ROLE OF POLICY COHERENCE AND INTERNATIONAL LABOUR STANDARDS

National polices to accompany retructuring activities are only one component of an overall policy whose objective is to make globalization fair, as the report of the World Commission on the Social Dimension of Globalization urges (ILO, 2004). In order to provide a response to certain aspects of concerns about the current phase of globalization, international instruments are indispensable. For example, at the global level, greater policy coherence in accompanying structural change is needed. Attempts have been made for some years by the World Bank to make an exit from the Washington consensus. This major player in the multilateral system is currently, like the ILO, seeking to match social policy measures to free trade measures. The OECD is in favour of accompanying free trade by job security measures. These moves, which combine adjustment and job security measures for workers, have some potential for cooperation between the multilateral players.

However, very often the international players still advocate diverging and contradictory policies.

Arguing in favour of a pragmatic model for governance of the internationalization of employment, Langille, in his paper *Better governance of the internationalization of employment*, calls upon the fundamental text of the Philadelphia Declaration (1944), which he describes as a possible "coherence convention". According to the author, "*it is not an insight of startling originality to point out that a core aspect of governance of the employment issue lies in basic global macroeconomic governance issues – particularly the management of the global financial system*". It is a matter of creating conditions for coherent governance, which is close to the deep political coherence dear to Amartya Sen between economic, political and social rights. It is up to governments to put this governance in place. And they therefore have a renewed role to play by favourizing the legitimacy of a plurality of players to act, and strengthening the possibilities for other regulations, by for example favourizing certifications. The public authorities are only one player among others. They must take responsibility for the coherence of policies and make effective the way forward sought today by this plurality of players (professional organizations, enterprises, NGOs, etc.). Langille believes that we are in a world where legal, centralized structures of command and control are becoming less and less important and where human capital is the critical factor and human resources policy is determining.

And the rules of the game need to be made more equal with and between developing countries. The countries of the South need a policy protecting them from unfair competition more than the countries of the North. Trade and international investments remains overwhelmingly dominated by the North. The countries of the North do not suffer the most from the negative effects of competition due to the advantages of the South in labour costs and working conditions, because they retain advantages in productivity and a competitive position in the value chain.

Fierce price competition is active in the emerging countries, intensified by the irruption of China on the world market. Respect for labour standards, especially for fundamental rights at work, could re-establish a balance in trade. The setting up of free trade unions in China would lead to a considerable increase in salaries.

The ratification and implementation of international labour standards sometimes comes up against obstacles. For several years now, the right to work has been criticized and questioned. In *The role of international labour standards for governing the internationalization of employment*, Werner Sengenberger points out that for orthodox free-market economists "*...interference in the labour market by "artificial" rules strikes against the "economic law"*. According to this argument, international labour standards would be ineffective and futile, or worse, they would do harm to economic progress. They will generate sub-optimal outcomes. "*The greatest damage to growth is in across-the-board labour standards that dictate either minimum standards or minimum conditions* *for higher and fairer wages*" (e.g. Sachs 1996)". Is this argument solid? Not in Sengenberger's opinion. He settles the question on the supposed arbitrage between employment and regulation. Improved international labour standards do contribute to greater productivity. It is the relationship between workers' rights, political and social stability and human capital that are attractive for foreign direct investment. The social tensions emerging in China could put this argument to the test.

The reason why international labour standards have been put in place since the founding of the ILO are still valid: non-regulated competition in the labour market results in negative effects on working conditions; rules and regulations that have legal force are needed to prevent destructive competition. Better still, international labour standards can improve economic performance by encouraging entrepreneurs to innovate, make productivity gains and drop less profitable activities.

Sengenberger sees international labour standards as global public goods, which meet criteria for fair competition and non-exclusion, and these qualities should pave the way for strengthened cooperative action. But recent times have seen the development of several obstacles to better regulated globalization based on decent work: the growth of shareholder capitalism, which gives capital pride of place over work; a good third of the global workforce unemployed or underemployed, which results from weak macroeconomic policies; fiscal and monetary constraints imposed by the international financial institutions on developing countries and by the ECB in Europe; and, finally, the decline in trade union membership and influence in most countries.

Philippe Waquet confirms this analysis in *The role of labour law for industrial restructuring* reminding economists that "*Labour law should not be dismissed as a procedural system designed to hamper the 'normal' development of a market organization process, nor should it be reduced to a second-rate financial compensation scheme designed to paper over the cracks resulting from the internationalization of employment and offshoring*". It is important to match freedom of enterprise with the right to obtain employment, as promulgated in the preamble to the French Constitution. In the same way, and contrary to what some economists claim, French law is not over-protective but in large part based on Community law as far as collective economic redundancies are concerned. But, social and human problems resulting from offshoring have not been adequately addressed, either in France or elsewhere.

In *The social dimension of globalization and changes in law*, Mireille Delmas-Marty points out that in nearly 100 years universalism has been both enriched by many laws (from 'soft' to 'hard') and impoverished (by fragmentation of these laws: the 1966 Pacts, regional strategies, codes of conduct, etc). She also turns to the impact of globalization, writing that "*From the legal point of view, globalization is not... associated with a world law which is already established, whose components could be described, but with the transformation of the field of law through the growing diversification of a law organized in a plural but rarely pluralist way*". She particularly stresses that normative spaces are increasingly negotiated between States that do not, or at least not fully, include the setting up of institutions, legislative and juridical executives, which would bring stability. Therefore, this variable-speed space, by lacking a proper judicial framework could become an 'à la carte' space in which each could introduce specific exemptions.

5. APPROACHES FOR IMPROVEMENT (1): CREATING CONDITIONS FOR BETTER GOVERNANCE OF EMPLOYMENT TO MAKE DECENT WORK A REALITY FOR ALL

No one will question the fact that progress achieved towards full employment at global level, an objective set by the international community at the Social Summit in Copenhagen in 1995[3] has not met expectations, as noted by the UN Secretary-General in his February 2005 report to the UN Social Development Committee.[4] The rate of youth unemployment in particular rose from 10 per cent in 1995 to 14.4 per cent in 2003. The subject of the quality of employment, an objective affirmed at Copenhagen and Lisbon in 2000 has been severely dented by the growing number of working poor (60 per cent of the 550 million working poor recorded globally are women) and by the growth of the informal sector. The growth of FDI and the global integration of economic and financial markets have moved faster than progress with global social governance, which currently cannot even manage the process in hand to the benefit of human beings. How can globalization be made fair and offshoring less traumatic for both individuals and economies? How to implement the ILO Decent Work strategy, which is based on the concept developed in Copenhagen (and already partially comprised in the declaration of Philadelphia and the employment convention of 1964) and places the possibility of productive work in conditions of freedom, security and dignity at the heart of sustainable development?

Several proposals were made in the papers presented.

One group aimed to better regulate trade between industrialized and emerging countries, and **to re-think the current economic model**. Thomas Palley proposed in-depth reform of the global growth model, led by exports and entirely dependent on the US playing the role of global buyer and borrower of last resort, and to move to a viable growth model in which domestic demand would play an important role. China should make a transition by abandoning its current strategy of growth based exclusively on exports and convert to a strategy led by growth based on domestic demand, and should re-value its currency. But, generally speaking, the whole world should revise its growth model. To achieve this, economic policies must give more space to demand, redirecting and increasing

---

[3] See the Copenhagen Declaration, commitment 3: Full employment: We commit ourselves to favourizing the realization of the full employment objective by making it a fundamental priority of our economic and social policies, and to provide all, men and women, with the possibility of giving themselves the means of sure and sustainable subsistence thanks to freely-chosen employment and productive work".

[4] www.un.org, report E/en.5/2005/6, paras. 140-160.

public expenditures, for example by introducing social insurance and education systems in countries that do not have them.

According to Thomas Palley, this all gives the ILO a clear mission. As the ILO is responsible for the development of full employment and decent working conditions – which implies action on exchange rates and macroeconomic policy – the ILO must become involved in currency exchange rates, financial architecture and economic policy issues.

A second set of proposals, drawing conclusions from the value chain approach developed by Cohen, aimed to speed up **the specialization of companies** at both ends of this chain by favourizing the development of sectors with *high R&D potential* on the one hand, and developing jobs (mainly unskilled) in the protected sectors on the other hand. From this point of view, the industrial fabric requires overhaul, in order to encourage mobility of resources and maintain dominant positions in the fields of research and technology by adequate R&D expenditure, so that high value added services can take over. This means developing an *industrial policy* based on national and especially European technology and pursuing a *policy of social cost exemptions on low salary jobs* and of accompaniment. Attention should also be paid to the means available to *regions*, not only to sectors and people, in order to assist affected regions to fight against the cumulative downward spiral of less jobs, less income, less infrastructure and general loss of attractiveness. This means helping regions where the level of industrial employment is high to profitably overturn the impact of international trade.

Several articles in this book dwell on the lack of alignment in global governance with a view **to strengthening the effectiveness of fundamental social rights**. Waquet points out that in the fields of trade and industry, the WTO exercises complete oversight concerning the respect of the rules of competition, but has no such function in social affairs, and it is inadmissible that the conditions in which workers are employed should not be guaranteed by effective and applicable rules.

Sengenberger denounces the fact that *"There is lack of a social dimension in the governance of the globalization process. Trade, economic and financial policy making is largely separated from labour and social policies. The first are put in the driver's seat, while the latter are placed on the back seat. In the employment policy field, "sectorialism" dominates, meaning that competencies are split between the IMF, the World Bank, WTO, and the ILO. Frequently, these organizations give incoherent, even conflicting policy advice to national governments (events where they join forces, as for example in the Cambodia project mentioned below, are rare). At the same time, the competencies are blurred, or overlap. Through its lending policies, the IMF interferes with labour market policies even though this is not within its mandate and although it has no technical competence in this field. There is a parallel lack of policy integration and policy coherence at the national level."*

This point is also stressed by Brian Langille who claims for more policy coherence both between international players and in the national context.

Mireille Delmas-Marty proposes going beyond the two dominant models of governance, on the one hand, 'the pyramid', a hegemonic, hierarchical and vertical model, and on the other, 'the network', a model of self-regulation which is developed through cross and horizontal interactions. She argues in favour of a flexible linkage between the legal, social and juridical, which would help avoid constructions that are too difficult to understand for the citizen, and, like Langille and Waquet, puts the accent on the role of politics to re-introduce a plurality of players, to identify their transnational strategies and to make the social dimension of globalization effective. The authors underline the imbalance between the legal bodies, the lack of symmetry between the collective bargaining preferences, and would like to 'provide teeth' to ILO Conventions, which, unlike the WTO, does not have an arbitration body nor powerful means of imposing sanctions against contravening countries, but which is based on the goodwill of States.

Globalization has restarted the debate on the necessity to go beyond the goodwill of States in matters of application of social standards. This question was raised, mainly by the United States, France and Belgium, when the WTO was set up in Marrakech in 1994. The opposition of a large number of developing countries ('*trade, not aid*') also saw coercive action in the framework of the WTO thrown out. In paragraph 4 of the Singapore final declaration (1996), trade ministers nonetheless expressed 'their commitment with regard to internationally recognized labour standards', insisting on the fact that the ILO was 'the competent body for setting up and managing these standards'. They agreed that the comparative advantage of low-wage developing countries should not in any way be put into question. In this context, the Declaration on fundamental principles and rights at work, adopted in 1998 by ILO member States, in the wake of the Copenhagen declaration, was a decisive contribution to the promotion of fundamental human rights at the workplace.[5] The 1998 Declaration contains a clause recalling in terms close to those employed in the Singapore declaration that these rights could not be used for protectionist reasons, which was a response to the main concerns of the developing countries. The Declaration takes from the ILO Constitution itself the obligation to put fundamental rights into action: it explicitly states that ILO member States are obliged by their very membership of the ILO to 'respect, promote, and carry out these rights in good faith and in conformity with the Constitution'. This link could have remained no more than a pious wish if the text did not link it up to a follow-up mechanism (on the one hand an annual reporting mechanism which reviews the situation of countries which have not ratified Conventions relating to fundamental rights, and on the other a global report every four years which reports progress made on each of these rights). There is therefore a sort of status quo on the issue of the social clause, following the renewed failure in dealing with the subject within the framework of the WTO conference in Seattle in 2000. This status quo is

---

[5] Eight Conventions cover the five fundamental rights of forbidding forced labour, the worst forms of child labour and discrimination, as well as granting the right to collective bargaining and freedom of association.

marked by the absence of a secretariat for fundamental rights concerning the disciplines in the multilateral trading system. The subject of the linkage between social standards and global trade rules is far from being solved, as the developments described in this book demonstrate. There are many reasons for this. Firstly because, without even modifying existing rights, the current regime of general exceptions with GATT and GATS (taken up by the WTO) would be perfectly capable of integrating certain fundamental social rights if cooperation mechanisms and the dormant dialogue between the WTO and the ILO were revived. Then, because the WTO has not exhausted the subject, the diversification of economic exchange and the proliferation of bilateral accords gives it multiple faces.

Mireille Delmas-Marty believes that internormativity would be clarified by recognition of fundamental rights as universal rights, which would make way for the foundations to be laid for possible commercial sanctions against countries which did not respect labour standards or new systems of interpreting them: *"the parties to a dispute before the WTO could raise an exception of incompetence and obtain a referral to an ad hoc organization placed under the auspices of the competent organization"*, such as the ILO, for example. She suggests 'adjustment techniques' for the application of standards, based on the variable indicator model implemented by the European Court of Human Rights. These margins of application of standards would not apply to core Conventions, but would be adapted to the social and economic context of the country and therefore would be evolutionary.

All authors called for greater involvement of the ILO in the implementation of labour standards and in the linkage with other international organizations in the quest for regulation and coherence.

Some authors also called for a revision in the way in which **legal responses could be made**: legal responses to issues regarding the internationalization of employment should be developed in cooperation with the sphere of action of multinational companies, Marie-Ange Moreau pleaded, i.e. to be in agreement on place, time and action: *"Such an approach requires us to reconsider the underlying concepts of labour law, which are rooted in the dualistic model of employers/workers or capital/labour, and spatially and temporally conditioned by the Fordist corporate approach, ignoring completely the transnational, web-type systems of organization favoured by the 'network economy'."* The main proposals firstly aim to give value to the comparative social advantages of enterprises of European origin. Today, the development of a European policy is required in order to create a systematic link between Community policies which highlight an area's attractiveness and employment in such a way as to put in place reciprocity of social costs at the European level and to help finance job conversion programmes.

A further approach proposed by Marie-Ange Moreau is the development of an active policy on fundamental social rights to ensure that they are not only a rampart against deregulation in the Union, but also a real **comparative social advantage** in the EU market. This pre-supposes that the firming-up of fundamental social rights proclaimed in the Charter will become an obligation for member States and a given in the open method of coordination.

Several authors pinned their hopes on the development of **a system of transnational professional relations** (Waquet, Moreau, Sengenberger). The more than 30 International Framework Agreements (IFA) that currently exist, concluded at global level between international federations of trade unions and multinationals clearly demonstrate that a new linkage between international level groups and actors with representation at the international level is being built. A new network grouping international federations, supported by trade unions and European enterprise committees, and a useful negotiating space for the promotion of the group and its development at the international level is being put into place (e.g. the agreement signed by Renault on fundamental rights, Rhodia agreement on corporate social responsibility, EDF agreement). Admittedly there are still only a limited number of these agreements and opposition to their development is strong (notably from UNICE), but the EU must create incentives for trade unions to negotiate at the transnational level and the implementation of a legal framework for transnational collective bargaining must become one of the responses to the challenge of globalization (Moreau).

The authors thus confirm that the condition for the setting of standards is the pledge of their efficiency – if the material and legal difficulties (lack of legal status of the international agreement, negotiating framework, etc.) encountered by these initiatives can gradually be resolved. The lifting of barriers to effectiveness and efficiency of standards could well be linked to getting round the gap between 'hard' and 'soft' law, thereby bringing politics back into play, which must accompany and guarantee the changes it has brought about.

6. APPROACH FOR IMPROVEMENT (2): GENUINE SOCIAL ACCOMPANIMENT

All the authors agreed on the need for better accompaniment of restructuring activities. Restructuring, of which offshoring is only a particular form, unsettles individuals and brings to bear on them the costs of what is most often a beneficial adjustment for society both in the medium and long term. Restructuring activities no longer appear what they once were – serious but isolated events.[6] In the current phase of globalization, they reflect a stage of permanent transformation. Hence the necessity to implement accompaniment arrangements for the duration. What does accompaniment involve and who does it concern? As to what it involves, the authors agree that the best method of promoting transitions to new jobs is to develop efficient active labour market policies. These must be seen as an essential tool in globalization policies.

---

[6] See JP Aubert and R. Beaujolin-Bellet: (2004), *Les acteurs de l'entreprise face aux restructurations: une délicate mutation*, Travail et Emploi, no. 100, October, and *Restructurations, nouveaux enjeux*, Revue de IRES, no. 47, 2005/1.

To be more precise, after having exhausted the virtues of preventive approaches, countries should develop:

–   Systems that personalize support and advice and individual follow-up for unemployed workers;

–   training systems, assisted employment and employment subsidies, on condition that they are targeted, directed to job finding and if need be, mandatory;

–   public employment services with sufficient means available (especially an adequate number of competent counsellors);

–   systems developed with a view to reciprocal obligations.

In some countries that are particularly advanced in this respect, mainly the Nordic countries, employees under threat of redundancy can make use of these services, training included, during their notice period.

The experts also agreed on the need for promotion of career security through prevention of downgrading of skills, improvement in mobility and employability development. Gazier declared that two points must be taken into consideration in order to make firm proposals: laid-off workers' dependence on their previous career as a solution to their problems; and the need for the active participation of those being retrained. The solution lies in anticipating and in working on employability. Several examples were provided: Netherlands Railways, which draws up a skills balance sheet every three years, positioning all employees on the labour market; if training is required to bring some employees up to the market level, the company is obliged to fund it, and the employee to follow it; national pacts in Europe; methods of agreement, etc; Austrian "employment foundations", where the redundancy notice is made six months in advance and where there are three types of sources for funding: public funds for employment policies, a significant share of around one-third of the retraining allowance received by the "leavers" and a very small contribution paid by the remaining workers to pay for the training schemes. Reclassification performance recorded has proved to be higher than average.

States that have chosen trade liberalization must show their capacity to build a credible redistribution system for employees. The experts underlined the need to put in place specific accompaniment systems for workers, similar to the US Trade Adjustment Act (Gazier and Torres). While evaluation does not demonstrate the full efficiency of this system, on the other hand, one of the positive aspects is that it strengthens public support for free trade. This compensation mechanism should be developed at European and possibly also at the global level.[7]

On the other hand, discussions have taken place on the issue of whether this type of assistance should be provided to those workers who are victims of offshoring only or to all workers who have experienced restructuring of their

---

[7] "A la recherche de la régulation perdue: quelles règles du jeu pour l'après-Cancun", article by J.M. Paugam and D. Tersen, Politique étrangère, 3/2004.

enterprise. There was no clear-cut agreement on this point. Arguments in favour of a wider system show that there is little difference between the two categories of workers and that workers and public opinion make no distinction between redundancies due to offshoring or due to other reasons.

The main conclusion is that there is an urgent need to face these problems both for the short and medium-term effects of globalization and the internationalization of employment, via appropriate labour market policies, by setting up permanent institutions to manage adjustments at local, national and international level, with a view to reintegrating workers in a stable way. Such institutions building requires the contribution of all socio-economic actors, especially the social partners. Such institutions should be considered as a public good and be accessible by all those affected by offshoring, whether the cause is global or any other. In future, the adaptation of workers to structural change must be seen as a right, which implies the duty to take up offers that ensure one's own employability.

GLOBALIZATION AND EMPLOYMENT

BY DANIEL COHEN[1]

1. INTRODUCTION

In the space of 50 years, between 1950 and 2000, the share of trade in GDP more than doubled and international trade continued to increase almost continuously throughout the period.[2] Despite this spectacular growth, it was not until 1973 that world trade figures returned, as a share of GDP, to their 1913 level. In the case of the United Kingdom, however, the turn of the century figures were only reproduced in the early 1980s.

This statistical finding would seem to show that the adventure of globalization began again in the 1980s from the point at which it had left off in 1913. This analogy is nevertheless misleading.[3] While post-World War II trade gradually regained its early 20th century level, its nature has until recently been very different from trade in the 19th century. In 1913, the United Kingdom – the leading trading nation of the time – imported wheat and tea and exported textiles. It traded largely with far-off and dissimilar countries. The proportion of western Europe's exports destined for the developing world continued to fall throughout the post-World War II period from 28 per cent in 1955 to 14 per cent in 1972. At present, exports from the wealthy to the poor countries account for only 2 per cent to 3 per cent of their GDP (whereas exports from the poor to the wealthy countries account for a percentage which is five times higher). As is well known from the works of Helpman and Krugman, trade is chiefly the preserve of the wealthy countries. It is only as we move into the 21st century that a genuine reversal seems to be taking place.

2. THE NATURE OF TRADE

Europe is a good example in this respect. The Europe of 15 accounts alone for 40 per cent of world trade. Two-thirds of its imports and exports are within Europe. France, Italy, the Netherlands and the United Kingdom are the main

---

[1] I should like to thank Cyril Nouveau for his valuable assistance.

[2] As an average for the OECD countries, it increased from 12.5% in 1960 to 20% in 2000.

[3] See "Is Globalization Today Really Different Than Globalization A Hundred Years Ago?", M. Bordo, B. Eichengreen and G. Irwin, NBER, June 1999.

trading partners of Germany, which is the leading European exporting power. There is less trade between Germany and the United States than between Germany and Belgium and Luxembourg. Most world trade is therefore a local type of trade, from the point of view of both products and trading partners. This largely continues to be the nature of trade today (see Table 1).

Table 1: Export and import structure by main regions of destination

		Destination of exports		Origin of imports	
		1990	2003	1990	2003
United States	Amount	393 106	723 611	517 020	1 305 250
	Developed countries	64.9	56.4	59.7	49.7
	CEEC and CIS	1.0	0.6	0.4	1.7
	Developing countries	33.8	43.0	39.8	49.4
Germany	Amount	409 261	742 020	346 461	596 449
	Developed countries	83.3	81.7	81.6	79.4
	CEEC and CIS	4.6	3.9	3.7	4.0
	Developing countries	11.9	14.2	14.6	16.5
France	Amount	216 396	386 394	234 439	390 008
	Developed countries	77.9	79.2	80.6	81.5
	CEEC and CIS	1.4	2.0	2.0	2.6
	Developing countries	17.3	17.5	15.0	15.1
United Kingdom	Amount	185 101	306 063	223 040	383 671
	Developed countries	81.5	80.6	85.1	75.6
	CEEC and CIS	1.0	1.6	1.0	1.6
	Developing countries	16.7	15.9	13.3	20.7
China	Amount	62 760	438 250	53 809	412 836
	Developed countries	35.7	56.2	51.3	43.5
	CEEC and CIS	3.7	2.4	4.8	3.3
	Developing countries	54.1	33.2	43.1	47.1

Amount: US$ millions
Structure as percentage.
Source: UNCTAD, 2004.

Most trade is still in ordinary products and between neighbouring countries whose consumers have similar tastes. This is "horizontal" globalization which increases the range of resources available to firms and consumers. "Old-style" globalization, understood in its 19th century sense of long-haul trade between dissimilar countries, has grown at a much slower pace than "local" globalization. Excluding trade with the other European countries, France's trade with the rest of the world, including the United States and Japan, accounts for less than 10 per cent of its GDP. The economist Jeffrey Frankel has determined a simple calculation (for the United States), which is just as applicable to Europe.[4] The

---

[4] Jeffrey Frankel: *Globalization and the Economy* in "Governance in a Globalizing World", edited by Nye and Donahue, Washington, DC: Brookings Institution, 2002.

European economy accounts for approximately one-quarter of the world economy. If it were perfectly integrated in the world, in the simple sense that its purchases and sales did not depend in any way on its trading partner's origin or destination, it would purchase or sell three-quarters of its goods abroad. In practice, purchases and sales account for only 12 per cent of its GDP. Calculating the ratio between the theoretical and the real figure gives a factor of 1 to 6. The reality is six times smaller than the fiction of a perfectly integrated world.

The activity of American multinationals perfectly illustrates the prevailing nature of world trade.[5] They have a world turnover of US$ 21,000 billion. They employ 7 million people. The activity of multinationals mirrors world trade of which they are also the main vector; 77 per cent of the sales of American multinationals in 1998 went to the OECD countries.

There is no doubt that the main interest of these multinationals is the consumers of the countries in which they set up, which explains why their foreign direct investment has long been in the wealthy countries themselves. This is still the case today, even though the leading recipient of direct investment is now China (see figure 1).[6]

It also explains why the longer the direct investment in a country, the more the country has increased its customs barriers; investment *in situ* is a way of getting round tariff barriers and reaching the consumer. This is why Japanese motor manufacturing firms stepped up their investment in the USA – in the early 1980s – in order to counter increasing US protectionism.

In the OECD's European countries, the activity of multinationals continues to be traditional. The proportion of exports by subsidiaries has remained stable over the last 20 years: around one-third of output is re-exported to other (European) countries. However, significant changes were gradually recorded for the emerging countries during the 1990s. While total employment in multinationals increased by only 25 per cent, it doubled in Asia in the ten years from 1989 to 1998. In China, there was a 53 per cent increase every year.

In the emerging world, multinationals are now setting up in countries where customs tariffs are low in order to use them as a platform for re-export. In East Asia, an average of 50 per cent of production is re-exported. This re-exportation takes place along a production chain that is becoming increasingly hard to track, chiefly to other Asian countries, before the end product is finally despatched to the United States. In 1995, the majority of American imports were intermediate products purchased by industrial firms.[7] In the European countries (France,

---

[5] Hanson et al., NBER, 8433, August 2001.

[6] As an average, between 1994 and 2003, net outgoing flows from the developed countries were equivalent to 2.3% of domestic gross fixed capital formation (GFCF). In the developing countries, net incoming flows were 7.5% of GFCF. From 1970-1979, the corresponding figures were 1% and 2.5%.

[7] In 1925, 90% of imports into the United States were still in two sectors: products for the agri-foodstuffs sector and raw materials for the industrial sector. Imports of semi-finished products for the motor manufacturing industry, for instance, accounted for no more than 0.02% of total imports. Its imports of capital goods in general accounted for no more than 0.4% of total imports.

Figure 1: Increases in foreign direct investment

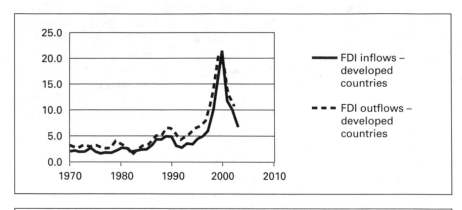

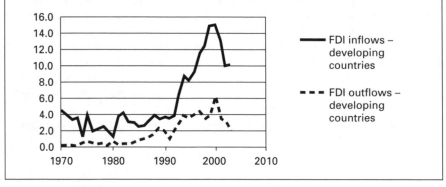

Source: UNCTAD
(http://www.unctad.org/Templates/Page.asp?intItemID=3277&lang=1)

Germany and the United Kingdom), over half of intermediate products are now imported.

The famous Barbie doll offers a striking illustration of the new nature of world trade. It illustrates what is being termed the "vertical disintegration" of the manufacturing process. The raw material, i.e. the plastic and the hair, comes from Taiwan and Japan; assembly takes place in the Philippines before moving on to lower wage areas in Indonesia and China. The moulds come from the United States as does the last coat of paint prior to sale ...

This "vertical disintegration of production"[8] characterizes the third wave of expansion of world trade since 1945, following the growth of intra-branch trade, then, from the 1970s, North-South trade. It has a great deal to do with the development of information technologies and is underpinned by a revolution in work organization.

---

[8] Feenstra, 1996.

Table 2 Vertical disintegration

Intermediate goods imported as a proportion of total intermediate goods of the industrial sector in the United States

1972*	5.7%
1979*	8.6%
1987**	12.4%
1990*	13.9%
1992**	13.9%
1997**	17.7%
2002**	22.1%

Source: *Feenstra-Hanson [1997]
**Burke, Epstein and Choi [2004]

3. INTERNATIONAL TRADE AND INEQUALITIES

The main intellectual model for assessing the effects of trade with poor countries on employment in wealthy countries has long been to contrast the employment of skilled workers with that of unskilled workers. Many studies have examined the supposed role that international trade played in growing inequalities in the wealthy countries in the 1980s and 1990s. With the notable exception of the works of Adrian Wood, the overwhelming majority of these studies concluded that trade was not in itself the main cause of wage inequalities (see the summary of this debate in the Annex to this paper).

In public debate in the Northern countries, the Southern countries are sometimes accused of unfair competition by artificially maintaining wages and working conditions at an excessively low level in order to attract international capital. This is called social dumping.

According to Marin (2004), the cost of labour in the Central and Eastern European Countries (CEECs) is 10 to 20 per cent of the cost of labour in Germany or Austria. However, this difference corresponds almost exactly to the difference in mean labour productivity between the countries: in this case wage differentials are therefore explained by the level of development and not by "social dumping" phenomena. As a result, it is possible to predict that these differentials will gradually be cancelled out.

It is nevertheless true that labour productivity in the subsidiaries of German and Austrian enterprises located in eastern Europe is much higher than this mean productivity, since it is equivalent to 20 to 60 per cent of productivity in the home country.[9] For enterprises which relocate, the drop in the unit cost of production is therefore 40 to 70 per cent (see Table 3). Bonnaz et al (1994) similarly find that the average price of imports from the developing countries is 2.1 times less

---

[9] There are two possible explanations for this difference: it may be that the Western enterprises "import" by bringing in capital and technologies enabling this productivity gain; on the other hand, it may be that there is a selection effect, as the sectors in which the foreign direct investment is made are those in which the recipient countries have a comparative advantage and for which the productivity differential is therefore below the mean.

than the price of equivalent goods produced in France. Yet the proportion of jobs lost through trade with the emerging countries is still small, accounting for only 6 per cent of the jobs lost because of "ordinary" restructuring, according to the Dublin Foundation.

Table 3   Relative wages and productivity in the countries of eastern Europe in comparison with Germany – 1990s

		Country	German multinationals
East	Wage	23.4	16.5
	Productivity	23.5	60.0
	Unit cost	99.7	27.6
South – East	Wage	10.4	18.6
	Productivity	11.4	37.7
	Unit cost	91.0	49.4
CIS	Wage	5.4	3.3
	Productivity	8.1	11.9
	Unit cost	67.0	27.4

East = Baltic states, Czech Republic, Hungary, Poland, Slovakia, Slovenia
South-East = Albania, Bosnia-Herzegovina, Bulgaria, Croatia, Macedonia, Romania, Serbia

"Country" shows the relative wage and productivity of the countries in question in comparison with Germany
"German multinationals" shows the relative wage and productivity of the subsidiaries of German enterprises in the countries in question, in comparison with the wage and productivity of parent companies in Germany
Source: Marin (2004)

The main reason why studies are hard pressed to find that trade has a significant effect on inequalities has to do with a simple statistic. Eighty per cent of trade is in industrial or agricultural products and only 20 per cent in services. The employment situation in the wealthy countries is the exact opposite. Industrial and agricultural employment accounts in practice for less than 20 per cent of total employment and services for close on 80 per cent. International trade is based on the congruent portion of employment.

According to some commentators, what is new in the debate on offshoring is more that all jobs are being opened up to the laws of world trade. In contrast to the jobs in industry which have been lost, and which are often relatively unskilled, the new factor is that many of the jobs at stake are highly skilled. Intel's CEO, Craig Barrett, paints a worrying picture: 300 million highly skilled Indians and Chinese, he explains, will soon be competing with American computer scientists. The Internet means that computer scientists, accountants, radiologists and even lawyers are now concerned. These fears mirror others, but what do the figures tell us?

While the prevailing assumption in the 1980s and 1990s was that trade with the countries of the South was prejudicial to unskilled workers in the countries of the North, the study by Forrester Research (2002), cited above, led to a wide-ranging debate in the United States on the threat that offshoring would pose for skilled jobs. With the development of the new information technologies, a variety of services can in practice be relocated, and not just the employees of call centres: the skilled jobs of computer scientists, consultants, architects and financial analysts also seem threatened. A study of Europe would provide very similar findings.

What is not certain, however, is that this offshoring of services, brought about by the development of information technologies, will have effects that differ substantially from other types of offshoring. In particular, there is no certainty that they will primarily concern the most skilled jobs. In this respect, a number of studies make it possible to reject the notion that the number of skilled service jobs in the Western countries could decline in the coming years.

Among the service jobs requiring information technology skills, it is the least skilled and the least well paid which are concerned by offshoring. Kirkegaard (2004) stresses that 57 per cent of service jobs threatened by offshoring (according to the Forrester projections) are in occupations in which the average wage is below the national average.[10] Arora and Gambardella (2004) reach a similar conclusion when studying the software sector: "much of what is being offshored to India is the production of software, rather than its design. There are two key resources required to remain the centre of innovation in software: access to talented designers, software engineers and programmers; and proximity to a number of large and technically sophisticated users. The US dominates on both counts."

Mann (2003) lastly stresses that, according to the Bureau of Labor Statistics' forecasts for the United States, the occupations covered by Forrester's study are those in which there will be the highest increase in the number of jobs in the United States in future years: the rate of growth of jobs for workers with information technology skills in the ten years between 2000 and 2010 will therefore be double the total growth of jobs in the American economy. The BLS nevertheless forecasts a downturn in jobs in some occupations, chiefly telephone operators and bank tellers. In the case of these jobs, the effects of offshoring are being heightened by the introduction of automated services.

4. THE VALUE CHAIN

To understand the scale of the change emerging in the 1990s, it is much more useful to analyse what changes are being made to a product's value chain rather than to look at the contrast between jobs in industry and the service sector.

We can look for this purpose at the notorious example of a pair of Nike trainers called "Air Pegasus". They are sold at US$70, more or less equivalent to EUR70. First question: how much does the person – probably a woman – producing them earn? Answer: US$2.75. This figure explains why people are so astonished by the difference between the price paid for these trainers in Paris or

---

[10] However, calculating the "average wage" of the jobs destroyed from the graph put forward by Kirkegaard, weighting the "average wage" of each category by the number of jobs destroyed in this category, provides an average wage for the jobs destroyed which is above the national average (some US$ 43,100, whereas the average wage is around US$ 36,000).

New York and the wage actually received by the person producing them somewhere in Morocco or Indonesia.

But let us continue to break down the cost structure. Producing the shoes does not just require labour, but raw materials as well: leather, rubber, etc. Machinery also needs to be bought, warehouses rented and invested capital paid for. The shoes then need to be exported. Before they are boxed, the trainers finally cost Nike US$16.5. This does little to resolve the mystery. How can a manufacturing cost of US$16.5 lead to a retail price to the consumer of US$70? The answer is in two stages. First, Nike runs phenomenal advertising campaigns. Promotion (including stars' fees and actual advertising campaigns) costs US$4.00 per pair. The labour of Nike's own workers (administration, sales representatives, etc.) as well as the firm's capital expenditure, payments on investments, storage costs and shareholders' remuneration, come on top of this. It is worth noting here that Nike is not a particularly profitable enterprise. The return on investment was 10 per cent in 2001. In total, the wholesale price of the trainers, i.e. the price at which Nike sells them to distributors, has now increased to US$35.50. The price of the shoes is therefore doubled by the cost of the distribution needed to get them on the feet of the end consumer. The personnel responsible for selling them have to be paid. This is supplemented by the rental of sales points, payments on the capital invested by the retailer which, here again, includes payments on investments, storage costs and shareholder dividends ... and so on.

These figures can therefore be summarized as follows. Articles such as Nike's "Air Pegasus" trainers cost as much to produce as social articles than as physical articles: Nike spends as much on promotion costs as it does on manufacture in Indonesia. These figures tend to show that what is being purchased is as much the image and the concept as the product itself. At the third stage of the pyramid, it costs as much to get the shoes on to the consumer's feet as it does to manufacture them in the full sense of the term. This is a fascinating example of the "new world economy": combining the production of an "intangible" (the brand), with an urban and global design, with a tangible output, i.e. the shoe which has come from very far away and, lastly, with a heavy and predominant proportion of services in the most limited sense: getting the product made in this way on to the feet of consumers in the places where they live.

As the example of the trainers shows, it is the two upstream and downstream activities of *design and marketing* of these articles which now occupy the key place. At one end of the value chain, an "intangible" good is produced: a chemical formula in the case of a drug, a brand or an image in the case of a sports shoe or an article of clothing.

The drug is nothing, however, without the doctor who, at the other end of chain, prescribes it and the brand of a sports article counts for little without the large store in which consumers can admire it, compare it with other articles and possibly buy it. The other end of the value chain includes "face to face" or F2F activities, to use the words of E. Leamer and M. Storper, paraphrasing B2B (Business to Business). These are activities acting as relays for and supplements to the intangible goods which they prescribe. These F2F activities are local. Ground rents cost them dear as they have to be in places in which people live. Their niches are local and they range from the corner shop that closes at midnight to the doctor who people are keen to have close by.

While globalization is helping these two ends of the value chain to prosper, it is, in contrast, increasingly tightening the noose around the intermediate stage, that of production. This is why it is misleading to contrast services and industry. Within the industrial sector, it is the most service-oriented activities of the industrial sector itself which are flourishing (in the wealthy countries) and production activities in the strict sense which are tending to be outsourced. Recent studies such as those by Maurin, Thesmar and Thoenig (2003) show that firms taking part in international trade are tending to reduce their production activities in the strict sense and focus on tasks geared more towards managing the new complexity of the value chain.

5. NEW WORK ORGANIZATION

Zara is an example of a firm illustrating the sometimes paradoxical effect of new information technologies on offshoring. Its founder, Amancio Ortega, was one of the pioneers of the use of new technologies in the textile sector. While Gap continues to follow the conventional model of four ranges per annum, Zara's stock is rotated much more rapidly and is renewed every two weeks. The time between design and execution is five weeks for Zara, while for Gap it is nine months. Zara's performance depends on an "armada" of 200 designers who produce 12,000 different designs every year. The basic idea is to play on consumers' impatience. If they like a product, consumers have to buy it immediately as they may not find it again. Zara manages fashions and consumer tastes in real time as a function of sales. Sales are linked to the ultra-modern factory in Galicia. If blue is not selling, red takes over. While Zara has stocks, they are only of raw textile products and not of actual clothing. The stores are supplied by lorry, except for the New York boutiques.

This example shows the extent to which the Internet revolution is not just a technical revolution in communications. It is primarily a revolution in work organization, but based on principles which predate it and to which it gives a new dimension.

According to Philippe Askénazy,[11] the objectives of work organization in the Internet age are: "adaptability to demand, reactivity, quality and in particular the optimization of the production process drawing in particular on all human competences. These objectives are reflected by growing multi-skilling on the part of employees and delegation of responsibility to hierarchically lower levels." The way in which this type of work organization complements the information and communication technologies is instantly apparent.

---

[11] P. Askénazy (2001): "La croissance moderne", Economica.

The information society enables producers to use flexible, "just-in-time" and "bespoke" methods vis-à-vis customers. Within production, the contraction of hierarchical levels makes it possible to delegate more responsibility to levels that were strictly supervised in the past, with the counterpart that workers are also more accountable for their performance.

These new production methods have not been created by the information technology revolution; to some extent, they take up methods tried out in the 1960s in Japan and associated with "Toyotism". IT nevertheless makes it possible to radicalize their use and create new applications in which the idea of "networking" of complex production units, within and outside the firm, is being developed. Only a few sectors initially started to reorganize their production methods in this way and it is the gradual spread of these methods to the whole of the economy that is likely to have played a part in the recent speeding up of total factor productivity. According to a survey of 1,000 American enterprises by the magazine *Fortune*, cited by Philippe Askénazy, 27 per cent were using such production methods based on autonomous teams in 1987. By 1996, 78 per cent were using these methods.

In these new management methods, outsourcing to subcontractors plays a major role. Firms are focusing on their comparative advantage, on the points at which their margins are best and particularly on the two ends of the chain as discussed above. From this point of view, it can be said that employment is itself being internationalized by a process which predates it and which is much more global than is suggested by the proportion of jobs actually offshored.

6. GEOGRAPHY STILL MATTERS

"Countries with good communications will be indistinguishable. They will all have access to services of world-class quality. They will be able to join a world club of traders, electronically linked, and to operate as though geography has no meaning. This equality of access will be one of the great prizes of the death of distance".[12] These optimistic words contrast strongly with the way in which economists perceive economic geography.

According to the estimate proposed by Tony Venables,[13] close on 50 per cent of interregional and international wage dispersion can be explained exclusively by geographical variables and remoteness from the main capitals. There are obviously some "anomalies" such as Australia, New Zealand, Japan, the United States, Singapore and Hong Kong, where "distance" alone is not enough to explain wealth. They show that the "tyranny of distance" (the title of a famous book on Australia) is not absolute. All the same, although the cost of distance has been declining sharply for two centuries, the world's economic geography

---

[12] F. Cairncross; "The death of distance 2.0: How the communication revolution will change our lives". Harvard Business School Press, 2000.

[13] Anthony Venables: "Geography and International Inequalities", London School of Economics, 2001.

is nowadays astonishingly similar to its actual geography. In this respect, Zara offers a telling example of the need to be "24 hours by lorry from its customers".

Economists who have examined these data in detail have been led to put forward what seems to be a surprising paradox: *far from dispersing economic life in space, the reduction of transport costs seems, on the contrary, to be conglomerating peoples and wealth*. This paradox can be explained by the re-interpretation of the nature of trade by Helpman and Krugman, which places economies of scale at the core of the analysis. Imagine that two previously isolated regions are suddenly connected by railway. The better developed region will then be able to capture increasing market shares by bringing its economies of scale into play. Because transport costs are smaller, it becomes possible in practice to supply goods to remote parts of the territory and not to have to manufacture them there. If the second region is not sufficiently equipped to react, it is quickly relegated to "primary" activities in which size is of little or no advantage.

If migration starts to take place, gradually depriving the poor region of its best assets, the chain of events takes an irreversible turn. As workers gather together, it is also easier for firms in the prosperous region to recruit, and for workers to find jobs. Knowledge and the social uses of existing techniques can therefore be more readily propagated. The drawbacks of bringing all these activities into one place – congestion, pollution or high rents – do not seem to be enough to offset the benefits of this urban conglomeration. Economists who have examined regional inequalities have shown that these principles are correct. When two cities are connected by high-speed train, it is the least populated city that suffers the consequences. In Europe, despite a general reduction of inequalities between countries, regional inequalities have been continuing to grow for 20 years.

The prospering region is able to pay higher wages than the poor region. It profits from the upstream linkages enabling a firm to share the same labour market or range of subcontractors with other producers, what Albert Hirshman has called "backward linkages". It also benefits from "forward linkages", those downstream linkages provided by proximity to consumers and knowledge of their tastes. The picture that this provides is one of a multi-purpose and prosperous "heart" and of hyper-specialist and poor neighbouring regions. In contrast to the Ricardian theory that it is good to specialize in a task, exactly the opposite is true here. What is good for an individual is not good for a region or a nation. If you use computers yourself, you want to be able to rely on the services of a nearby computer producer. If you are in the labour market you want to have a very wide range of outlets. It is the prerogative of the centre to have such a range of choice available, and the curse of the fringes that they are deprived of this range of choice.

It can therefore be seen that the main effect of reduced communication costs is both to strengthen the centre and step up competition between the fringes. This development is very well illustrated by the veiled rivalry between Mexico and China. The free trade agreement signed in 1992 established Mexico as the

United States' subcontractor. Since this agreement, Mexico has in practice become a re-export platform through what are known as the maquiladoras. Whereas only 10 per cent of the output of American firms located in Mexico was re-exported to the United States in 1982, 40 per cent of their local output is now being re-exported. Most Mexican employment is now located along the border with the United States, whereas in the 1980s it was concentrated largely in the Gulf of Mexico region. US multinationals now import 30 per cent of their needs from their Mexican or Canadian subsidiaries. China, however, although further away but much cheaper, has seen a similar development. In the early 1980s, multinationals in China exported only 20 per cent of their output. The figure has doubled since then. Finding out how far China will go to dislodge Mexico from places that it has struggled to gain is central to the current debate in Mexico. Despite its geographical proximity which means that it is "24 hours by lorry" from its customers, Mexico feels threatened. It is afraid that the eastern coast of China will become the world's workshop, or at least that of the United States. The forces of "conglomeration" in a country of the South are also illustrated here. China is itself on the way towards organizing a new centre-fringe duality between its eastern seaboard and its 800 million or so poor peasants. Inequalities between the two groups have almost doubled in the last 20 years (from 1 to 2 to 1 to 4).

This rivalry between the fringes is not just the preserve of poor countries. Even within the wealthy countries it steps up the contrasts between regions. Looking therefore at the role played by trade in industrial employment, the first key point to note is that this problem concerns the French regions in a very imbalanced way. Their levels of industrialization may in practice vary in a ratio of one to two. The Nord-Pas de Calais, for instance, has an industrial employment rate of 25 per cent while the corresponding rate in the Ile de France region is below 14 per cent. If the general reasoning that, in a given country, a job lost as a result of offshoring is regained elsewhere is fairly accurate, there is nothing to say that a job lost in the Nord-Pas de Calais will be regained there. The industrial region has to struggle to turn the forces of international trade to its profit.

This is undoubtedly not an impossible task. The fact that the Japanese firm Toyota has set up in the Nord-Pas de Calais, to continue with this example, has helped the region's motor manufacturing industry to regain some of the jobs lost in textiles. The region's iron and steel industry is relying on the Chinese market to make up for the European market's lack of vitality. All of which confirms the potential benefits of globalization for those able to control them. The battle is nevertheless fierce and could be lost, not in the absolute as the neo-mercantilists think, but to other French regions. Industrial regions have to fight on two fronts which are to some extent at odds with one another. They have to remain competitive with respect to their international rivals, which imposes a degree of wage restraint. At the same time, however, they have to remain attractive to the younger generations tempted by other, more dynamic French regions, making it necessary for them to keep wages high.

7. WHICH POLICIES OF ADJUSTMENT?

Whatever the actual scale of the changes globalization brings, consideration has to be given to how to regulate it. There are two fundamental questions here: how to develop and apply global labour standards, and how to support workers threatened by globalization?

Global labour standards

For the emerging countries on the path to convergence with the wealthy nations, growth itself is not everything. Albert Thomas, the first Director-General of the ILO, always said that growth is not enough to guarantee an improvement in the lot of workers. Labour standards and environmental standards are essential to ensure harmonious human development. But who should decide what these standards should be? Global labour standards often run the risk of being interpreted by the poor countries as hidden forms of protectionism. This was, incidentally, why the poor countries condemned the Seattle negotiations. Yet it is not principally a North/South issue: rivalry between the emerging countries themselves is a fundamental aspect of the problem.

The abolition of the Multi-Fibre Arrangement (MFA) will cause a lot less concern in Northern countries, which no longer have many jobs in this sector, than it will in countries like Morocco, Tunisia and Mexico. Now that there are no longer any common ground rules in the Southern countries, there is a risk that they will lose ground in a certain number of important social or ecological areas. They themselves need to develop their own labour standards if those standards are to be successful.

There are a number of different aspects to consider here.

International labour standards primarily pursue the same aims as fundamental rights. Combating all forms of forced labour falls into this category. Another example is the right to belong to a trade union, which aims to give workers representation (something which the "contract" of employment, enshrining the workers' subordinate position, negates). The idea here is to regulate relations between people on a different register from relations between things – regardless of the economic cost, it might be added.

However, not all labour standards fall into this category. Many of them are designed to achieve a better economic and social balance.

Take, for example, paid leave, or the duration of the working week. Both of these are major gains for workers and have usually been achieved through hard bargaining. Yet it does not follow that labour has benefited at the expense of capital. Hours not worked are not paid, just as increases in social contributions are most often quickly clawed back from workers' net wages.

This does not detract from the merits of these measures, but it does show that labour demands often need to be backed up by labour standards, in that they require a cooperative approach. The most mundane example of this is giving everyone Sunday off. If some firms give their employees Monday off, and others Tuesday, it becomes difficult for couples to have a family life.

The abolition of child labour (even when interpreted directly as a fundamental right) is another example of a measure that needs to be supported by labour standards if it is to be effective. Banning child labour also presupposes that society undertakes to send children to school. This involves a complex, collective approach, but in the end everyone wins: the children themselves, their parents, and the companies that employ them later on.

In all these examples what is most often needed is for the Southern countries to abandon rivalry among themselves, which is preventing them from finding better cooperative solutions. If tripartite cooperation is needed to achieve the appropriate regulation of working time, for example, even if this is ultimately paid for by the workers themselves, rivalry between countries competing in world trade can delay the development of that regulation.

The idea is not to export standards from the North, but on the contrary to encourage the Southern countries to adopt standards that will help them to put aside rivalry, not in general, but in the areas that harm the moral and human integrity of their workers. (Promote constructive, not destructive, competition.) The damaging effects of growth on the environment clearly fall into this category.

Who will ensure that labour standards are respected? Who will support plans to introduce them? Progress has been made in the field of trade because institutions already exist that are capable of regulation (WTO) and can penalize countries that do not obey the ground rules. In areas other than trade the same rate of progress has not been achieved, and the problem for the ILO today is to enforce compliance with the principles it introduces. A supranational body is urgently needed to ensure that fundamental rights are observed and to exert the leverage that the constitutionalization of fundamental rights can provide. Global governance will in future have to give some thought to links between the WTO and the ILO and to harmonizing the views expressed by the IMF, the World Bank and the WTO.

It is also interesting to look at what is currently happening with transnational labour relations. The conclusion of global agreements thanks to international federations shows that new links are being formed between international-scale groups and actors that have a representative role at international level. This switch to a transnational negotiating model will be possible if two conditions are met: if agreements are actually signed, and if a legal framework is established for transnational collective agreements.

How can we help more specific victims of globalization?

According to the conventional conception international trade enables an efficient international division of labour provided that, in each country, workers are re-allocated between sectors. In this respect, labour mobility and continuing training have to be promoted in order to make the most of the potential offered by the re-allocation of tasks.

This approach to the problem opens the door to measures targeted on individuals. This is one of the main starting points in the debate on flexi-curity.

It is not specific to international trade, however. If a sectoral approach is followed, the main focus of a policy of adaptation is one of speeding up the specialization of the firms at both its ends: the development of sectors with a high R&D potential needs to be promoted and jobs (especially unskilled jobs) need to be developed in the protected sector. This is the path that is instinctively being taken by a country like France, which seeks both to pull off a high-technology industrial policy (Beffa report) and to implement a targeted policy of exemptions of low-waged and local jobs from social security contributions (Cahuc-Debonneuil report). Here again, the measure is general in scope, and is targeted not at those actually involved in global trade, but at those who might benefit from it.

If the geographical approach is taken to the effects of trade on employment, it must be noted that international trade is perfectly capable of creating jobs in one region and destroying them in another. There is no guarantee that the same jobs will be involved. Old industrial areas are under greater threat here than dynamic regions with a strong tertiary sector. The stress has to be placed on the resources available to regions rather than on individuals or sectors as in the two previous approaches. A region which wishes to adapt has to offer the new (physical and human) infrastructure that the post-industrial world needs. It could be envisaged that the State or Europe, via the structural funds, continue to pay the occupational tax or its equivalent to the region affected by offshoring, at least for a certain period, to help it to combat the downward spiral: fewer jobs, less revenue, less infrastructure and general loss of attractiveness.

Like TAA in the USA, which were designed to compensate for the effects of international trade on employment in America, the idea of setting up compensation funds for workers who are the victims of offshoring also offers some interesting prospects. The US scheme is an old one (Trade Adjustment Act, 1962) and provided income assistance and re-employment services for workers directly affected by trade liberalization. The eligibility criteria were initially very strict, but the scheme really took off once they were relaxed, and it has now helped two million workers since it was set up. In 1993, under the North American Free Trade agreement NAFTA, it was opened up to workers in subcontracting companies and suppliers, as well as those whose companies had relocated to Canada or Mexico (200,000 have received help on this basis).

This sort of scheme has the twofold advantage that it directly compensates those harmed by trade policies, and, perhaps above all, it helps to teach us about the effects of trade. We can count the number of people affected, we can bring the phenomenon down to scale, and we can also perhaps find out more about poorly understood aspects, such as the geographical concentration of jobs lost.

8. CONCLUSION

The good news from the last 30 years is that we have seen a reduction in global poverty: 40 per cent of the population lived on less than one dollar a day in 1981, whereas the figure is now down to 20 per cent. On the other hand, inequalities have increased considerably between the two extremes, and we are now seeing a worsening gap between the most successful and the least successful countries. The poorest countries are getting poorer. We need to get away from the idea that economic openness is enough for growth. The poor countries suffer from a lack of infrastructure and access to education, as well as problems in accessing markets in the wealthiest countries (internal transport costs in Africa). Yet openness is vital, otherwise growth strategies will soon be stifled.

The whole debate is about preserving globalization as the driving force of global growth, while at the same time protecting what makes it liveable. If we fail to find a credible response to the concerns it generates, we cannot rule out a protectionist backlash. It is a vital step in the process of regulation for the Southern countries themselves to think about labour standards (child labour, working conditions, environmental standards) in order to prevent social decline in the emerging countries. Giving the countries of the North instruments of solidarity towards workers who lose jobs because of offshoring is another vital step, which also has the great advantage that it counts the people affected and un-demonizes the phenomenon itself.

EFFECTS OF INTERNATIONAL TRADE ON THE LABOUR MARKET IN WEALTHY COUNTRIES

1. JOBS DESTROYED

1.1 Employment balance of trade in goods and services

Method aspects

In the standard theory of international trade, it is generally supposed that countries have full employment: the effect of openness is to re-allocate the labour force between sectors within each country without changing the total number of jobs.

Taking a different approach, it is possible to work out the employment balance of foreign trade: the idea is simply to evaluate the number of domestic jobs needed to produce exported goods and services, and the number of domestic jobs that would be needed to produce imported goods and services. The difference between the two is the balance.

While an evaluation of the employment content of exports raises few problems, several methods can be envisaged to measure the employment content of imports, leading to different results. Assuming that France imports 100,000 shirts from a country E for a total value of EUR1 million, is the job content:

- the number of workers needed to produce shirts worth EUR1 million in France? (content by value)
- the number of workers needed to produce 100,000 shirts in France? (content by volume)

The second method obviously leads to a higher estimate of the employment content of imports. From a theoretical point of view, choosing the correct counterfactual situation depends on the price elasticity of the demand for shirts, whose price would increase if they were produced in France: using a Cobb-Douglass demand function, the amount spent by consumers on a product does not vary with the price of this product, and the content by value method is correct. The content by volume method assumes zero elasticity, and is therefore an upper limit on the employment content of imports. In practice, the employment content of imports from the developing countries is modified by a ratio of 1 to 2 depending on whether the estimate is by value or by volume (which corresponds to the price difference between a product produced in the home country and the same product imported; see Bonnaz et al (1994)).

Wood (1995) argues for a third method. In his view, it is possible to consider that there is complete specialization in trade between wealthy and poor countries. In this case, the shirts that France imports are goods differing from the shirts which are produced in France. As a result, only data from the foreign country can provide information on the production function of the imported shirts and the number of workers needed for their production. Wood therefore starts from the number of workers needed to produce 100,000 shirts (worth EUR1 million) in country E, and makes two adjustments, the first to take account of the difference in the relative price of factors between France and country E, and the second to take account of the drop in demand brought about by the increased cost of the shirts that production in France would entail. The two elasticities that need to be introduced (elasticity in the demand for factors as regards relative prices and elasticity in the demand for the product as regards price) are the key hypotheses in this estimate. Wood's reference estimate uses relatively low elasticities (0.5), which increase the estimated employment content of imports from the developed countries. The effect of trade on employment remains high with elasticities of less than 0.9, but declines rapidly thereafter. Wood's method, which is very dependent on these hypotheses, has not been taken up to any great extent in the literature especially as, according to the estimate by Baldwin (1993) (cited by Bonnaz et al (1994)), only 14 per cent of American imports of manufactured products cannot be substituted by national production.

Estimates of the employment content of trade generally lead to relatively insignificant balances.

In an industrialized country, the unit employment content of industrial imports from the developing countries is always greater than that of exports to these countries, with a ratio varying between 1 and 4/3 (see the review of the literature drawn up by Jean (2001)). As the amount of trade with the developing countries is low, the employment balance of foreign trade equilibrium is low: less than 1 per cent of employment in industry and 0.5 per cent of total employment (Fontagné and Lorenzi (2005)).

To obtain more substantial deficits, account has to be taken of any trade deficit, and the method of content by volume of imports used to measure their employment content. Even then, the results are never as much as 2 per cent of total employment (Jean, 2001).

1.2 The issue of spin-off technical progress

Among the criticisms of the method of the employment balance of trade, is one that relates to the failure to take account of the technical progress brought about by international competition which may lead enterprises to reduce the number of workers per unit of production without this openness actually giving rise to goods flows. In this case, the corresponding jobs destroyed are not taken into account by the method described above. Moreover, this method underestimates the employment content of imports if this is calculated from the productivity of national enterprises in the sector that have survived, and are therefore the most productive.

Cortes and Jean (1997) attempt to evaluate the extent of this technical progress brought about by international trade, by regressing apparent labour productivity by sector for three countries (France, United States, Germany) in respect of various variables, including the penetration rate.

They obtain the following result:

- an increase of one point in the rate of penetration of imports in a given sector leads to a rise of 0.7 per cent in apparent labour productivity in this sector if the imports come from wealthy countries, and 1.3 per cent if they come from poor countries;
- a quarter of the productivity gains recorded between 1977 and 1993 can be explained by import growth, representing a gain of 13 per cent in apparent labour productivity;
- in contrast, increasing trade does not have much of an effect on the relative skilling of the labour force (in the case of France, trade accounts for less than 10 per cent of the increase in average labour skilling in industry between 1977 and 1993).

Calculating the effect on employment of the technical progress brought about by trade is not obvious. According to Wood (1995), the effects measured by the employment content of trade needs to be more or less doubled; starting from a deficit of 10.8 per cent of industrial jobs measured by the employment balance method, he therefore obtains a total loss of 20 per cent of jobs in industry, concentrated among unskilled workers.

According to Jean (2001), "The linkage [between international trade and technical progress] means an appreciable upgrade in the assessment of the scale of the effect of international competition on labour markets in the industrialized countries. On the basis of the research we have mentioned, it seems reasonable to say that international trade may account for between 10 to 40 per cent of the increasing inequalities observed over the past 20 years or so in many industrialized countries, in terms of wage or employment. At the same time, the effect is not linked solely to North-South trade: it is also due substantially to trade between the advanced countries."

1.3 Number of jobs concerned by offshoring

Offshored jobs

While the "employment deficit" that international trade has caused in the developed countries is low, is increased offshoring changing the situation?

Estimates of the number of jobs "offshored" are in most cases extrapolations from interviews with the managers of enterprises or press articles. Kirkegaard (2005) therefore takes the data of Bronfenbrenner and Luce (2004) as a starting point: from a review of the relocations announced by the English-speaking news media between January and March 2004, the authors give a figure of 40, 000 jobs offshored from the European Union (EU-25) during this quarter. Kirkegaard multiplies this figure by four to obtain an estimate of the annual number of jobs offshored, i.e. 160, 000, which, in relation to the 116 million private-sector jobs in European Union, represents an annual rate of 0.14 per cent.

Starting from enterprise survey data, covering 80 per cent of foreign direct investment from Germany in the 1990s, Marin (2004) estimates that 90,000 German jobs were lost in Germany between 1990 and 2001 following offshoring to the CEECs, corresponding to 0.26 per cent of total employment in Germany.

Lastly, the Forrester Institute (2002) estimates that 3.3 million service-sector jobs will be offshored from the United States by 2015. In Europe, the Forrester Institute (2004) estimate is 1.16 million service-sector jobs by 2015. Kirkegaard (2005) relates this latter figure to Europe's 56.7 million service-sector jobs and thus obtains an order of magnitude of offshored jobs of 2 per cent.

Net effect: positive?

The effects of offshoring on employment are not just limited to the jobs relocated. Offshoring in practice brings about productivity gains that may pave the way for increased domestic production.

By way of example, two studies have tried to measure the net effect of offshoring on employment in the developed countries:

– drawing on an extensive database covering enterprises in Germany and Austria which invested directly in the CEECs in the 1990s, Marin ([2004) regresses employment in the parent company with respect to several variables, including the amount of wages in the foreign subsidiary. She finds that a wage decrease in the subsidiaries leads to an increase in employment in the parent company, which she interprets as a productivity gain effect for the parent company.

– Amiti-Wei (2004) find, for the United Kingdom, that an increase in the proportion of services imported in all the inputs of a sector does not reduce employment in the sector, but tends in contrast to increase it. They interpret this result in the same way as Marin.

GLOBALIZATION AND ITS IMPACT ON JOBS AND WAGES

BY MICHEL FOUQUIN

1. INTRODUCTION

Opposition to globalization has been steadily increasing since the Seattle summit in 1999. Its critics feel that the process of globalization is dominated by the leaders of the wealthy countries and by major companies and multinational banks, that people are never consulted in any way, and that the developing countries are completely marginalized. The anti-globalization movement, representing "civil society", and the leaders of the developing countries have realized the scale of the challenges presented by globalization and are trying to develop and impose alternative solutions for a fairer and more sustainable globalization. Systematic opposition is gradually giving way to the idea of reform.

This report attempts to define the characteristics of globalization and its impact on employment, separating the problems of the North from those of the developing countries.

2. GLOBALIZATION IS NOT A NEW PHENOMENON, BUT ENTERED A NEW PHASE AFTER 1990

If, like the eminent French historian, Fernand Braudel, globalization can be dated back to the 15th century, and if we accept that the global economic system had already reached its apogee before the World War I (in terms of international capital flows), we have never had the feeling as we have today that every country (except perhaps in the most isolated regions of the world) and every sector (except perhaps traditional public services in the various countries) have been directly and profoundly affected by the phenomenon. Individuals themselves, both as consumers and producers, experience globalization on a daily basis. The scale and depth of globalization are in a way such that its consequences are new: it seems that one single economic system – the market economy system – has to prevail, with one single corresponding political system – democracy – that is supposed to be the culmination of the history of humanity (thus realizing Fukuyama's vision of the end of history). However, past experience has shown that, while the liberal, 19th century form of globalization produced extraordinary wealth, it came at the cost of intolerable poverty, and ultimately ended in World War I, the world recession of 1929 and World War II.

Our aim here is not to give a political assessment of the current phase of globalization, but to look at some of its consequences in terms of jobs and wages.

3. WHAT IS THIS NEW WORLD?

The world of certainty is over

– After World War II, countries equipped themselves with the tools they needed to control the outside world, and large companies devised strategic plans that were meant to guide their policies in the long term.

– After 1973, the world of relatively reliable economic forecasting disappeared. The world before floating exchange rates and oil crises, the world of East versus West (up to 1990), of colonizers and colonized, disappeared once and for all, coming to a full stop with the break-up of the USSR.

– The failure of centralized planning, which had been unable to make the transition from managing shortages and a war economy (USSR) to the mass consumer economy, meant that there was no radical alternative to the market economy system. The latter became the central reference, while the necessary regulations and restrictions on competition are solely intended to make up for times when the market itself cannot guarantee fairness.

– The abandonment of the fixed exchange rate system, which removed strict controls on capital movements, in turn allowed the services sector to be opened up to international investment. Prior to this, services, which accounted for up to 75 per cent of all economic activity in the developed countries, had been protected from international competition.

– The paradox, therefore, is that while the world has become more uniform because of globalization, it has also become less predictable in economic terms. Because the basic parameters of the international economy have become so volatile, governments are being forced to rely on short-term policy adjustments at the risk of losing legitimacy, given that they are supposed to take the long-term view of the future of their countries.

The role of the dominant countries was and still is crucial, but is waning

The role takes various forms, depending on the field in question.

When the United States unilaterally decided to remove the dollar from the gold standard in 1973, it effectively imposed a system of floating exchange rates on the rest of the world, which until then had been linked to the dominant currency by fixed exchange rates. Currencies were all ipso facto either in the floating system or became linked to the dollar. European resistance to floating exchange rates took the form of the European exchange rate mechanism, culminating in the single currency that was supposed to maintain cohesion in the Euro zone and keep open the option of federal development. But the Euro is still floating against the dollar and has not yet succeeded in competing with the dollar as an international currency. Similarly, the monetary coordination projects in Asia still appear to be a very long way from offering an alternative solution to the role of the IMF in the event of a crisis. The same applies to Latin America, where the trend is to dollarize.

When the US decides to deregulate air transport, then telecommunications, then the computer sector, it contributes towards destabilizing those sectors in the rest of the world. Other competing developed countries can only either opt for new, fairly ineffective forms of protection, or follow suit in their own way, sometimes successfully (telecommunications, air transport), sometimes not (computer industry).

Having said that, if the strategy of the dominant country or company did not work for those adopting it, it would quickly be abandoned. The gradual abolition of public monopolies in telecommunications has promoted the extraordinarily rapid growth of the new technologies and a reduction in prices for such services.

Unlike these previous examples, the organization of international trade is the product of international negotiations between sovereign States. Trade globalization is first and foremost a decision freely taken by sovereign States to eliminate obstacles to international trade in goods, services and capital brick by brick, in the name of economic efficiency. The decision to set up the WTO, reached following extremely lengthy negotiations in the Uruguay Round, was the product of an intergovernmental agreement between the GATT member States. It is true that up until Seattle the USA and Europe dominated the negotiations, but current developments in the balance of power within the WTO show that the developing countries, brought together in the G20 for middle-income developing countries and in the G90 for the poorest countries, are able to steer international negotiations so that greater account is taken of their interests.

The impact of globalization on the working of the world economy

Within this new world economic system the effects of economic and political upheavals spread rapidly, and the fact that there are so many potential major crises makes them difficult to predict. The first quality that States, companies and employees need to have is adaptability and flexibility in coping with unexpected crises. Crises tend to come on a very large scale. Take exchange rate crises, for example: the US$ / EURO (or ecu before 1979) rate has been fluctuating between 0.8 and 1.30 since 1979 without the slightest sign of settling at an even value; the most we know is the size of the fluctuation margins. Energy prices (from 1955 to 1968 oil prices in dollars were decided by the major companies and remained entirely fixed), the fall of the Berlin Wall and the opening up of China to the world are all upheavals which challenge the long-term trends in the world economy, but which also consolidate the globalization movement.

Globalization is speeded up by technological progress

However, technological progress is only rarely the origin of globalization. Technology is not the driving force here. It offers new solutions and prospects for new markets, but in itself it is nothing if it does not respond to pre-existing social demand. The integration of the financial markets and in particular the almost total unification of the foreign exchange markets, where currency supply and demand are constantly in balance as if there really was a single global market, are the best example of this. The supply of radically new technologies is progressing at its own rate. The Internet, for example, was invented in response to the US Defense Department's concern to protect its communications systems from nuclear attack, so it is hard to see how this is an effect of globalization. But civil society has seized upon this tool and put it to widespread use, as we all know. The effect of globalization has been the lightning acceleration of the use of a technology designed for national defence. Generally speaking, globalization is greedy for information and communication technologies (ITCs) and finances the R&D needed for their development.

Technological progress produces its own specific effects. In particular, as we will see later, it seems that the growing demand for skilled labour is greater the more widespread ITCs become. In that sense technical progress has a major social impact.

4. GLOBALIZATION REDUCES ABSOLUTE POVERTY

The impact of this new globalization

One of the main features of this new phase of globalization has been the emergence of extremely large developing countries such as China and India.

In 1981, according to World Bank estimates, 40 per cent of the world's population lived on less than one dollar a day (the official poverty line). By 2001,[1] this figure had fallen to 21 per cent. This remarkable progress was the result of vigorous economic growth of 5 per cent per year in 25 developing countries with a total population of three billion people (including China and India). Of those countries, some – Botswana, Chile, China, Korea, Thailand – have even succeeded in doubling their per capita GDP in the space of a decade.

The main reasons for this performance have been progressive economic reforms, an average reduction in customs tariffs of 34 per cent, macroeconomic stability keeping inflation in single figures, the priority given to education, the encouragement of local and foreign investment, and political stability. This has enabled these countries to make the most of their main asset – their sizeable populations – with an explosion in exports of highly labour-intensive manufactured goods. In 1980, only 25 per cent of their exports were manufactured goods, compared with over 80 per cent today. In the services sector there has been a similar development: services used to account for only 9 per cent of their exports, but have now increased to 17 per cent.

Access to the global markets has been made easier by international investment, which has provided wider access to the most advanced production technologies, and by the reduction in transoceanic transport costs. It is now

---

[1] The World Bank indicator is a very rough approximation of reality, but it has the advantage of attempting to give a universal measurement. The absence of reliable surveys in the poorest countries is just one of the problems involved here. However, we can assume that although measuring the level of poverty is difficult, the trend it has followed over time is less debatable.

estimated to cost less to transport freight from Shanghai to Le Havre than from Le Havre to Paris.

It is important to note that the growing and successful involvement of the emerging countries in world trade is more the effect of sound domestic policies than the result of their commercial policy in the strictest sense.

But this is not enough

Alongside the impressive results for some countries, we can see that the majority of countries are continuing to stagnate, and, even worse, some are declining in absolute terms.

Table 1 shows the ILO's estimates for employment, growth and the active population in the major regions of the world. From these figures we can deduce a productivity indicator (relating growth in production to growth in the active population), which allows us to measure how efficiently labour is used. In the long-term improvements in labour productivity are the only thing (apart from oil or other profits) that helps to improve living standards.

Table 1: Employment, growth and productivity (1993-2003)

	Employment Rate		Active Pop.		GDP		Productivity	
	1993	2003	93-03	98-03	93-03	98-03	93-03	98-03
LATIN AMERICA	59.3	59.3	2.3	2.0	2.6	1.4	+ 0.3	− 0.6
EAST ASIA	78.1	76.6	1.3	1.2	8.3	7.1	+ 7.0	+ 5.9
SOUTH-EAST ASIA	68.0	67.1	2.4	2.6	4.4	2.2	+ 2.0	− 0.4
SOUTHERN ASIA	57.0	57.0	2.3	2.3	5.5	5.1	+ 3.2	+ 2.8
MIDDLE EAST	45.4	46.4	3.3	3.1	3.5	3.6	+ 0.2	+ 0.4
SUB-SAHARAN AFRICA	65.6	66.0	2.8	2.7	2.9	2.9	+ 0.1	+ 0.2
EASTERN EUROPE	58.8	53.5	− 0.1	0.7	0.2	3.8	+ 0.3	+ 3.1
INDUSTRIALIZED ECONOMIES	55.4	56.1	0.8	0.6	2.5	2.3	+ 1.7	+ 1.7

Source: ILO, Global Employment Trends, January 2004, and author's own calculations.

Over the period 1998 to 2003 we can see that only three regions recorded good results:

East Asia, with a record 5.9 per cent per year, had the best results;

Eastern Europe, with 3.1 per cent per year, underlined the success of the reforms carried out since the fall of the Berlin Wall and the decision to join the EU;

Southern Asia recorded an increase of 2.8 per cent, largely thanks to the improvement in India's performance.

South-East Asia recorded good performance over a longer period, from 1993 to 2003; the fall-off in its results between 1998 and 2003 is accounted for by the impact of the 1997-1998 financial crisis and, later, the effects of SARS.

The results for Latin America, on the other hand, are declining, while the Middle East and Sub-Saharan Africa are stagnating and losing ground compared with the wealthiest countries, which are continuing to progress at a rate of 1.7 per cent per year, close to the secular rate for the American economy.

According to the World Bank, in 2000 1.2 billion people were living on less than one dollar a day; in the 1990s economic growth in all the developing countries, including the least productive, was only 3.5 per cent per year. In order to halve poverty by 2015, it needs to increase to 5-6 per cent per year.

One of the major problems relating to poverty lies in the inadequate development of Sub-Saharan Africa, despite the fact that it receives much higher levels of aid than Latin America and Asia. The main reasons for its stagnation are the exceptional periods of drought experienced in Zimbabwe, Zambia, Malawi and Swaziland, the fall in the prices of goods exported, the fact that 40 per cent of children do not attend school, and the very rapid increase in the population despite AIDS, which affects 25 million people and reduces life expectancy by ten years in many countries. Numerous armed conflicts affect 20 per cent of inhabitants, and poor governance and corruption among the elite still persist.

For these countries, the World Bank's equation that openness is good for growth, and growth is good for reducing poverty, seems not to work.

One of the main obstacles to the development of exports from Sub-Saharan Africa, apart from the fact that they largely comprise primary products, is the cost of domestic and international transport, in other words the massive shortage of infrastructure, particularly ports. It has been noted (T. Meyer, S. Zignago) that the poorer a country is, the more difficulty it has in accessing markets in the developed countries, despite all the measures taken to make access easier for them. It should also be stressed that some primary products such as cotton or sugar are often subject to measures which discriminate against these countries.

5. FROM POVERTY TO INEQUALITY

Globalization increases inequality

Economic inequalities are increasing on all fronts, and particularly between rich and poor countries: in 1960 the combined GDP of the 20 wealthiest countries was 20 times that of the 20 poorest countries; by 2000, the ratio had doubled from 20 to 40 times.

Globalization tends to discriminate between the poorest countries and the intermediate countries.

If absolute poverty is being reduced in the world, and if this reduction seems too slow and the African problem remains a stumbling block, what is the situation with inequality? As we saw earlier, if we simply compare the two extremes of distribution among all the countries in the world, we can see that the income gap is widening. What would happen if we compared all countries, using per capita GDP measured at constant prices and at a purchasing power parity exchange rate for a given year? And if we looked at each country as an observation? The result is what is known as the indicator of inequality between countries, shown in the graph below. If we want to focus on population, we can also weight the previous result by the population of each country to give the indicator of international inequality.

We can see that the indicator of inequality between countries has increased almost constantly since 1960, whereas the indicator of international inequality fell between 1980 and 2004. How can we reconcile these two results? China is one of the main reasons for this divergence. If we exclude China from the two indices, the first remains practically the same, while the second shows the inverse trend, with international inequality increasing. Of course, neither of these indicators takes account of the effect of internal inequalities, which could still call our diagnosis into question.

Graph No 1: International inequality and inequality between countries

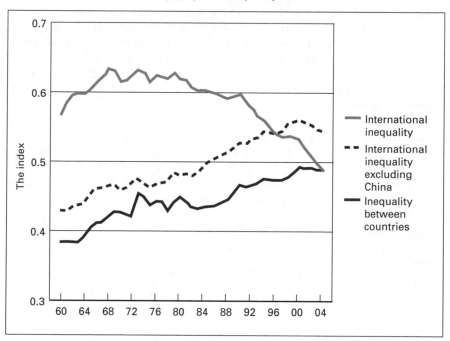

Source: CHELEM-CEPII, March 2005

China as one of the central players in globalization: a successful example, and a threat to the rest of the world?

China's performance since 1978 has been exceptional by any measure, and it is now upsetting the balance of global trade and finance.

China's own statistics may be open to criticism, but at least they give us a sense of scale. So if overall long-term growth is officially put at over 9 per cent per year, we can be sure that growth, correctly measured, is at least 7 per cent,[2] an exceptional rate in itself. The western media are haunted by the image of China as the world's factory, capable of producing the most simple goods ("junk") to the most sophisticated (computers and missiles), with an almost inexhaustible reserve of poorly paid labour, leaving the least skilled workers in the rest of the world in poverty. What is the real position?

China's progress is only socially sustainable if a large number of Chinese benefit from its growth. It appears that real wages (wages deflated by consumer price inflation) are rising at an annual rate of at least 5 per cent. This is, admittedly, less than global growth, but it is far from negligible. This wage trend is also consistent with the development of household consumption, which would not be possible without growth in wages.

Is mass underemployment compatible with growth in wages? The answer is yes, at least for those who have the good fortune to be in the modern sector. On the one hand, we can see that there are certain controls on worker mobility, even if they are being relaxed in order to allow workers from the poorer provinces to go and work in those that are wealthier. But on the other, we know that farmers do not become manual workers, much less skilled manual workers, overnight, which reduces the supply of labour for the modern sector. Only young people are leaving the countryside en masse for cities and supposedly better living conditions.

Having said that, in some factories the working conditions are staggering: at busy times the weekly days off are cancelled and the daily working hours are longer. It seems that this is exceptional, however. Companies working for western clients tend to be rather more restrained, because their western partners do not want to risk condemnation. It should also be pointed out that unacceptable work situations are found even in developed countries.[3]

---

[2] For a critique of China's statistics see Fouquin, Lemoine eds., "The Chinese Economy", Economica, 1998.

[3] "Real wages have continued to decline in NYC garment factories in the 1990s, a trend that started in the 1970s and accelerated in the late 1980s with the passage of IRCA. Wages in Chinatown have fallen about 30 per cent in the past 5 years. The federal minimum wage is US$5.15 per hour and the official UNITE minimum wage is between US$6.72 and US$8.15 per hour. However, garment workers make between US$2 and US$6 per hour and older, slower workers make even less. Nearly all manufacturers pay by piece rate. In turn, many contractors, even in unionized shops, pay their workers by piece rate, which is reduced if the worker produces fast. The piece rate system is known to intensify the pace of work and impose longer hours on workers. Nonpayment of wages and overtime is extremely common in NYC garment factories, and contractors often shut down shop and re-open under another name to escape liability for labor claims.

Hours

In the past two decades, working hours in NYC garment factories have steadily increased, especially in Chinatown and Brooklyn factories. This trend, again, coincides with the passage of IRCA. Many workers work 6 to 7 days a week, 10 to 12-hour days and 80-hour weeks are not unusual. In addition, home-work and child labor have become more common. During busy-order, rush periods, "owners even ask workers to put in 24 hours straight or face lay-off." Officially, workers are entitled to overtime if they work over 40 hours a week (or 35 hours a week if they are unionized) and one day of rest if they work six full days a week. In practice, however, overtime is rarely paid, whether factories are unionized or not."

Testimony by Peter Kwong before the US House Education and the Workforce Committee; 31 March, 1998.

Internal inequality is still growing

The unequal development of the regions in China shows that opening up the economy greatly benefits those regions that have most contact with other countries. The knock-on effect is eventually passed on to the economy as a whole and therefore reduces poverty at national level; but this goes hand in hand with growing inequality.

Agricultural regions are lagging behind urban regions, the provinces of the interior and coastal regions.

While China and India were still cut off from the global economy, the proportion of the population living in rural areas remained more or less stable and dominant. When China and India opened up their economies, this triggered a radical social transformation. In China, the proportion of farm workers in the active population fell from 65 per cent in 1984 to 42 per cent in 2003 (Graph 2).

Graph No. 2: Agricultural, Primary Workers, 1984 – 2003 in China
(% of Total Active Labor)

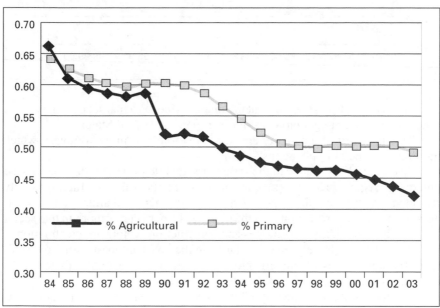

The decline of the rural population is synonymous with economic development. Productivity, or more precisely the annual added value produced per worker, is several times higher in industry than in agriculture. Similarly, underemployment is structural in rural areas – given the seasonal nature of farm work – while it tends to be more occasional in urban areas.

As a result, the wage trend is more favourable in urban areas than in rural areas, producing greater inequality (Graph 3). While China was one of the most

Graph No. 3: Urban and Rural Incomes, 1978 – 2003 in China
(yuans per capita)

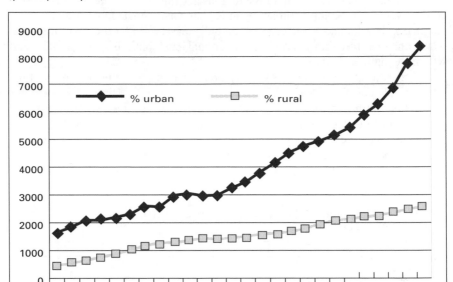

egalitarian countries in the world at the time of Mao, as a market economy it has now become as non-egalitarian as, for instance, the United States.

This urban-rural inequality encourages workers to move to towns, which has dramatic social implications.

Another radical change to the system, the disintegration of the State-owned enterprise sector, has brought mass lay-offs in its wake. In fact, officially recorded industrial employment in China has not increased although China has announced annual growth rates in the order of 15 per cent or more in this sector for over 20 years. Only the services and construction sectors are creating jobs.

Areas that are largely rural and far from the coast are least likely to benefit from the advantages of globalization. In Yunnan, for example, there are 17 million poor, i.e. 50 per cent of the rural population.

Another problem posed by China's more international orientation is its competition with other developing countries, especially in the clothing sector since the abolition of quotas on 1 January 2005. We know that industrialization often begins with the emergence of a clothing export sector. This is true of Bangladesh, Thailand, Sri Lanka, Turkey, Tunisia, Central America, the European countries in transition, etc. China's competitiveness may well put the development bases of certain poor countries at risk. However, countries that are close neighbours of China, such as Viet Nam, can offset their losses of exports to developed countries by gains in relation to the Chinese market, while other Asian and South-East Asian countries rich in raw materials benefit from the rise

Graph No. 4: Rural poor in China in 2002

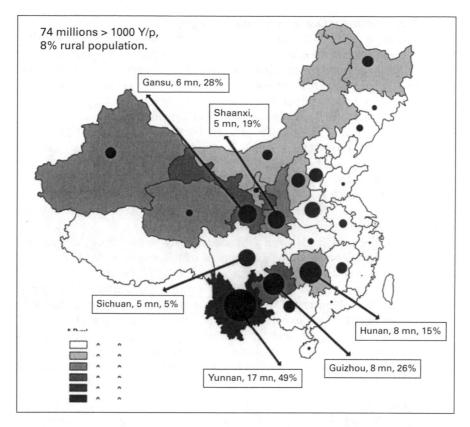

74 millions > 1000 Y/p, 8% rural population.

Gansu, 6 mn, 28%

Shaanxi, 5 mn, 19%

Sichuan, 5 mn, 5%

Hunan, 8 mn, 15%

Yunnan, 17 mn, 49%

Guizhou, 8 mn, 26%

in raw materials prices, although there is the risk of a dangerous downturn in the longer term.

Is India following in the footsteps of China?

In India, which is some 20 years behind China, growth has slowly been improving. For the time being, India's strategy is directed far less at the international market. It is under less constraint here than China because as one of the founder members of the GATT it can apply the GATT rules designed to enable poor countries to protect themselves from international competition. Today it remains one of the most protectionist countries in the world. It is also hesitant to accept foreign investment, which accounts for ten times less than in the case of China.

On the other hand, it has managed to develop high-level data-processing service activities, which are a major source of international revenue. Nonetheless, experts estimate that if India wants to speed up its growth, it will have to open up its economy more widely, encouraged in this respect by its longstanding rivalry with China.

5. INEQUALITY IN DEVELOPED COUNTRIES

Effect of globalization or of technical progress?

Since the mid-1980s there have been signs of a worsening of the distribution of incomes in some developed countries, which is particularly marked in the United States and the United Kingdom. There have been many studies and controversies about the reasons for this inequality. The decline in the living conditions of the least-qualified workers seems to be a general phenomenon in the OECD countries. The unemployment rate among unqualified young people, who are, therefore, also the lowest paid, is two or three times higher than that of those with qualifications (OECD, Employment Outlook); job insecurity has also increased in nearly all developed countries.

Two main reasons for this have been put forward: on the one hand, competition from the emerging countries (i.e. globalization), and on the other, the spread of information technologies, which allow the most routine tasks to be automated and call for higher skills in that area.

In 1997, Feenstra and Hanson published a study on the impact of trade and technology on the comparative development of the wages of American blue-collar and white-collar workers over the period 1972-1990. Their findings confirmed the importance of the technical factor in explaining the widening gap between the two categories of workers: the impact of the technical factor is 50 per cent higher than the impact of trade, assuming endogenous prices.

Another study suggests that competition from emerging countries speeds up productivity rises in the rich countries' most vulnerable sectors, while seeming to have little impact on employment, which tends to run counter to analyses of offshoring.

Is growing inequality inevitable?

Generally speaking, there is no systematic growth of global inequality between employees (measured by the D9/D1 ratio, i.e. by relating the wages of the first decile of the poorest to those of the last decile of the richest) in the developed countries of the old European continent. Graph 5 shows the trend of wage inequality.

At most we see a regular progression of the indicator in the Netherlands, on the basis of what are in fact very low levels of inequality, and a decline in France since 1990. The inequality level is low and tends to remain so in all the Scandinavian countries: a slight rise in Denmark and Sweden, falling in Norway and Finland since 1989. Finally, despite a long period of stagnation, Japan is maintaining a low level of inequality.

In the case of France[4] with its high level of redistribution, we find that the gaps between what are known as primary market incomes are growing while income inequality after redistribution remains stable. Hence we can conclude that redistribution policies can correct the primary effects of technological

---

[4] The following data are taken from the CAE report 'Economic Inequality' by T. Atkinson, M. Glaude and L. Olier.

Graph 5: Trend of the spread of wage rates

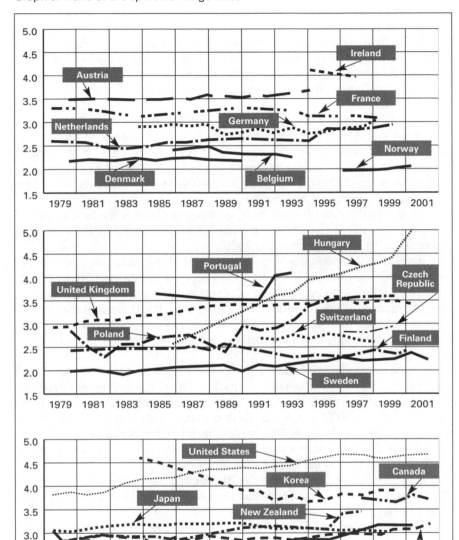

a) The ratio D9/D1 is between gross wages rates at the threshold of the 9th to 10th decile and those at the threshold of the 1st to the second decile. For France and Italy net wages.

b) Data has been estimated for years with no data available for Austria, Canada, Finland, Hungary, Ireland, New Zealand and Portugal.

Source: OECD data base on wages

change or of globalization. Yet it is questionable whether such a policy is sustainable in the long term, and in particular whether the rise or maintenance of high unemployment are sustainable.

An analysis of the trend of primary market incomes in France (active employment and replacement incomes) shows that the inequality between employees' incomes worsened during the 1990s: the income of the first decile fell by 3.2 per cent compared to average income, while that of the richest rose by 0.3 per cent.

In fact the poorest households lost out while the average-income categories were more able to maintain their relative position. This is largely a result of the polarization of households with or without employment. The proportion of saturated households (i.e. two jobs per household) rose from 55 per cent to 62 per cent between 1982 and 1999 while the proportion of households with no job at all rose from 3 per cent to 5 per cent.

After redistribution, the ratio between the upper limit of the first decile and the lower limit of the last decile fell from 4.8 in 1970 to 3.5 in 1984 and then remained stable at 3.4 until the year 2000.

Redistribution increased over the same period, which led to a 50 per cent rise in first decile incomes in the 1970s, 70 per cent in 1990 and 90 per cent in 1996. This reflects the introduction of a number of minimum social benefits: income support (Revenu Minimum d'Insertion, RMI), one-parent family allowance (Allocation de Parent Isolé, API), etc. The various allowances are playing an increasingly important part in redistribution, while the impact of taxes is falling.

At the same time, inequality is tending to grow in the less developed countries or countries in transition such as the Eastern European States. Hungary started out with one of the lowest inequality levels in 1986 (2.5), only to rise to level 5 in the year 2000, which is equivalent to that of the United States. In fact, this rise in inequality began in 1986, before the fall of the Berlin Wall. In Poland, the rise was also quite sharp, but only began in 1990, with the start of transition. It is now higher than in the United Kingdom.

Among other developed countries, the United States easily heads the list. There too, the rise in inequality began very early on, in 1981 if not before, as shown by the graph below.

More extended series relating to the United States show that income inequality fell between 1947 and 1978, while the purchasing power of the minimum wage remained the same between 1960 and 1978. Conversely, the fall in the purchasing power of the minimum wage that began in 1979 and remained very marked until 1989 was accompanied by a sharp growth in inequality.

It may be added that if data on American households' assets are taken into account, not only is the inequality even greater than in the case of income, but the trend of assets substantially worsened this inequality between 1983 and 1989, this time to the detriment in particular of the middle classes.[5]

---

[5] Wolf (2004).

Graph 6: Income inequality among American households and minimum wage

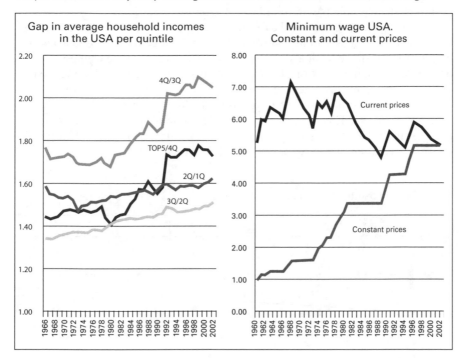

Gap in average household incomes in the USA per quintile

Minimum wage USA. Constant and current prices

Confusion between de-industrialization and relocation

Many media and politicians – Ross Perot in the United States and Jean Arthuis in France, for example – have repeatedly pointed to the risk of emerging countries, which are accused of practicing social dumping, 'siphoning off' developed countries' jobs.

They are usually confusing the process of de-industrialization and the phenomenon of relocation.

Offshoring accounts for only 10 per cent of the fall in the number of industrial workers in France, which is one of the major foreign investors; the decline in industrial jobs is mainly the result of the scale of rises in labour productivity, the slowdown of demand for manufactured goods and the tendency to outsource some jobs that are not the core activities of industrial enterprises, such as accounting and legal services. Jobs counted as industrial then become services jobs, although their purpose is always to contribute to the smooth running of productive activities.

At the same time, competition from Southern countries tends to speed up the endeavour to lower unit costs and to transform productive processes. In particular, some industries can break down production processes into unskilled labour-intensive segments and segments that are more intensive in the use of capital and skilled labour. In that case, the fall in transport costs facilitates trade in intermediate products within industrial groups.

There appear to be few real cases of out-and-out offshoring to major emerging countries such as China. On the one hand most of the rich countries that invest in, for example, China, do so in order to gain access to the Chinese domestic market. Genuine cases of offshoring occur in Hong Kong, where almost all industrial jobs have disappeared, and also in Taiwan and South Korea. In this case, Chinese exports replace the exports of the first generation of newly industrialized countries! This is very marked in the clothing sector (Graph 7) where the growth of the Chinese net surplus reflects the decline of the net surplus of the first generation of newly industrialised countries (NIC1).

Graph No. 7: Position of each clothing market

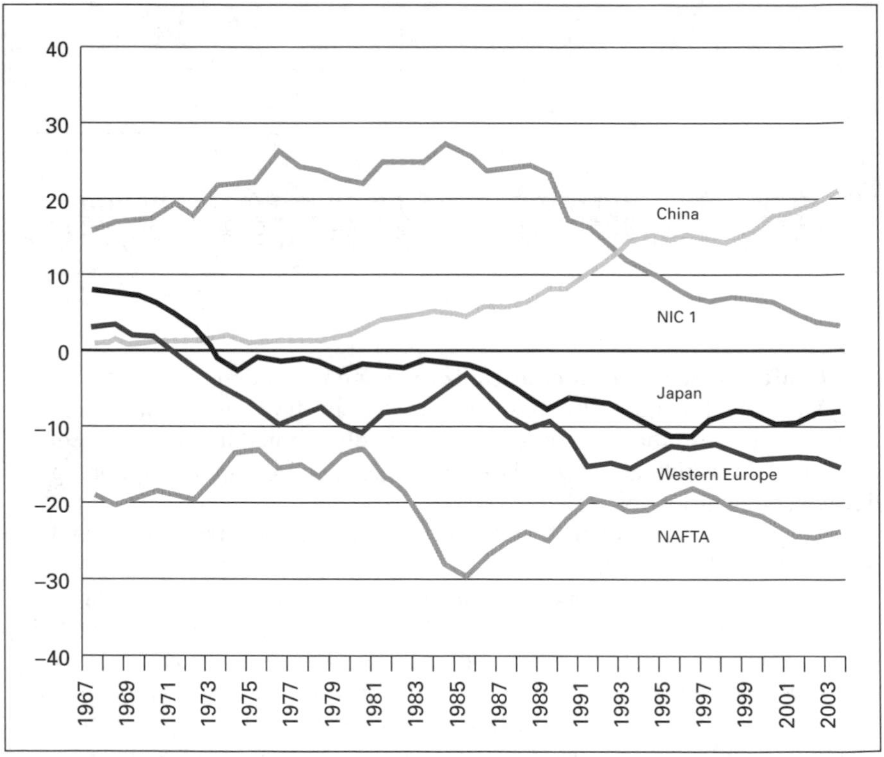

Source: CHELEM – CEPII 2005

A study by the BEA (Bureau of Economic Analysis) (Hanson 2002) concludes that multinationals still have a strong tendency to produce and create jobs in the United States. Multinationals accounted for about 75 per cent of domestic production according to BEA's last survey in 1999, i.e. the same level

Table 2: Activities of US affiliates in various emerging countries

Country	Net jobs added by foreign affiliates in 1989 – 2002	% of sales by foreign affiliates to local customers, 2002
Mexico	514,200	64%
China	269,200	71%
India	83,300	87%
Poland	71,200	72%
Malaysia	52,800	44%

Source: BEA (Bureau of Economic Analysis)

as ten years earlier, in 1989. This finding confirms what has been observed in the French case. However, the ratios relating to American employment show a relative decline, from 79 per cent to 73 per cent, in domestic employment in the parent companies, compared with employment abroad. Moreover, half of the investment went to western Europe, as it did ten years earlier. Investment to the Asian Pacific countries rose from 15 per cent to 17 per cent over the same period.

Horizontal investment has been the dominant form of American firms' investment over the past 50 years, i.e. they have largely preferred access to the local market. In some industries, however, such as electronics, industrial machinery and motor vehicles, where production can be fragmented, there has been a tangible rise in vertical investment. In the particular case of the motor vehicle industry, this is due to relocation to neighbouring Mexico.

This type of investment is highly sensitive to costs, be they wages, taxes or tariffs.

6. INTERNATIONAL MIGRATION

While globalization goes hand in hand with greater freedom of movement of goods and capital, it would seem that, conversely, manpower movement remains highly regulated. These restrictive and protectionist policies are justified by the fear that the inhabitants of poor regions will migrate on a mass scale towards rich areas. The current difficulties facing international negotiations on the liberalization of services illustrate the difficulty of reaching an agreement on these issues, in particular labour mobility. The Bolkenstein directive in Europe is another case in point.

In relation to international migration today, Table 3 shows that it has accelerated very markedly since 1997, according to all the available sources. The only notable exception is Germany, which saw an exceptional increase in migrants at the turn of the 1990s, although it is now reverting to a more normal rate. Japan and Korea, which were traditionally very closed to migration, are becoming increasingly open. In terms of proportion of the working population, the rates vary from 22 per cent for Switzerland to 0.3 per cent for Japan, via 9 per cent for Germany, 5 per cent for France and the United Kingdom, and 3.8 per cent for Italy and Spain.

In high-immigration countries such as the United States, Canada and Australia, immigrant workers account for, respectively, 15 per cent, 20 per cent and 25 per cent.

These immigrants come from countries in transition such as Russia and Ukraine, who go mainly to Germany, and from countries such as China and India, whose destination is Asia and America. At the same time, there is still mass emigration from Latin America towards North America and Spain.

Table 3: Immigration
(Gross immigration flows in thousands; annual averages)

Data drawn from population registers	1993-1997	1998-2002	Data drawn from residence permits or other sources:	1993-1997	1998-2002
Germany	775	654	Australia Permanent entries	84	90
Austria	50	70	Temporary entries	97	235
Belgium	53	65	Canada Permanent entries	227	214
Denmark	22	60	Temporary entries	60	78
Spain	50	265	Korea	44	115
Finland	8	9	United States Permanent entries	829	856
Hungary	14	19	Temporary entries	827	1202
Japan	236	318	France	89	136
Luxembourg	9	11	Greece	n.a.	8
Norway	19	29	Ireland	16	29
Netherlands	75	87	Italy	41	254
Czech Republic	6	15	Mexico Permanent entries	40	40
Sweden	46	41	Temporary entries	27	25
Switzerland	86	88	New Zealand	43	40
			Poland	0	18
			Portugal	6	47
			United Kingdom	215	359
Total	1449	1730	Total above	2645	3746

Source: OECD International Migrations, report 2004

7. CONCLUSION

The emergence of new countries, including the two giants China and India, in the global economy was largely made possible by the open market policies they pursued. This is a very positive trend for the global economy, but other trends do pose problems. A large number of poor countries remain untouched in the long term by the overall progress, and policies of openness are ineffective or inadequate there. Two key factors appear to make the difference. The quality of institutions is one crucial factor: if the market economy is to work, it needs a relatively efficient legal and bureaucratic framework. The other factor is the quality or simply the existence of basic infrastructure. In both cases, the solution is not primarily economic but political: the resolve of rich countries to provide efficient funding and to support political reforms aimed at better control of public activity.

Among the 'successful' countries, there is also the risk of an unfair distribution of created wealth, as also of choosing options that seriously harm the environment.

The developed countries are facing a rise in exclusion. The potential for progress still looks very strong, but the machinery of exclusion looks stronger than ever as a result of the pressure produced by the nature of technical progress and the competition from the newly emerging countries. Safety nets alone cannot combat exclusion. If they are generous they lay too heavy a burden on the only employed members of the working population, thus creating a kind of vicious circle. If they are inadequate, they produce a population of working poor that harks back to an earlier era, restoring credit to the theory of the inevitable impoverishment of the masses.

SERVICE JOBS ON THE MOVE – OFFSHORE OUTSOURCING OF BUSINESS RELATED SERVICES

BY BARBARA GERSTENBERGER
AND R. ALEXANDER ROEHRL

1. INTRODUCTION

In recent months, the debate over 'offshoring', a concept that was introduced only a few years ago, has moved to the top of the political agenda and has received a significant amount of media attention. In 2004, *The Economist* featured 87 articles relating to issues on outsourcing and offshoring, 46 of which focused on the outsourcing of services. A search on Factiva, a database of newspaper clippings, found more than 12,000 articles that made reference to outsourcing or offshoring for Europe (compared with more than 22,000 articles for the US).

This debate has been fuelled by figures outlined in the widely quoted 2002 Forrester Research study, which claimed that by 2015, 3.3 million white-collar American jobs would be transferred 'offshore' to low-cost countries like India.[1] In Europe, the focus has been on the migration of IT-related service jobs to Eastern Europe, and also on increased offshoring to Asia. To date, however, the statistical and methodological basis of such estimates, by private companies, is not entirely satisfactory.[2]

While the relocation of production activities and the associated loss of manufacturing jobs is not a new phenomenon, either in the US or Europe, increased global competition in the high-skilled white-collar job sector has become a major concern in the developed countries. Increased offshore outsourcing has been facilitated by a number of contributing factors: the Internet, infrastructure improvements in developing countries, and a dramatic decrease in data transmission and international transport costs. As a result, service-based companies are now saving costs by hiring workers abroad to fulfill tasks previously carried out in-house. Initially, outsourced tasks tended to be standardized, back-office functions, which often do not require face-to-face

---

[1] In a 2004 follow-up study – based on a survey of 100 companies specializing in business process outsourcing and 1,800 leading IT firms in the US and India – Forrester concluded that offshore outsourcing was accelerating and that 542,000 IT jobs could be lost by 2015, i.e. about 50,000 jobs per year. See John McCarthy, 'Near-Term Growth of Offshoring Accelerating', Forrester Research, May 2004.

[2] Such estimates are similar in nature to estimates provided by these same companies on the potential implications of e-commerce in the mid-1990s.

contact with the customer or other employees. However, more recently, even jobs in highly specialized professions – such as architecture and radiology – are subject to offshore outsourcing, the argument being that all tasks that can be telemediated can, in principle, be outsourced offshore.

How significant is this threat? Although some of the projections paint a bleak picture, it is virtually impossible to find reliable data on the number of jobs that have already been moved offshore; forecasts for the future are even more dubious. One of the problems in finding reliable data is the lack of a clear definition. 'Offshoring', 'outsourcing', 'offshore-outsourcing', 'relocation' are just some of the terms that are being used interchangeably, to describe the same phenomenon, i.e. moving tasks performed in a domestic company across a national border.

The European Restructuring Monitor (ERM),[3] which provides data in the next section of this paper, uses the term 'relocation' to describe restructuring activities that involve a shifting of production or service tasks across a national border, regardless of whether or not the process is of an intra-company nature. The geographical dimension of these shifts is, therefore, the key distinguishing element. The ERM also includes a category for 'outsourcing', which is reserved for the legal dimension of the shifting of tasks, i.e. the supply of tasks by an independent company ('subcontracting') *within* a country.

In a status report on the outsourcing of ICT and related services in the EU – prepared for the European Monitoring Centre on Change (EMCC)[4] in 2004 – this distinction between the geographical and legal dimension of shifting jobs is maintained. Both dimensions are, however, brought together under the term 'offshore-outsourcing'. This term refers to any shifting of tasks, initially performed in-house, across national borders, and these tasks are either performed abroad by affiliates of the parent company or by independent suppliers. The main findings of the status report are presented in the second part of this paper.

The scarcity of reliable statistical data has resulted in an increased demand for 'anecdotal' evidence from companies, on their practical experiences with outsourcing and on their motivations, as well as lessons learned in the process. In March 2005, the EMCC organized a seminar, 'Offshore outsourcing of business services – threat or opportunity?' at which three multinational compa-

---

[3] The European Restructuring Monitor (ERM) is a tool designed to provide a quick overview of restructuring activities in Europe and of their employment consequences. It provides information on individual restructuring cases and allows for the compilation of statistics comparing countries, sectors and types of restructuring. All information is based on the analysis of daily newspapers and the business press, in the EU15 and in three of the new Member States: the Czech Republic, Poland and Slovakia. From April 2005, monitoring will be extended to the EU25 and to Bulgaria and Romania. Further information is available at: http://www.emcc.eurofound.eu.int/erm/

[4] The European Monitoring Centre on Change (EMCC) is part of the European Foundation for the Improvement of Living and Working Conditions, a Dublin-based European agency. Created in 2001, the EMCC's task is to support key actors in the understanding, anticipation and management of change. As well as developing monitoring tools, the EMCC conducts sectoral and case study research, and organizes the exchange of practical experience. The results of EMCC activities are available at: http://www.emcc.eurofound.eu.int

nies and one SME shared their past experiences and strategies for the future. Section Three of this paper presents the highlights of this seminar.

2. DATA FROM ERM

The ERM is an online information database on restructuring activities, reported in national media and through other sources. A network of correspondents covering the 25 EU member States, in addition to Bulgaria and Romania, gathers information on company restructuring cases leading to the creation or loss of at least 100 jobs. Equally, the ERM monitors restructuring cases involving sites of at least 250 employees, where 10 per cent of jobs have been lost due to restructuring. ERM correspondents make contact with these companies, in order to verify the published information and to obtain additional facts. The project has been running since late 2001 and so far the feedback has been positive in relation to coverage, particularly since 2003. One downside, however, has been the necessary foregoing of coverage of small and micro enterprises, as well as of smaller job reductions. Nevertheless, the ERM's approach has the advantage of creating a rich, up-to-date source of case studies, best practices and qualitative information on trends in the various work environments, at a time when there has been a lack of comprehensive national statistical reporting on restructuring. For subsequent policy responses, such qualitative information is even more important than quantitative information.

Data from the ERM indicates that the relocation of production and service activities is certainly not the main cause of job losses in the EU. Graph 1 shows the overall announced job losses (and job creations), recorded by the ERM each month, between January 2003 and February 2005, by type of restructuring in the EU15, the Czech Republic, Slovakia and Poland.

More than 80 per cent of announced job losses (almost 1,080,000 jobs) were due to internal restructuring, stemming from the need to adapt to technological change, from changes in consumer demand and from changes in work organization. In comparison, less than 5 per cent of job losses (around 63,000) were clearly attributable to the company's decision to relocate its production activities. In other words, of the 50,000 jobs lost on average each month, due to restructuring activities in the 18 countries monitored, less than 3,000 were lost due to relocation. These numbers compare well with aggregate top-down estimates, such as those of the EU, which predict that roughly 150,000 new jobs are lost and created each month in the EU25. It is important to note, however, that the smaller firms – which is where most employment is located – are not included in this sample.

It should also be noted that the overall number of job reductions due to restructuring activities increases linearly (rather than exponentially) over the period observed, which implies a roughly constant number of job reductions per month. This is also true in relation to relocation activities, as no significant increase in job losses due to relocation can be observed. The ERM also shows that it is predominantly the larger companies (with an average of 8,800 employees)

Graph 1   Major announced job reductions each month by type of restructuring
(Jan. 2003 – Feb. 2005) (EU15+3)

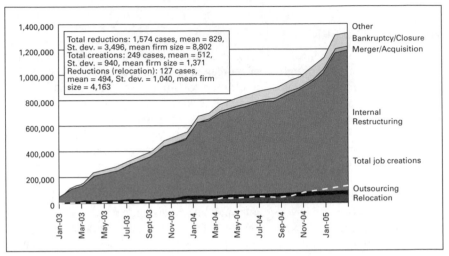

that engage in restructuring activities most actively, and that have the most dramatic employment consequences (an average 800 jobs lost at a time). The average size of companies that relocate is also relatively large (around 4,200 employees). Job creation, as recorded by the ERM, takes place in the smaller of the large companies (with an average of approximately 1,400 employees).[5]

Graph 2 examines the gross employment loss due to restructuring of the different countries, between the first quarters of 2003 and 2005. For the 18 EU countries analysed, gross announced job reductions accounted for 0.6 per cent of total employment, over the relevant time period. Country differences are significant in terms of the extent, nature and effects of restructuring on the labour market. Belgium was the hardest hit with announced gross job losses amounting to over 2 per cent of total employment, and this was followed by the UK and France. Major differences exist between the Benelux countries (Belgium, the Netherlands, Luxembourg). There was no common trend either between the four central, large economies – France, Germany, the UK and Italy. 'Peripheral' countries also show significant differences. Considering that the UK and Germany were the only two EU countries with a net employment loss between 2003 and 2005,[6] it is tempting to make conclusions about the effect of labour market flexibility. However, one should be cautious about making such interpretations, based on short-term data of only two years.

---

[5] In contrast to job reductions, the coverage of job creation cases by the ERM is clearly not as extensive. Good news is simply less newsworthy than bad news. In addition, a large proportion of job creation cases occurs within very small firms with ten or less employees.

[6] See online EUROSTAT Chronos database, April 2005.

Graph 2   Share of announced job reductions (2003 Q1 – 2005 Q1)
in total employment in 2004 Q1

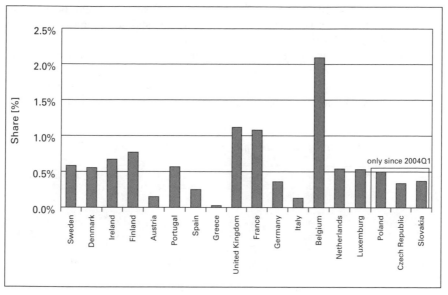

Table 1: Distribution of cases and employment effects, by sector (2003)

Sector	Number of planned job reductions	% Planned job reductions	Number of planned job creations	% Planned job creation	Number of cases	% Cases
Textiles and leather	3008	13.31%	0	0%	8	17.78%
Electrical	2110	9.34%	0	0%	6	13.33%
Post and telecommunications	3344	14.8%	0	0%	5	11.11%
Metal and machinery	1337	5.92%	0	0%	5	11.11%
Motor	990	4.38%	0	0%	4	8.89%
Financial services	7350	32.52%	0	0%	3	6.67%
Chemical	240	1.06%	0	0%	3	6.67%
Glass and cement	225	1%	0	0%	2	4.44%
Food, beverage and tobacco	650	2.88%	60	100%	2	4.44%
Hair and beauty care	1200	5.31%	0	0%	1	2.22%
Extractive industries	350	1.55%	0	0%	1	2.22%
Energy	976	4.32%	0	0%	1	2.22%
Construction and woodworking	90	0.4%	0	0%	1	2.22%
Commerce	42	0.19%	0	0%	1	2.22%
Information technology	90	0.4%	0	0%	1	2.22%
Consultancy business services	600	2.65%	0	0%	1	2.22%

Looking at the distribution of restructuring cases and employment effects by sector, it is interesting to note the high number of job losses in the financial services sector. In Table 2, the 7,350 announced job losses outlined for financial services was the result of a decision by three UK based companies – Norwich Union, HSBC and Prudential – to move their call-centre and back-office functions to India, Malaysia and China. It should be noted, however, that the majority of relocation cases have occurred in the manufacturing sector.

A comparison between figures for 2003 and 2004 shows that extrapolating trends, observed in one year (or one quarter), can be somewhat misleading.

Table 2: Distribution of cases and employment effects, by sector (2004)

Sector	Number of planned job reductions	% Planned job reductions	Number of planned job creations	% Planned job creation	Number of cases	% Cases
Metal and machinery	3835	16.49%	350	40.18%	13	16.88%
Motor	2810	12.08%	100	11.48%	12	15.58%
Electrical	2373	10.2%	0	0%	10	12.99%
Post and telecommunications	1687	7.25%	221	25.37%	10	12.99%
Food, beverage and tobacco	1653	7.11%	0	0%	7	9.09%
Chemical	1629	7%	0	0%	7	9.09%
Textiles and leather	1503	6.46%	0	0%	5	6.49%
Commerce	115	0.49%	200	22.96%	2	2.6%
Health and social work	550	2.36%	0	0%	2	2.6%
Glass and cement	3000	12.9%	0	0%	2	2.6%
Transport and storage	200	0.86%	0	0%	1	1.3%
Performing arts	150	0.64%	0	0%	1	1.3%
Financial services	3300	14.19%	0	0%	1	1.3%
Consultancy business services	210	0.9%	0	0%	1	1.3%
Information technology	70	0.3%	0	0%	1	1.3%
Construction and woodworking	101	0.43%	0	0%	1	1.3%
Pulp and paper	76	0.33%	0	0%	1	1.3%

In 2004, the number of job losses in the financial services sector was much lower at 3,300. Nevertheless, these job losses are significant, particularly as they relate to one specific case – Norwich Union in the UK – where job losses were announced after the company decided to move more of its jobs offshore.

Overall figures for 2004 confirm that even though relocation is not necessarily the number one cause of job loss in Europe, the number of relocation cases has increased significantly, from 45 in 2003 to 77 in 2004.

Also, a word of caution in relation to the broad category of 'internal restructuring': as other organizations that monitor newspaper reports on company

Graph 3 Quarterly job reductions due to offshore outsourcing by sector (EU15+3)

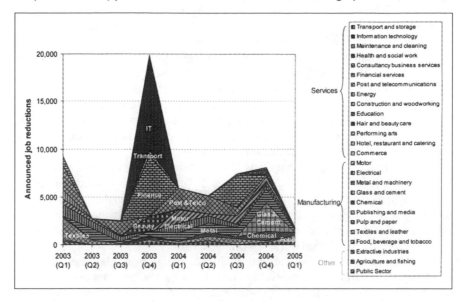

restructuring have confirmed, companies are becoming more circumspect about announcing their relocation plans. As Bronfenbrenner/Luce claim in the Multinational Monitor, '…corporations that lay off workers in the United States and expand operations in India may try to deny or obscure a direct link between the two events'.[7] The same reluctance to unveil offshoring plans, due to the harm that it could cause to the company's public image, can be assumed for European companies. It is therefore quite likely that a number of the restructuring cases recorded in the ERM, which involve the relocation of jobs, are actually cloaked under the term 'internal restructuring'.

Graph 3 shows the quarterly time profile of announced job reductions due to offshore outsourcing. The upper areas depict the job reductions in the services and the lower areas manufacturing sectors. Due to the small number of larger cases, there are significant fluctuations in the amount of job reductions.

The significant number of cases recorded by the ERM, involving the relocation of service jobs, has been a sufficient motivation to examine in greater detail the issue of outsourcing, at a sectoral and company level.

3. OUTSOURCING OF ICT AND RELATED SERVICES IN THE EU

The biggest challenge in accurately analysing the current situation, and in anticipating future developments, is the lack of reliable statistical indicators on offshore outsourcing of services. Trade statistics are problematic, since it is

---

[7] http://www.thirdworldtraveler.com/Corporate_Welfare/Offshoring.html.

much more difficult to track the movement of intangible goods across borders. Also, intra-firm trade is not reported separately/explicitly in most official trade statistics, which makes it difficult to distinguish between movement of services within an organization and between companies.

One alternative approach is to look at the employment statistics, in particular, of sectors that provide a good indication of present and future trends.

The status report, 'Outsourcing of ICT and related services in the EU', draws on a body of existing research carried out over more than two decades, addressing 'offshore information processing', 'trans-border teleworking', 'the new global division of labour in information services' and other related issues, all essentially dealing with the same phenomenon.

The approach of the authors was to first identify which service jobs were, in principle, 'offshorable'. The authors used data from the UK Labour Force Survey which, since 1996, has been collecting data on whether people work remotely using a telecommunications link and a computer, as part of their job. By definition, the tasks performed remotely can be telemediated and can, therefore, in principle be carried out in an offshore office.

Using the NACE classification system, the two sectors identified as being most at risk of offshore outsourcing (or providing the best opportunities for outsourcing) were NACE 72 'computer and related activities' (data processing, hardware and software consultancy, and other computer-related activities), and NACE 74 'other business activities' (call-centre activities, secretarial, translation, accounting, auditing, tax consultancy, etc). Using EUROSTAT data, the authors of the report subsequently examined the distribution of employment in these sectors and found that they account for 1.3 per cent (NACE 72) and 6.3 per cent (NACE 74) of European employment. In the enlarged EU (excluding Poland), both sectors together employ 13.7 million workers.

An analysis of employment trends in these sectors shows no evidence of net job loss between 2000 and 2003, despite significant shifts in employment. On the contrary, with the exception of Denmark, there was a net growth in employment in these sectors, in all member States, with no job losses recorded in the 'other business activities' sector in any of the States. Employment growth for this sector was much higher in the new member States: in the Czech Republic, employment in the sector grew by 90 per cent during the period 2000–2003. This suggests that there is a considerable amount of relocation of jobs to the EU.

A partial explanation for this positive picture is Europe's language diversity and the wage differentials within Europe, which offer a wider range of options for companies planning to relocate their services. Also, many jobs have already been outsourced to Europe from the US and other parts of the world. The growth of the two sectors – ICT and other business activities – is a reflection of the general trend to outsource (i.e. subcontract) ICT and ICT enabled functions; this in turn has resulted in a general employment shift to these sectors from other parts of the economy and, increasingly, from the public sector.

Does this mean that offshore outsourcing does not pose a threat to employment in Europe? Based on information collected by the ERM, it is clear that offshore outsourcing has frequently resulted in individual cases of quite dramatic job cuts within a particular company. To date, it is still rare for offshore outsourcing to be associated with actual redundancies, as job losses tend to be seen in the context of normal workforce fluctuations. However, it is quite clear that many previously secure jobs have come under greater threat, due to the possibility of offshore outsourcing. Also, the organizational change is likely to have an impact on skill requirements (language and communication skills, for example) thus creating a risk of exclusion among those who lack up-to-date skills.

Lastly, even though offshore outsourcing is increasingly becoming a more common business practice, it is still associated with a high risk of failure, and the potential benefits tend to differ between companies and countries. A comparison of US and German cost savings shows that, on average, the US economy gains US$1.12 to US$1.14 for every US$1 of corporate spending transferred to India, while Germany loses EUR 0.2 for every Euro of corporate spending transferred to India or eastern Europe. The authors of the EMCC status report attribute this difference to potentially higher coordinating costs for German companies, due to greater language and cultural differences, and lower re-employability of German workers.

To understand the risks associated with offshore outsourcing, it is necessary to learn more about companies' strategies, their motivation for outsourcing service activities and their past experiences. In a seminar organized for members of its Company Network in March 2005, the EMCC explored corporate strategies related to the offshore outsourcing of business services. ABN AMRO (The Netherlands), Elcoteq – Personalijuht (Estonia), T-Systems (Austria) and Siemens Business Services (SBS, Ireland) presented their company strategies and assessed their experiences with offshore outsourcing. The following section provides an overview of the highlights of this seminar.[8]

4. OFFSHORE OUTSOURCING OF BUSINESS SERVICES – THREAT OR OPPORTUNITY?

Clearly, the decision to outsource or offshore business activities is not taken lightly. It is generally viewed as a long-term process with numerous obstacles and decision points along the way. The relocation of jobs is not always an explicit strategy, but may form part of a wider company restructuring process, set up for efficiency reasons and taking into account the global nature of modern markets.

Such company restructuring may involve the concentration of business activities in shared services centres – specialized profit units that serve the whole firm and that may eventually provide the same services to external companies. The shift to a shared services unit implies a critical assessment of all organiza-

---

[8] A full seminar report and the four case examples are available on the EMCC Portal http://www.emcc.eurofound.eu.int/exchange.htm

tional aspects, including staff availability, skills, costs, ICT infrastructure and working procedures. This assessment may lead to the conclusion that it is more cost-effective to outsource part or all of the work. Once that decision is made, the question arises to whom and where the work will be outsourced. In a globalized economy, where a large part of the world has become a market place for trading of business-related services, remote locations increasingly present themselves as viable destinations.

Mix-and-match global sourcing

Business service providers like SBS and T-Systems offer tailor-made solutions to companies wishing to outsource. This may involve routine programming jobs or an entire business process, encompassing technical infrastructure and management. When designing business solutions for their customers, service suppliers are constantly searching for the best deal for each component of that service. Because the capacity and knowledge for any specific activity is now available in several places, the service provider has more flexibility to combine different capacities. At the same time, risks can be spread.

Globally organized service providers 'mix and match' the available service delivery capacities from different countries, both inside and outside their own group, and combine them in a variety of ways, to deliver the required service package. Each solution will have its unique costs, benefits and employment impacts. A client company might, for instance, require employees working at the 'end of the chain' to be in direct face-to-face contact, or require that part of the work should remain 'in Europe'. Alternatively, they might demand particular highly specialized staff, even at a higher price, or conversely ask for the service at the lowest possible cost, regardless of who provides it. The skills base, wage and non-wage costs, language skills, time zone, culture and stability of the region are among the factors most often taken into account when preparing a customer-specific package.

Being organized on a global scale themselves, such service providers are important catalysts for the overall globalization of the economy. Needless to say, the 'delivery capacities', including those of the service providers themselves, are in permanent competition – particularly those companies that are both providers and customers of business services.

Follow the customer, follow the sun

Another major reason for service providers to offshore is the decision by client companies to reorganize on a global scale and to require the same flexibility from its subcontractors. The global relocation of production activities is not a new strategy. Because products and services are increasingly intertwined, however, moving one often implies moving the other, despite the ability of ICT to bridge time and distance. When companies outsource much of their business services, the relocation of their production activities implies that the related service must also be mobile: customers go global and service providers must follow suit.

T-Systems customer-oriented offshoring strategies:

The 'follow the sun' principle, enabling 24-hour service provision, has led to the operation of network control centres in Chicago, Frankfurt and Tokyo.

The 'follow the customer' principle involves following big customers to destinations such as China, as well as operating high-cost plants in most western European countries, where customers are located. Their presence in high-cost locations is also related to the need for special skills or the importance of corporate responsibility.

Software development is offshored to St. Petersburg in Russia because of wage costs and available skills. St. Petersburg is regarded as a nearshore facility, since staff can be flown in on demand within a couple of hours. Many customers located in Europe have to be supplied locally. As a result, only about 35 per cent of total software programming is offshored to India.

Offshore outsourcing has therefore become a core strategy for large service providers. Typically, the services they offer tend to 'move up the value chain', starting with delineated and standardized tasks, and gradually including more activities, until a full business process is provided. The provider of this package thus becomes a strategic partner for the outsourcing company. This sometimes triggers a further trend of 'reverse offshoring'. Such a trend can be illustrated by some of the larger Indian service providers, who started off as subcontractors in routine software programming and now operate as full business process providers, and who are sourcing globally themselves, including moving some activities 'back' into Europe.

It is clear that the growing interconnectedness of companies, resulting from the trend of outsourcing business services, accelerates the globalization of the economy. In a sense, offshore outsourcing is a self-triggering process for both the customer and the provider.

Large and global, or small and local?

Of course, more 'traditional' corporate logistics still apply to the outsourcing of business services. A fast growth in a company's activities can encourage outsourcing, as internal capacity becomes limited and major investment cannot be justified. Some activities are simply better and more cheaply provided by specialized firms that possess the necessary infrastructure and skills. This is not a new phenomenon. At national level, this economic mechanism has always been important for employment growth and that is why the current increase in outsourcing is not, by definition, a threat to national labour markets. On the contrary, it may offer opportunities for local endogenous business growth.

The provision of business services is not necessarily a monopoly of larger players. Local, small firms can offer the advantages of proximity and local contacts, as regular face-to-face contact, required to fine-tune procedures, solve problems or share knowledge, is often neglected when going offshore. Therein lies the strength of local players. The outsourcing of HRM functions by Elcoteq and OÜ Personalijuht, for example, illustrates how such processes may require considerable cooperation and communication to build up trust and mutual understanding.

In the case of Elcoteq Tallinn, the HR manager reports that a discussion about outsourcing at an HR conference inspired them to look for an external solution, to address the impact of rapid company expansion. For OÜ Personalijuht, the contract with Elcoteq demonstrated that there was a mature market for outsourced HRM activities, providing the opportunity for further international growth. This has resulted in a decision by OÜ Personalijuht to open a subsidiary in Lithuania. The next step in their growth strategy will be to develop a new payroll administration service in Finland.

The outsourcing of highly specialized or non-standard work, requiring frequent fine-tuning, creates a niche for smaller players, when the market is mature for both the outsourcing company and the service provider. For the smaller local service provider, this may provide the initial impetus for going global.

Social dialogue
In relation to the key success factors of offshore outsourcing, there is general agreement about the importance of involving stakeholders and informing employees and their representatives about the plan and processes involved. Unfortunately, this is sometimes as far as the agreement goes. Fully respecting the rules and principles of social dialogue requires the involvement of employee representatives and/or trade unions from the beginning, not only by providing information about plans and decisions, but also through consultation and negotiation, in order to agree on strategies to manage the impact on employees.

In some cases, employers and unions have reached agreement on how to prevent lay-offs, promote re-skilling, reorientation and internal mobility of redundant employees and to compensate for financial losses. The so-called 'employability agreement' of ABN AMRO provides an example of such an agreement.

Agreements on how to manage the impact of company restructuring on employees are rarely straightforward. In relation to offshore outsourcing, there are a number of difficulties. Firstly, decisions are not always taken in the country where the majority of jobs are affected. National boundaries may also limit employment reintegration schemes. Also, although unions may not oppose outsourcing, as reallocation might be possible at national level due to outplacement initiatives, problems may arise if there is a general reduction in jobs within a specific occupational group. If an entire department or business function is outsourced, internal reallocation may not be possible because there are no jobs with similar competency profiles remaining. In ABN AMRO, there is a fear that finding employment for workers in future reorganization or offshoring projects will become increasingly difficult. Reorientation is also easier for younger

The basic aim of ABN AMRO's employability policy is to prepare employees for future developments, by optimizing their employability. This is regarded as a shared responsibility of the employee and the bank. The employability agreement covers career development (a personal development plan, offering training and educational programmes and, if needed, guidance via the employability centre) and reorganization (a selection and matching or assignment procedure, and guidance via the employability centre in finding a new function, and financial arrangements). In the employability centre, an employee is granted 18 months to find a new position within the bank. Failure to do so leads to termination with financial compensation. The longer somebody stays in the employability centre, the lower the financial compensation will be in the event of subsequent dismissal. The employability agreement includes a 'right to return' for an outsourced employee, exactly two years after their transfer. In the two outsourcing projects undertaken under this agreement, about 10 per cent of affected employees made use of this right. Many of these were older workers.

employees who can find jobs on the external labour market but may be harder for older workers.

To anticipate the impact of restructuring and to manage change effectively, the early involvement of employees is seen as crucial: to prepare reorientation, to prevent the atmosphere deteriorating and to avoid resignations by key employees who feel that their jobs are at risk. Generally, it is the most highly qualified who leave on their own initiative when job insecurity grows, and this can have damaging effects for all concerned.

5. OUTLOOK

Looking back, offshore outsourcing of business-related services is only the latest of a number of interrelated processes, directly linked to technology change, which in turn have led to changes in the location of production. The sum of these processes is often referred to as 'globalization'. The late 19th and early 20th century witnessed an earlier wave of globalization, which was characterized by rapid increases in capital flow and increased trade in raw materials and finished products (such as textiles). The current wave of globalization,[9] which began after World War II and which seemed to accelerate from the 1980s, has witnessed large increases in intra-product trade, capital flows and, increasingly, trade in services.[10] Common causes for these processes include continuing technological improvements, particularly in transport and communications, which have in turn altered the world's economic geography. As in the past, special interest groups representing those most affected by this change have tended to lobby for

---

[9] See, for example, the work on economic geography by Overman, Venables and Krugman, and on production systems by Feenstra, Hanson, Choi, Kimura and others.

[10] See Amiti and Wei: *Fear of service outsourcing: Is it justified?*, NBER 10808, September 2004, http://www.nber.org/papers/w10808.

political constraints on the cross-border flows mentioned above, particularly during times of rapid technological change.[11] In the past, such lobbying attempts have been successful, whenever the costs and benefits of globalization were too unevenly distributed; hence the recurring 'waves' of globalization.

What does economic history then tell us about the nature of current offshore outsourcing of business-related services?

Firstly, it is likely that government policies regarding offshore outsourcing of business-related services will have far-reaching consequences that will go far beyond the economic issue at hand.[12] The major processes of economic globalization are closely linked. For example, a significant part of offshore outsourcing of services is directly or indirectly linked to similar outsourcing of manufacturing services. One might argue that without these links, the well-known 'international fragmented production systems' would never have emerged to the extent that they did, on a regional and global level. In general, although the current nature and extent of globalization is not necessarily inevitable, the underlying technological changes could continue regardless. Such technological changes have the potential to ever increase the overall potential benefits of increased globalization.

Secondly, at any point in time and space, there appears to be an 'optimal' level and type of offshore and onshore outsourcing. Once political constraints are lifted, an 'adjustment process' begins towards the new equilibrium. 'Over or under-shooting' of this equilibrium can result in huge costs and employment effects. Signs of this are already visible in relation to intra-product trade. Although the share of intra-product trade has only reached about one-third of world trade in goods, there are already signs of saturation in relation to offshoring processes. Japanese multinationals, for example, have recently started to expand their domestic manufacturing capacity once again. In contrast, offshore outsourcing of services is still only at the very beginning of its adjustment process worldwide. Therefore, it is futile to extrapolate from today's trends what will happen in future decades, given various policy options. In particular, it is difficult, if not impossible, to forecast the exact 'saturation point' of the current adjustment process. Nevertheless, there are good reasons to expect that, under any conceivable circumstances, offshoring will affect only a small share of jobs in business-related services (which currently account for about 55 per cent of total employment in Europe). Recent studies on offshoring of services suggest the persistence of limitations, in the form of indirect transaction costs, and the continuing importance of geographical and human proximity.[13] Never-

---

[11] See, for example, the work on the history of economic globalization by Williamson, O'Rourke, Spree and others. In particular: Williamson: *Globalization, Convergence and History*, Journal of Economic History, Vol. 56, No.2, 1996.

[12] Also possibly beyond the economic issues.

[13] For example, a 2005 ZEW showed that, while 87% of companies have outsourced IT services, only 6% of them used offshore outsourcing. The remaining 94% used onshore outsourcing.
See http://www.zew.de/de/topthemen/meldung_show.php?LFDNR=443& KATEGORIE=2.

theless, the expected adjustment period could be potentially shorter than in the case of goods trading, because of lower capital intensity and the fact that political constraints have only recently intensified the process. This rapid pace may pose a formidable challenge for decision-makers. The current unprecedented media-attention given to the trend to offshoring, and the exaggeration of this trend by both employers and employees, reflects somewhat how social partners have used this issue as a bargaining tool, rather than an unprecedented growth in offshoring.

Thirdly, while the overall long-term benefits of trade in business-related services is undeniable, the costs and benefits are not equally shared by all groups of people, regions or countries. As labour is the least mobile aspect of production in the early 21st century – mainly because of political constraints – it is also expected to lose or gain the most in the process.[14] Increasing competition among countries and regions, to attract investment by global multinational companies (see, for example, the recent introduction of the flat tax in some eastern European countries) has led to concerns about a race 'below the bottom' in this 'new systems competition;[15] as a result, there may not be sufficient capital to pay for related infrastructural costs, and regulatory systems could, as a result, be eroded. Efforts such as those of the ERM, need to be strengthened, therefore, in order to deliver the hard facts that are lacking in relation to these issues.

Fourthly, in recent years, smaller countries and those on the 'periphery'[16] have tended to grow much faster than the larger 'core' economies. This is particularly true for some of the more peripheral European countries[17] and it mirrors a similar phenomenon that took place during the previous wave of globalization in the late 19th and early 20th century. This is partly due to the fact that peripheral economies can suddenly benefit from unfettered access to larger 'core' markets, which were previously more restricted. Such a straightforward insight debunks a popular myth that the recent success of 'peripheral' countries is direct evidence of the fact that certain labour market policies, promoting greater deregulation, will lead to successful economic results similar to those of 'core' countries.[18] Since the 1990s, Europe has also increasingly experienced a shift in skills-intensive production, particularly in business-related services, from the 'core' countries to Eastern Europe[19] and Asia. Again, this is not surprising, as

---

[14] Based on the assumption of continued migration restrictions.

[15] See Hans-Werner Sinn: The New Systems Competition, NBER 8747, 2002, also at: http://www.nber.org/papers/w8747 .

[16] The term 'periphery' is used in various ways. For the purpose of this paper, the 'periphery' simply refers to economies at a significant geographic distance from the markets of the most technologically advanced countries, i.e. larger 'core' economies.

[17] For example, Sweden, Finland, Ireland and Spain.

[18] This is not to say that flexibility would not lead to better results. Yet, deregulation of labour markets is not necessarily the key to improvement, as reflected by the huge labour market differences between countries such as Ireland, Finland and Slovakia.

[19] See Dalia, Marin: *A Nation of poets and thinkers – less so with Eastern enlargement?* University of Munich, Paper 2004–06, April 2004, available at: http://epub.ub.uni-muenchen.de/archive/00000329/01/EasternEnlargement-munich_discussion_papers.pdf.

companies in these core countries tend to offshore production that is less transport-intensive. It should be noted, of course, that the definition of what constitutes 'the economic periphery' naturally changes over time. Thus, a long-term view of the role of developing countries and economies in transition is important.

In addition, the work of the EMCC[20] (ERM, 2004) and others has clearly shown that, in terms of job losses and job creation, offshore outsourcing currently represents only a tiny proportion of more general company restructuring processes (including bankruptcies) that lead to higher productivity, long-term economic growth and new jobs. It is also against this more general background of restructuring that any policy action on offshoring should be seen.

Finally, there is a need for a clearer and more coherent vision on how to tackle the issue of offshoring of business-related services, by companies, social partners, local and national governments, as well as by international organizations. For the reasons already outlined, this vision should encompass a more realistic view of broader restructuring processes and globalization. If time scales and the geographic dimension are explicitly taken into account, much could be learned about the prospects for labour markets, working conditions and the 'European social model', under the various policy options available. Further lessons could be also be learned, at the international level, from the success and failures of subnational regional development policies and institutions.

Is there a single set of 'optimal' policy options for each type of stakeholder that should be pursued by all countries? The trend to increasing international specialization through offshore outsourcing suggests that there is not one particular set of 'optimal' options. Instead, it appears that every stakeholder – whether a company, organization or government – will need to find its own optimal model. For example, there is no doubt that countries like France, Germany or Japan will have higher labour costs than China and many other countries, for at least another generation. Therefore, strategies that focus, for example, mainly on reducing direct and indirect labour costs to make industry more 'competitive' in these countries may be doomed from the outset.[21]

---

[20] See also other related EMCC products at: http://www.emcc.eurofound.eu.int/

[21] In this respect, lessons could be learnt, at international level, from the successes and failures of sub-national regional development policies and institutions.

TRADE, EMPLOYMENT AND OUTSOURCING: SOME OBSERVATIONS ON US – CHINA ECONOMIC RELATIONS

BY THOMAS I. PALLEY

1. INTRODUCTION

This paper examines the trade, employment and outsourcing dimensions of the current US–China economic relationship. The paper begins with an analysis of the US trade deficit and China's contribution to this deficit. Thereafter, the paper turns to an examination of the recent job creation record in the US economy, with a particular focus on manufacturing. The enormous trade deficit and the recent poor job creation record frame the relationship with China.

The paper reports estimates of the number of US jobs lost as a result of the trade deficit with China. Other US concerns include (i) the impact of exchange rates and the trade deficit on investment spending, (ii) the impact of global labour arbitrage on wages, (iii) the impact of offshoring R&D activities on future US technological leadership and standards of living, and (iv) future prospects for offshoring previously non-tradable services.

These problems link with the current global economic model that emphasizes export-led growth and has the US playing the role of global buyer and borrower of last resort. This model is probably unsustainable. US and Chinese policymakers must initiate a transition to a new economic model or risk a damaging economic downturn when the contradictions of the current model surface. China must revalue upward its exchange rate against the dollar as part of the global process of restoring sustainability to the US current account. China must also shift away from its existing model of export-led growth to a model of domestic demand-led growth. This will require macroeconomic domestic expenditure switching policies and policies that address low wages and growing inequality of income in China.

2. OVERVIEW: US CONCERNS REGARDING THE ECONOMIC RELATIONSHIP WITH CHINA

US–China economic relations are currently dominated by the massive US goods trade deficit with China. Concern over the deficit has been amplified by the feeble private sector employment recovery in the wake of the recession of 2001. Especially problematic has been the employment performance of manufacturing, which entered recession before the national economy (July 2000 vs. March

2001) and continued losing jobs through to February 2004. Moreover, since February 2004 there has been minimal job expansion in manufacturing.

The trade deficit with China is widely viewed as a significant factor in manufacturing's poor employment performance. In addition to these short-term job concerns there are growing concerns about the long-term implications of China's economic development strategy for future US standards of living and the international competitiveness of the US economy. These long-term concerns relate to (i) the shift of US manufacturing R&D activity, (ii) displacement of manufacturing investment spending from the US to China, and (iii) offshore outsourcing that has companies shedding activities in the US and shifting them to China.

3. THE US TRADE DEFICIT

The US goods and services trade deficit rose to a record US$617.5 billion in 2004, and equalled 5.6 per cent of GDP. The overall deficit increased by 24.4 per cent. Imports grew by 16.3 per cent while exports grew by 12.3 per cent. Table 1 provides a breakdown of the deficit in terms of goods and services exports and imports. The driving factor behind the growing trade deficit is the goods trade deficit, which increased 21.7 per cent in 2004. The US runs a surplus in services trade, but this surplus is small relative to the goods trade deficit. Moreover, the surplus in services trade fell 4.9 per cent in 2004, continuing a trend that began in 1998. In 2004, imports of both goods and services grew faster than exports of goods and services. The US goods trade deficit now equals almost 6 per cent of GDP, and many analysts believe it to be unsustainable at this level.

A geographical decomposition of the trade deficit shows that the US is running deficits with every major region of the global economy, and all of these regional deficits worsened in 2004. Table 2 provides a regional breakdown of the deficit. The goods trade deficit with China is especially problematic as it now constitutes the single largest component of the deficit (24.9 per cent), and it also grew at a far faster rate (30.5 per cent) than the overall goods deficit (22.4 per cent) in 2004. The goods trade deficit with China increased by US$37.9 billion in 2004. China therefore accounted for almost one-third (31.8 per cent) of the worsening of the overall goods trade deficit, which increased by US$119.1 billion.

The China deficit should be viewed as part of a broader Pacific Rim problem, with the deficit with Pacific Rim countries representing 43.4 per cent of the overall goods trade deficit. China represents 57.3 per cent of the Pacific Rim trade deficit, and the increase in the deficit with China in 2004 accounted for 72.9 per cent of the increase in the deficit with Pacific Rim countries. The bottom line is that the US has trade deficits with all major regions of the globe. The problem is particularly acute with regard to Pacific Rim countries. China is the single largest contributor to the deficit, and its contribution is growing fast.

A final US trade concern with China is the deficit in advanced technology products (ATP) trade. ATP trade is widely viewed as an indicator of leading edge

Table 1. US trade deficit decomposed into exports and imports of goods and services.

	2004 (US$ billions)	2003 (US$ billions)	per cent change 2003-04
Exports of goods	807.6	713.1	13.3
Exports of services	338.6	307.4	10.1
Total Exports	**1,146.1**	**1,020.5**	**12.3**
Imports of goods	1,473.8	1,260.7	16.9
Imports of services	290.1	256.3	13.2
Total Imports	**1,763.8**	**1,517.0**	**16.3**
Goods trade balance	**−666.2**	**−547.6**	**21.7**
Services trade balance	**48.5**	**51.0**	**−4.9**
Goods & Services trade balance	**−617.7**	**−496.5**	**24.4**

Source: United States Department of Commerce and author's calculations.

Table 2. Regional composition of the US goods trade deficit

	2004 Goods Trade Balance (US$ billions)	Percent share	2003 Goods Trade Balance (US$ billions)	Percent share	Percent Change 2003-4
Total (balance of payments basis)	**−666.2**		**−547.6**		**21.7**
Adjustments	**14.7**		**15.2**		
Total (census basis)	**−651.5**	**100.0**	**−532.4**	**100.0**	**22.4**
North America	**−110.8**	**17.0**	**−92.3**	**17.3**	**20.0**
Canada	−65.8	10.1	−51.7	9.7	27.3
México	−45.1	6.9	−40.6	7.6	11.1
Western Europe	**−114.1**	**17.5**	**−100.3**	**18.8**	**13.8**
Euro area	−82.9	12.7	−74.1	13.9	11.9
Pacific Rim	**−282.5**	**43.4**	**−230.5**	**43.3**	**22.6**
Japan	−75.2	11.5	−66.0	12.4	13.9
China	−162.0	24.9	−124.1	23.3	30.5
OPEC	**−71.9**	**11.0**	**−51.1**	**9.6**	**40.7**
Rest of the World	**−72.2**	**11.1**	**−58.2**	**10.9**	**24.1**

Source: United States Department of Commerce and author's calculations.

competitiveness. The US has a rapidly growing trade deficit in ATP trade with China, and imports from China are growing over three times as fast as exports. Table 3 provides data on US ATP trade and the ATP trade deficit with China. The US trade deficit in ATP in 2004 grew by 38.1 per cent in 2004, while the ATP deficit with China grew by 72 per cent. ATP imports from China grew 55.4 per cent in 2004. The ATP deficit with China (US$36.3 billion) now accounts for almost the entire national ATP deficit (US$37.0 billion). ATP exports are growing slower than ATP imports, and this problem is extreme when it comes to China.

Table 3. US ATP trade with the World and China.

	US$ Billions 2004	US$ Billions 2003	% Change
ATP – Exports	201.5	180.2	11.8
ATP – Imports	−238.5	−207.0	15.2
ATP – Trade balance	**−37.0**	**−26.8**	**38.1**
ATP – China Exports	9.4	8.3	13.2
ATP – China Imports	−45.7	−29.4	55.4
ATP – China trade balance	**−36.3**	**−21.1**	**72.0**

Source: Department of Commerce and author's calculations.

4. THE US EMPLOYMENT PICTURE

The magnitude of the US trade deficit is of concern in its own right owing to the potential danger it poses to global financial stability. In particular, there is a danger that financial investors may lose confidence in the US dollar and US financial assets, and a sudden rush for the exits could then trigger a rapid destabilizing decline in the value of the dollar and a spike in global interest rates.

Additionally, US citizens and policymakers are concerned about the employment impacts of the trade deficit, and the deficit is widely viewed as being a significant factor in the US economy's recent extended tepid job creation performance. Table 4 contains details of this performance. US private sector employment last peaked in December 2000, and it remained below that peak level in March 2005 – 51 months later. The US economy went through an extended 31-month job decline that lasted from December 2000 to July 2003. In the 20 months since then, there has been net job creation of 2.1 million, equal to 105,000 jobs per month. However, the economy has still not recovered its previous employment peak despite massive monetary and fiscal stimulus and continuing labour force growth.

The picture in manufacturing, the sector most impacted by goods trade with China, is even more dismal. Manufacturing entered recession before the national economy and manufacturing employment last peaked in July 2000 at 17.33 million jobs.[1] Thereafter, employment declined for 43 consecutive months, bottoming in February 2004 at 14.28 million jobs. Manufacturing therefore lost 3.05 million jobs, equal to 17.6 per cent of total manufacturing jobs. Since February 2004 manufacturing employment has risen a mere 30,000 jobs, and it is at levels last seen in the early 1950s.

There is widespread belief that the trade deficit is significantly responsible for this weak job performance. The massive monetary and fiscal policy stimulus

---

[1] In some regards manufacturing's downturn can be dated to March 1998 when employment growth in the sector came to a halt as a result of the East Asian financial crisis. The devaluation of East Asian currencies put US manufacturers at an enormous competitive disadvantage, which they have laboured under since. In 1998, China did not devalue its currency. However, massive inflows of FDI into China since then have enormously expanded China's export capacity and strengthened its export competitiveness, and it is FDI-based exports that are now driving the US trade deficit with China.

Table 4. Recent employment trends in the US private sector and manufacturing.

	Private Sector Employment	Manufacturing Employment
Last Peak	December 2000	July 2000
Employment at Peak	111.7 million	17.33 million
Last Trough	July 2003	February 2004
Employment at Trough	108.3 million	14.28 million
Months of employment decline	31 months	43 months
Jobs lost	3. 4 million	3.05 million
Jobs lost as percent	3.0%	17.6%
Current employment – March 2005	111.2 million	14.31
Jobs lost since peak	0.5 million	3.02 million
Jobs lost as percent	0.4%	17.4%
Months since last peak	51 months	56 months

Source: US Bureau of Labor Statistics and author's calculations

enacted by US policymakers, combined with consumer spending financed by higher equity and house prices, should have made for massive domestic job creation. Instead, much spending has leaked out of the US economy in the form of spending on imports.

Not only has consumer spending been redirected away from domestically produced goods, manufacturing investment has also probably suffered. First, competition in the import-competing sector of manufacturing reduces profitability, which constrains spending. Second, firms have closed down plants and transferred production offshore so that new investment spending associated with these plants takes place outside the United States. Third, firms may have expanded existing offshore capacity rather than US capacity. All of these channels contribute to job weakness in manufacturing, and all of these channels are germane to US-China economic relations.

5. MEASURING TRADE DEFICIT-RELATED JOB LOSSES

The trade deficit drains large amounts of spending out of the US economy via spending on imports. The immediate impact is that jobs are created in the country producing imports rather than the in United States. Using a disaggregated multi-sector input-output model, Scott (2005) provides estimates of the number of jobs embedded in the US trade deficit. These jobs are calculated on the basis of the current direct and indirect labour input needed to produce the deficit in goods trade, and they can be viewed as the lost job opportunities resulting from the deficit.[2]

---

[2] Scott's approach is to decompose the goods trade deficit by product category and then use disaggregated industry input-output measures to calculate the number of jobs needed to produce output equal to the trade deficit for that product category. Over time, the required labour input falls as a result of productivity growth, so that the lost job opportunity count depends on the year in which the count is done.

Table 5. US Trade & Jobs: the Numbers for NAFTA and China

	1993 $ billions	2002 $ billions	Change $ billions	Job impact	Multiplier (jobs/$billion)
Nafta Exports	144	227	83	794,174	9,568
Nafta Exports	−175	−342	−168	−1,673,454	9,961
Nafta Exports	−30	−115	−85	−879,280	
	1989 $ billions	2003 $ billions	Change $ billions	Job impact	Multiplier (jobs/$impact)
China Imports	6	26	20	217,500	10,875
China Imports	−12	−152	−140	−1,556,800	11,120
China Imports	−6	−126	−120	−1,339,300	

Source: Economic Policy Institute & author's calculations

Table 5 shows Scott's estimates of the lost US job opportunities embedded in the trade deficits with Mexico and China. There are 9,961 jobs embedded in each billion dollars of imports from Mexico, and 11,120 jobs embedded in each billion dollars of imports from China. In general, trade with China is more labour intensive than trade with Mexico, and this applies to both imports and exports. Between 1993 and 2002 the trade deficit with Mexico grew by US$85 billion, which represents 879,280 lost job opportunities. Between 1989 and 2003 the trade deficit with China grew by US$120 billion representing 1,339,300 lost job opportunities. Assuming the composition of trade remained unchanged in 2004, the 2004 trade deficit with China of US$162 billion now represents 1,808,055 lost job opportunities. Finally, looking to the future, China's trade surplus with the US shows signs of growing. Almost 60 per cent of China's exports are produced by multinational corporations operating in China, and the last several years have seen record levels of multinational foreign direct investment (FDI) in China. This FDI is now coming online, and it will add productive capacity to China's export machine.

These job numbers represent "lost job opportunities" rather than "lost jobs." Many jobs have been lost as factories have closed and production has shifted to China, constituting explicitly lost jobs. However, in addition the job opportunities measure captures jobs that were created in China to produce imports and which could have been created in the US instead.

The input-output methodology provides a first stab at estimating the jobs impact of the trade deficit. However, it both undercounts and over-counts job losses. Regarding undercounting, it misses jobs that are lost because of expenditure multiplier effects. Thus, when a plant closes, household incomes are reduced, which reduces spending and causes further job losses. Second, it does not count jobs that are lost because firms reduce investment spending owing to import competition, and nor does it count jobs that are lost because US firms divert investment spending to China. Third, it does not count job losses that may result from China contributing to lower US wages, which reduces household spending.

Balanced against this, the input-output methodology misses job gains from trade. First, it misses jobs that may be created because imports lower prices, which in turn frees up household income to be spent on other goods. Second, imports may lower firms' input costs, which then enables them to increase production and employment.

6. TRADE DEFICITS, THE EXCHANGE RATE AND INVESTMENT

An important element in the trade deficit debate is China's exchange rate, which is widely held to be 15-40 per cent undervalued against the dollar. Exchange rates have important effects on goods flows and employment. First, exchange rates affect exports and imports. An under-valued yuan makes US exports more expensive to Chinese buyers, reducing jobs in US export industries. It also makes Chinese imports cheaper to US consumers, displacing employment in US import-competing industries. The estimated 15–40 per cent undervaluation of the yuan is tantamount to a subsidy for imports from China and a tax on US exports to China.

Second, an under-valued yuan makes China-based production more attractive by lowering Chinese costs measured in dollars. This encourages firms to shift production to China and to locate new investments there. Third, an overvalued dollar undermines the profitability of US manufacturers, which reduces manufacturing investment, costing jobs and hindering growth in the manufacturing sector. On the positive side, an under-valued yuan makes Chinese imports cheaper which benefits consumers. It also benefits firms using imported Chinese inputs.

Empirically, there is strong support for the proposition that exchange rates impact business profitability and investment spending. Using annual US time series data for the period 1973-2001 in a simultaneous equation model of manufacturing profitability and investment, Blecker (2004) reports a total elasticity of US manufacturing investment with respect to the real value of the dollar of about –1.0 to –1.3. That implies a one per cent increase in the real value of the dollar reduces manufacturing real investment by between 1 and 1.3 percent. This study is for the overall value of the dollar. However, one can reasonably surmise that under-valuation of the yuan versus the dollar will have a qualitatively similar directional impact and the impact will be largest in industries competing with China.

There is considerable evidence that China's currency is under-valued relative to the dollar. As shown in Table 2, the deficit with China represents almost 25 per cent of the US goods trade deficit. It is the largest deficit with any single country and exceeds both the North American and Western European regional deficits. It is also the fastest growing component of the deficit except for the OPEC deficit (which is driven by high oil prices). Measured by the

Table 6. US Import/Export ratios

Country	2001	2002	2003	2004
China	5.32	5.66	5.36	5.67
Canada	1.33	1.30	1.32	1.35
Mexico	1.29	1.38	1.42	1.41
EU-15	1.38	1.57	1.63	1.62
Japan	2.20	2.20	2.27	2.38

Source: Commerce Department and author's calculations.

Table 7. Alternative measures of China's Trade Surplus.

	1999	2000	2001	2002	2003
China's trade surplus with the US:					
– Chinese data (US$ billions)	23.5	30.9	29.4	44.1	60.3
– US data (US$ billions)	68.9	84.2	84.1	104.2	124.9
China's global trade surplus:					
– Chinese data (US$ billions)	37.7	35.4	35.3	45.1	
– 43 partner data (US$ billions)	140.4	171.6	170.3	189.9	

Source: Fair Currency Alliance.

import/export ratio (see Table 6), the deficit with China is the most lopsided of all major manufacturing trading partners.

China seeks to refute these charges regarding under-valuation by claiming that it is only running a small global trade surplus, and that this is evidence that the yuan is not under-valued. However, China's data appears to be highly unreliable and it consistently reports its surplus with the United States as being about half that reported by the US customs service. In this connection, an exercise carried out by the Fair Currency Alliance showed that China also under-reports its surplus compared to the numbers reported by its top 43 trading partners. This under-reporting is evident in Table 7. In 2002, China reported a goods trade surplus with its 43 largest partners of US$45.1 billion, but these partners reported combined deficits with China of US$189.9 billion. In 2003, China reported a goods trade surplus with the US of US$60.3 billion, but the US reported a deficit with China of US$124.9 billion.

Foreign exchange markets are also sending clear signals that China should revalue. There has been constant upward pressure on the yuan for several years that has compelled the Chinese Government to intervene (sell yuan) and acquire dollar securities to prevent appreciation (see Table 8). Other East Asian governments have also intervened to prevent their currencies from appreciating, reflecting the fact that currency undervaluation is a Pacific Rim phenomenon. As a result of this foreign exchange market intervention, China's official foreign exchange reserves have risen from US$154.7 billion in 1999 to US$573.9 billion in November 2004 (see Table 9).

Table 8. Annual Official Chinese, Japanese, Taiwanese, and South Korean Foreign
Exchange Purchases (US$ billions)

Year	China	Japan	Taiwan	S. Korea
2000-01	46.6 billion	40.5 billion	15.5 billion	6.6 billion
2001-02	74.2	63.7	39.4	18.3
2002-03	116.8	201.3	45.0	33.7
2003 – Nov 04	170.6	166.3	37.2	

Source: IMF Financial Statistics and author's calculations.

Table 9. China's Official Foreign Exchange Holdings.

	1999	2000	2001	2002	2003	2004*
China's FX Reserves (US$ billions)	154.7	165.6	212.2	286.4	403.3	573.9

Source: IMF Financial Statistics.
* Data to November 2004.

Table 10. Changes in major currency exchange rates.

	January 2, 2002	January 19, 2005	% Change
Euro	1.11	0.76	31.5%
Japanese yen	132.02	102.52	22.3%
Canadian dollar	1.60	1.23	25.0%
Chinese yuan	8.28	8.28	0.0%

Source: Board of Governors of the Federal Reserve and author's calculations.

The fact that the US is running large trade deficits with every major region of the globe suggests that a generalized depreciation of the dollar is required. Table 10 shows that all major currencies, with the exception of China, have allowed their currencies to adjust upward. This is despite the fact that China accounts for almost 25 per cent of the US goods trade deficit.

China's failure to adjust its exchange rate is cause for concern by all – not just the United States. As the largest contributor to the US current account deficit, Chinese exchange rate adjustment must be part of the process of restoring sustainability to the US current account. China's refusal to adjust frustrates this process rendering Chinese policy a "global public bad" that exerts negative externalities on the entire global economy. With the yuan pegged to the dollar, China's currency is depreciating against the yen and the euro as the dollar weakens against these currencies. This threatens to cause manufacturing weakness in the European and Japanese economies. China's failure to adjust is also causing an exchange rate "logjam" effect as other East Asian countries (Taiwan, Korea) refuse to revalue for fear of losing competitiveness vis-à-vis China. Finally, as China rides the depreciation of the dollar it poses problems for other developing countries whose currencies are appreciating against the dollar. This risks a developing country growth slowdown that could turn into a developing country financial crisis.

7. OTHER LABOUR MARKET CONCERNS – OUTSOURCING AND WAGE STAGNATION

Another cause of US unease over China is offshore outsourcing of jobs. Outsourcing involves taking jobs that were previously performed within companies and having those jobs performed by an external supplier. This rearrangement of work has been going on within the US economy for a considerable period, but it now increasingly involves transferring work outside the United States. Most importantly, it now increasingly includes service work which was previously non-tradable. Forrester Research Inc. (McCarthy, 2004), predicts that the total number of US jobs outsourced by 2015 will reach 3.4 million. Previously, labour market insecurity from globalization was restricted to blue-collar workers. Outsourcing of service work has expanded this insecurity to include white-collar workers.

Aside from conceptual issues related to the definition of offshore outsourcing and why it differs from standard multinational production shifting, there is the problem of measuring the extent of the phenomenon. The US Bureau of Labor Statistics (2005) maintains a survey tracking extended mass layoffs, and part of this survey tracks layoffs involving movement of work out of the country. In 2004, there were 4,879 reported mass layoff events involving 956,327 workers. Of these, 357 events involved movement of work and 53,923 workers were affected. Approximately 30 per cent of the 357 events involved movement of work outside the US and 16,073 workers were impacted by this offshoring. This represents 1.7 per cent of all mass layoffs. Mexico and China were cited 52 per cent of the time as the destination to which work moved.

According to the BLS, offshore outsourcing is a minor phenomenon. However, there are severe problems regarding the completeness of the BLS mass-layoff survey. First, the survey only covers companies with more than 50 workers **and** where at least 50 workers filed for unemployment insurance. The survey therefore misses layoffs with a small count and layoffs at companies with less than 50 workers, as well as the many instances when workers do not qualify for unemployment insurance.[3] Second, offshore outsourcing is not just about lost jobs. It is also about lost job growth – for instance when a company develops its offshore production capacity or increases its orders from a foreign supplier. Lastly, the report does not identify mass layoffs related to companies shrinking or closing due to foreign competition. This conclusion regarding the

---

[3] Qualification for unemployment insurance (UI) is governed by strict rules concerning continuity of an individual's employment history. Approximately 40% of unemployed workers in the U.S. receive unemployment insurance at any time. However, the pool of unemployed includes workers who have been unemployed for longer than six months, and some of these may have initially received UI but this benefit expires after six months.

inadequacy of BLS statistics on offshore outsourcing has been confirmed by a recent US General Accountability Office (2004) report to the US Congress.

Bronfenbrenner and Luce (2004) provide an alternative assessment of the extent of global outsourcing based on an extensive media-tracking exercise that examined a broad array of media sources for news of firm and job relocations for two periods, 1 January 2004 to 31 March 2004 and 1 October 2000 to 30 April 2001. The main findings of their study are that: (1) Production shifts out of the US particularly to Mexico, China, India, and other Asian countries have increased significantly over the last three years. (2) The pace of job shifts to China has accelerated considerably, and job shifting to India has grown at an even faster pace – albeit from a much lower base. (3) During the first three months of 2004 there were 58 shifts to China documented across a range of industries as compared to 25 shifts to China during a similar period in 2001. (4) Nearly 100,000 jobs will move from the US to China as a result of production shifts in 2004 based on extrapolating the data collected during the limited period of the study. (5) The authors estimate that their media tracking methodology probably only "captures approximately two-thirds of production shifts to Mexico and about a third of production estimates to other countries". Accordingly, "in 2004 as many as 406,000 jobs will be shifted from the US to other countries compared to 204,000 jobs in 2001," of which nearly a quarter will go to China. (6) Production shifts, with consequent employment loss, have spread across the economy and now affect sophisticated manufacturing industries, services, and information technology. (7) All regions of the country are impacted by these shifts, with the Mid-West being especially hard hit. (8) Companies engaged in production shifts "tend to be large, publicly held, highly profitable, and well established." (9) The principal motive for production shifts to China is cost reduction rather than producing for the Chinese market. (10) The number of jobs lost because of production shifts far exceeds that reported by the Bureau of Labor Statistics in its report on mass layoffs due to overseas relocation. (11) Trade adjustment assistance to workers laid off owing to overseas job relocation is poor, covering less than one-third of the cases where production shifts occur.

Adverse wage and income distribution effects of trade deficit induced job losses and outsourcing are another cause of concern in the US–China economic relationship. However, estimates of the specific China contribution to lower US wages and a worsened US income distribution are not available. At the theoretical level, neo-classical trade theorists (Stolper and Samuelson, 1941) have long recognized that even if trade expands national income it can alter the distribution of income. In particular, for northern economies such as the US, global free trade tends to adversely impact wages and the wage share. This is because trade increases the effective supply of labour by embodying southern labour supplies in traded goods imported from the South. There is solid empirical evidence to support this proposition. Krugman (1995) estimates that 10 per cent of increased US income inequality is attributable to trade. Cline (1997) estimates that wage inequality increased by 18 per cent between 1973 and 1993, and trade contributed to 39 per cent of the increase. Palley (1999) estimates that trade accounted for 27 per cent of the increase income inequality between 1980 and 1998. With regard to wage levels, Kletzer (2001) reports that workers finding reemployment after losing their jobs as a result of trade dislocations, suffered a 13.2 per cent decline in wages.

The problem of increased global labour supply has recently been emphasized by Freeman (2004). In 1985, the global economic world consisted of 2.5 billion people. In 2000, as a result of the collapse of communism, India's turn from autarky, and China's shift to market-capitalism, the global economy encompassed 6.6 billion people. In 2000, the global labour force consisted of 2.93 billion workers: without these changes it would have consisted of 1.46 billion workers. In effect, there has been a doubling of labour supply that promises to put downward pressure on wages in northern economies for a very considerable period, and this downward pressure is amplified by the developments (technological, institutional, and policy) associated with globalization.

Moreover, Freeman suggests that this downward wage pressure is likely to move up the northern wage distribution and increasingly impact white-collar and higher skilled labour. This is because Asian nations, especially China, are raising their educational accomplishment and knowledge work is increasingly tradable. These developments are evidenced in the increased production of Asian and Chinese Ph.D.s, the increased share of Asian and Chinese high-tech exports and published scientific papers, and the flood of FDI into China. Indexes of technology capacity also show China gaining rapidly.

These knowledge and technology issues in turn relate to the earlier discussion of investment, and they also link with the issue of FDI and shifting of R&D activity to China. These developments promise to raise global output and developing country output and wages. Corporations also stand to do well. However, on the negative side they may (i) undermine the engines of productivity and standard of living growth in the US to the extent that they substitute and displace such activity in the US, and (ii) they may deepen wage pressures in the US by increasing the competitiveness of much lower paid Chinese workers at a time when more and more goods and services are becoming tradable.

Finally, not only does globalization have labour supply effects that impact wages, it also has adverse wage bargaining effects. These bargaining effects are documented by Bronfenbrenner (2000) in a study examining the impact of NAFTA on US labour markets. Bronfenbrenner's study looked at plant closing threats for a random sample of more than 400 National Labor Relations Board union certification election campaigns that took place between 1 January 1998 and 31 December 1999. She found that threats of plant closing were a pervasive part of campaigns and that plant closing threats significantly lowered the union election win rate (38 per cent with threat versus 51 per cent without threat). The use of closure threats is unrelated to company financial condition, and it is significantly higher in mobile industries compared to immobile industries (68 per cent versus 36 per cent). Though such threats are illegal, unions were unable to obtain remedies against such practices. The bottom line is that globalization combined with ineffective labour laws has created a climate enabling employers to illegally threaten plant closures to avoid unionization. This is contributing to the decline of unionization, with consequent adverse impacts on wages and income distribution. Although a study about NAFTA, the same qualitative logic regarding bargaining power probably applies to China-sensitive industries in the United States.

8. THE US TRADE DEFICIT AND THE CURRENT GLOBAL ECONOMIC MODEL

The US trade deficit, employment, and wage outcomes are connected to the current global economic model, of which China is an important component. This model has developing countries (including China) relying on export-led growth and running trade surpluses. Western Europe and Japan have also looked to run trade surpluses as a source of aggregate demand for their economies. The other side of this export-centred model is the United States, which plays the role of borrower and buyer of last resort, thereby contributing the demand that keeps export-led growth alive.

As long as the US maintains this role, the model is sustainable. However, there are two problems, the first which concerns the United States, and the second the entire global economy. With regard to the US, the model places significant short-term stresses on the US economy as well as in the long run. Though the US benefits from an inflow of cheap imported goods, which raise living standards in the short-term, this inflow comes at the price of massive de-industrialization and erosion of the manufacturing base. In the short term, the cost is manufacturing job loss and weak investment spending that has contributed to the weak recovery from recession. Longer term, the US risks a debilitating erosion of its manufacturing base that will lower US standards of living by (i) undermining future productivity growth and technological leadership, and (ii) undermining the US's ability to maintain a sustainable trade balance which will in turn will weaken the dollar, create adverse terms of trade impacts, and force policymakers to operate the economy at less than full employment in order to maintain financial stability.

The second problem with the model concerns its sustainability, and if the model implodes the entire global economy will be adversely impacted. Problems for the global economy will only emerge when the US eventually runs out of the financial steam that supports its role of buyer of last resort. There are two scenarios in which this is likely to happen. The first is if foreign investors lose their appetite for US financial assets. This would cause US asset prices to fall and interest rates to rise, bringing an end to the US consumer-driven expansion and causing a global economic slowdown as borrowing costs rose around the world. The second scenario is if US borrowers cut back on their borrowing either because they feel over-extended or because banks start to restrict the flow of new credit because they think borrowers are over-extended. In either case, US spending will contract, and contraction will quickly spread globally as export-dependent economies confront falling demand.

The conclusion is that many of the problems afflicting the US economy are a product of the current global model of export-led growth with the US as buyer of last resort. This model is probably unsustainable and it therefore carries the risk of a future severe global economic hard landing. The core challenge is how to shift from a model of export-led growth, predicated on the US playing the role of buyer of last resort, to a sustainable model of domestic demand-led growth. China is directly relevant to this challenge. It has become a global manufacturing powerhouse, and its size now means that its exports are contributing to the massive US trade deficit, creating financial fragility and undermining the US manufacturing sector. These developments threaten to eventually stall the US economy, in turn triggering a global recession that will impact all – including China. China must therefore transition away from its current export-led growth strategy to a domestic demand-led growth strategy.[4]

9. SOLUTIONS AND IMPLICATIONS FOR THE INTERNATIONAL LABOUR ORGANIZATION

The above analysis suggests that the global economy faces a difficult transition period, and failure to effect this transition will have costs for all. As buyer of last resort, the US has been fuelling global economic growth, and many countries would like to see this continue. However, there are two reasons why it cannot. First, as documented above, the model is exerting significant stress on the US economy and that stress will probably generate politically induced change. Second, even if no US political response is forthcoming, the model is unsustainable and stands to implode under its own debt dynamics.

To avoid a future global economic meltdown China must significantly re-value its currency upward. This is needed to prevent continued structural deterioration of the US economy. Developing countries also need this measure, as they are being competitively undermined by China's pegging of its currency to a depreciating dollar. The same holds for Western Europe and Japan, who have until recently been insulated from China by a strong dollar to which the yuan was pegged. China also has self-interest in taking this step because it will avoid a global slowdown that would wreak havoc on China's export dependent economy. Additionally, an upward re-valuation of the yuan would help restore internal economic balance in China and choke off accelerating inflation pressures.

Second, policymakers around the world, including China, must work cooperatively to change the existing paradigm of export-led growth to one of domestic demand-led growth. The details and requirements of such a policy programme are beyond the scope the current paper.[5] Broadly speaking, policy

---

[4] The policies needed to effect such a transition, and the political obstacles to achieving such a transition, are discussed in Palley (2004).

[5] The problems of export-led growth and the case for domestic demand-led growth are explored in Palley (2002, 2003).

must re-engineer the pattern of demand. This will involve expenditure switching programmes, increased government spending, social insurance systems that reduce the incentive for excessive precautionary saving, and labour standards that contribute to higher wages and improved income distribution.

These observations have direct implications for the ILO. Labour standards must surely be a part of a world with fair and full employment. However, achieving fair and full employment in the era of globalization requires attention to exchanges rates and the structure of macroeconomic policies that determine whether growth is export or domestic demand-led. The ILO's mission is achievement of fair and full employment with decent work, and that means it must inevitably engage with the issues of exchange rates, financial architecture, and macroeconomic policy, because these directly and forcefully impinge on its mission.

USING ACTIVE AND PASSIVE EMPLOYMENT POLICIES TO ACCOMPANY GLOBALIZATION-RELATED RESTRUCTURING

BY BERNARD GAZIER[1]

1. INTRODUCTION

Job losses resulting from industrial restructuring are as old as capitalism itself. As we begin a new millennium the debate on the corrective measures that need to be taken is more relevant than ever, but is now to be seen in the context of globalization. The growth of international trade and direct investment abroad, and the resulting increase in the interpenetration of economies on a global scale, are viewed in most countries as an opportunity, but also as a major threat to worker security. Hardly a week goes by without the announcement of redundancy schemes or offshoring.

This paper is intended to present an overall, though by no means exhaustive, view of the various economic and social policy measures that have been taken to limit the negative impact of restructuring resulting from globalization. Despite the many reports produced on the subject recently (see bibliography at the end of this book), it remains a difficult issue to get to grips with, for various reasons.

First of all, when we look at how jobs have developed, it is not easy, nor is it always justified, to separate what are, strictly speaking, the effects of globalization from the effects of "local" changes: the spread of new technologies, company mergers and the effects of intra-national competition are all powerful determining factors in destroying and creating jobs, and a firm's decision to try to remain competitive by shedding some of its workforce may often have its origins in both national and international competition. The process of globalization itself is far from being as homogeneous or as uniform as some people claim, and it uses many different channels, both direct and indirect. This paper will try to confine itself to job losses that are directly or indirectly attributable to globalization (such as job losses resulting from the closure of an industrial site), without disguising the relatively arbitrary nature of this restricted approach.

A further reason is that we are witnessing – in different countries and at different times – a profusion of different initiatives that are too numerous and

---

[1] The author held a number of discussions with Peter Auer during the writing of this report. He would like to thank Mrs. B. Einhorn at the Documentation Centre of the Institute of Labour Social Sciences (University of Paris 1) for her extremely valuable help in obtaining documents.

too various to analyse, and that are also highly complex, heterogeneous and evolving. We therefore need, strictly speaking, to combine a legal point of view, a political science or organizational sociology point of view, and an economic point of view. This paper will mainly take an institutional-economic viewpoint, while also taking other perspectives into account. Work should also begin on less well-known practices in Asia and Latin America. However, in view of the gaps in the information we have been able to assemble, this report will confine itself to illustrating the wide range of policies adopted and taking a look at how they have developed historically.

Another reason is that the various mechanisms accompanying restructuring that can be observed in a given country at a given time form a fairly coherent group and are located in a particular regulatory, institutional, economic and social context. The way they operate and their significance thus depend both on their combined effect and on the framework in which they are found. We will examine both the existence and development of individual mechanisms and the overall policies which are the implicit or explicit result of their existence and their combined effect. It is then necessary to carefully consider how they are applied and in particular how the actors concerned, chief among them the workers under threat and the social partners, are involved in decision-making and monitoring.

Lastly, studying and evaluating these mechanisms requires us to focus on the time dimension, both as regards the anticipation of restructuring processes and their development and conclusion. The dramatic nature of what is at stake, particularly for the least-skilled workers who often find themselves in long-term unemployment or suffer major loss of income, sometimes gives the impression that these are isolated crises relating to solidarity that is itself localized. It is undoubtedly one of the benefits of recent political developments that greater account is taken of the previous career paths of the workers affected as well as of their careers in re-employment. Since it is often the fate of workers who are the victims of restructuring that they are widely scattered, it is difficult to obtain an overview of the effects that can be ascribed to any given mechanism.

The rest of this paper is organized as follows: Section 1 takes a step back and presents a few historical, comparative elements. Section 2 examines the range of tools available and the role of the public employment service. Section 3 describes and discusses two general trends that have emerged over the last decade, "proceduralization" and "activation". Section 4 is devoted to recently formulated policies on employability and career path security, and to the various approaches that, to a certain extent, allow the workers concerned and all the parties affected to be involved in the concerted management of restructuring resulting from globalization.

2. INTERNATIONAL DIVISION OF LABOUR, MECHANICS OF RESTRUCTURING AND PUBLIC MEASURES: A FEW HISTORICAL AND COMPARATIVE MILESTONES

When we examine the growing number of studies today on the risks associated with offshoring and competition between developed countries and low-wage countries, what is striking is the absence of a historical perspective in most of the analyses. This may be at least partly explained by the fact that restructuring and job losses often come in waves, and the feeling of urgency tends to focus attention on estimating the likely scale of the job losses in the short and medium term and criticising media announcements of mass redundancies. As far as the current wave is concerned, the discussion is focused on sectors such as textiles and the automobile industry, and also on the innovations offered by the "relocatable" tertiary sector, such as activities suitable for mass computer processing (see in particular the European Community's estimates (2004) (Section 5) for Europe and Tejada and Swaim (2004) for the OECD countries).

However, earlier analytical reports (see, for example, McKersie and Sengenberger (1983), Sengenberger (1989), or Tronti et al (ed) (1999) demonstrate that actors in several earlier periods experienced the same sort of distress as a result of a similar process. Thus, McKersie and Sengenberger (1983), referring to the 1970s, describe in terms that are still immediately relevant, a radical change in the international division of labour (p. 41), characterized by the arrival of new Asian competitors (Japan and Korea, on that occasion) with up-to-date means of production, low or very low wages, lower rates of unionisation, less stringent labour and environmental standards, and cheap energy and raw materials. The first sectors affected by this "new" competition in 1970 were textiles, clothing, electrical and optical equipment, later followed by shipbuilding, steel production, the automobile industry, and mechanical and electronic engineering. Apart from the emergence of the "relocatable" tertiary sector, and the fact that workforces have declined in many of the sectors concerned in the developed countries, there is thus remarkable continuity with the pressures felt more than 30 years ago.

Studies of company closures or job cuts resulting from international competition, greater investment abroad or the choices made by the multinationals should thus go further back, probably to the 19th century. These processes form part of the general dynamics of job creation and destruction and the adaptation of businesses to new conditions. The cycles of "rationalization" in the 1920s and of automation in the 1950s in the developed countries are proof that periodic accelerations occurred that were perhaps similar to what we are seeing today.

We can look at the context in which the first collective reactions to this process appeared, and what policies were pursued in the first measures taken. There appear to be three determining factors in triggering public intervention. First, the existence of large companies forced to lay off large numbers of workers. Second, the impossibility of staggering these job losses over time, so that they appear massive and sudden. Third, the geographical concentration of the job losses, making them even more visible and generating losses of dependent activities. Coal mines are a typical example of large-scale job losses which have major local knock-on effects, but which have sometimes been able to be staggered over time. From the 1950s onwards, Europe's coal mines faced competition from sources of energy such as oil, as well as from other areas of the world where mining was cheaper. As M.I.A. Bulmer (1981) points out, between 1960 and 1970 the UK's coal mines saw their workforce drop from 602 000 to 287 000. Of the 300 000 jobs axed, only 60 000 were redundancies that happened in the final stages, when the Coal Board had exhausted its retirement and early retirement options. In this very dramatic case there was no major upheaval and public measures were limited.

The experience of the European Coal and Steel Community (ECSC) makes an interesting comparison with this first case (Ambrosi et al., 1967). It shows that the public authorities, both national and international, were much more involved, and that the birth of Europe, the concerted introduction of a common market and the development of ways of preventing and curing the resulting job losses were inextricably linked. Established by the Treaty of 18 April 1951 between the Federal Republic of Germany, Belgium, France, Italy, Luxembourg and the Netherlands, the ECSC came into force on 25 July 1952 and was a forerunner of the European Economic Community established by the Treaty of Rome of 25 March 1957. It established a common market for steel, coal, iron ore and ferrous scrap, as well as the concerted management of production centres and tariffs. By the end of the 1950s production surpluses and excessively high costs were evidence that coal was in crisis. In 1960 the ECSC experts proposed to halve French coal production and to close all non-profitable mines within ten years. The French Government highlighted the social repercussions that this would have and the need to maintain energy independence, and was allowed to introduce two phased reduction plans, each of 10 per cent in five years, conditional on capping extraction costs.

The implementation of this considerably watered-down measure came up against a wide range of different production conditions. The least profitable and most isolated mines were forced to close, leading to difficult and sometimes swingeing redevelopment measures during the 1960s. In order to ease the crisis, a number of ECSC loans were provided to make it easier to set up new industrial estates. The French Government granted retirement pensions to workers with over 30 years' service, redundancy payments to workers aged over 45, and travel and resettlement allowances for those forced to move home.

Most of the typical ingredients involved in the use of various public policies and company measures to accompany restructuring are to be found in this historical experiment, which was largely conducted in a context of strong, yet painful economic growth: preventive measures affecting the very conditions in which businesses operate, the attempt to ensure that changes happen gradually, the use of "age-related" measures, but also "active" measures promoting geographical and/or occupational mobility, reindustrialization subsidies, etc. European policies rapidly moved away from measures to slow the very process of restructuring, while the rest proved much more lasting.

The wide range of experiences of restructuring resulting from globalization is obviously found worldwide, occurring in Latin America as well as in Asia, where surplus workers are often laid off without public intervention or compensation from the firm involved in the restructuring. In the Brazilian truck industry, for example, Mercedes, long established there, introduced massive redundancies during the 1989-1992 recession, before relaunching its activities and completely reorganizing its 40-year-old production lines (Bresciani, 2001).

The former Communist countries deserve a special mention, first of all because the structure of the labour market and the operating rules in their societies showed no open unemployment, but instead a form of "labour hoarding" within firms themselves. Fazekas et al (1990), in a comparison of two restructuring in Hungary and France, examine how the Hungarian authorities used State subsidies to maintain earlier production structures pending more favourable conditions. The internal management of workforce surpluses disappeared in Hungary with the fall of Communism, there were massive job losses and open unemployment appeared. However, labour hoarding did not disappear everywhere and remains a persistent and paradoxical feature of the behaviour of restructuring companies in Russia, as Koumakhov and Najman (2001) and Schwartz (2003) show. The adjustments then tend to switch to wage levels, which fall or are sometimes deferred or even not paid at all. A final recent example, also in the automobile industry, shows how western investors can now buy a company and radically modernize it. In 1999, Renault bought the Romanian manufacturer Dacia and axed 12,000 jobs in order to reorganize the plant at Pitesti. In 2001, it set up an in-house labour reintegration department with 32 specially-trained Dacia workers, supported by two experts from the Renault Group's "Employment Initiatives" unit, to draw up professional experience statements and promote occupational reorientation. An assessment carried out in April 2004 (Développement durable Renault, 2004) shows that 5,000 workers found redeployment solutions, 1,815 were seconded to suppliers, a business "nursery" was set up, and the company is now recruiting around 100 highly skilled workers a year while at the same time providing rapidly growing training opportunities. The social measures taken should not, however, conceal the dramatic nature of the adjustments made.

3. THE RANGE OF TOOLS USED

Few reports have clearly focused, in a broad international perspective, on studying the instruments that have been developed and used to accompany restructuring. In an empirical and comparative perspective the highly detailed report a) by McKersie and Sengenberger (1983) provides a good starting point, and may be contrasted with b) the recent selection made by Tejada and Swaim (2004). The analyses offered by Auer (2001) and Hansen (2002) reproduce and expand the range of tools available, as well as providing practical advice for decision-makers.

Between interventionism and laissez-faire: developments during the 1980s

According to McKersie and Sengenberger (1983), the range of tools has expanded in a number of cumulative stages. Towards the middle of the 20th century there were three instruments that were first used to deal with restructuring and relocations: *subsidies* to maintain activity and employment, the options offered by the process of natural *wastage* of the workforce when it is not renewed, and *early retirement schemes* to accelerate wastage where the rate was too slow. According to the authors, this combination dominated restructuring in the developed countries between the 1950s and the 1970s. They give a striking example of this deliberately staggered management with job losses in the coal industry in Belgium, where the Government allowed the industry to cut 100 jobs a month, and the public authorities provided financial coverage for all losses (op. cit. p. 14).

The authors describe the huge variety of instruments available in the early 1980s in the framework of three main options, the first two of which were *laissez–faire* with a few minor corrections, and *prevention*, which involves controlling or even blocking economic adjustment. These are two opposite extremes. In one case the harmful effects on employment are directly accepted and may result in optional corrective measures being taken, while in the other efforts are made to avoid such effects. In one case State involvement is minimal, while in the other it is maximal. A third option is what they refer to as "*integration* strategy", which is half way between the two others and includes most of the measures examined.

As far as the public authorities are concerned, the *laissez-faire* option merely involves providing unemployment insurance. The authors give the example of the textile industry in the USA during the period from 1940 to 1960.

The preventive option is, logically, more diverse. It starts with protectionist measures designed to shelter the activity in question from global competition either temporarily or permanently. The end of the Multifibre Agreement in January 2005 brought concerns for what remains of the textile industry in the West, which has faced competition from Africa and Asia for 50 years and has managed/deferred its programmed disappearance by combining plant closures with protectionism. In the long run it is likely that only firms that have cornered specialized niches will survive in this sector both in Europe and in North America.

Beyond protectionism, permanent or temporary subsidies to maintain production have been very widely used in countries as far apart as Australia and the UK, for example, to try to stabilize employment in sectors under threat. In some cases massive State aid has led to the company concerned being nationalized, as happened with the French steel industry in 1988. Permanent aid has been criticized because it costs the taxpayer a lot of money and it risks putting off adjustments that will turn out to be necessary anyway, but some governments have used them persistently, like Australia with the textile, clothing, footwear and automobile industries.

In other countries, aid has remained a temporary measure and has involved preparing the conditions for a recovery, such as by training workers on reduced hours (partial unemployment). However, intervention has also consisted of subsidizing activity or stockpiling. One striking example given by McKersie and Sengenberger (1983) was Sweden during the 1976-77 recession, where the Government granted very substantial credit guarantees for shipbuilding and financed stockpiling in the steel and wood pulp industries. For wood pulp alone the stocks represented 1.4 million tonnes of raw materials, or half of the world's stocks (ibid., p. 61).

Without denying the benefits of this interventionist option, the authors stress the costs and disadvantages involved, and focus on the development of the third option (integration strategy), which consists of trying to link capital mobility with worker mobility by redirecting the latter to dynamic sectors through the application of manpower policies both within companies and on the labour market, as well as regionally. They feel that Germany and Japan provide the best examples of this approach.

Within companies the range of instruments includes stopping recruitment and the use of early retirement schemes, while work-sharing is regarded as a temporary expedient. The secondment of surplus workers to subcontractors is largely peculiar to Japan. The authors briefly criticize the use of early retirement schemes, noting that this runs counter to the growing trend towards prolonging working life. They also stress that, if practiced on a voluntary basis, there is a risk that it will deprive firms of their most highly skilled workers, and they extend this criticism to all programmes offering scope for voluntary departure (op. cit., p. 83). Lastly, there are instruments for personnel planning and concerted management planning. Among the examples given is Nippon Steel between 1970 and 1980, which went from 85,000 workers to 70,000 without lay-offs, by reassigning many workers to other sectors of activity and "lending" a thousand workers to the automobile industry that was then in full expansion.

Measures outside the company begin with subsidies given by the public authorities to employers hiring workers made redundant by sectors that are restructuring. In August 1980 in Japan, for example, employers giving permanent jobs and training to workers from the textile, steel, aluminium and shipbuilding sectors received grants of a half to a third of the worker's wage (in the case of SMEs) and were entitled to have part of the training costs refunded (op. cit., p. 89-90). It is interesting to note that in the account given for 1983 training and retraining courses organized by the last employer are only briefly mentioned (ibid., p. 90-91).

The authors continue with a brief description of intermediaries, created by the job-cutting company or not, which represent a "community body" allowing all the various local actors to be involved in managing the redeployment process. Their main role is to disseminate information and to act as extra job placement agents for workers who are the victims of restructuring. Likewise, companies may themselves encourage or even organize the geographical mobility of their surplus labour, as is seen in the USA but almost not at all in Europe.

Lastly, they describe the use of redundancy payment schemes, comparing countries where this is practiced intensively, such as the USA and the UK, with countries where it is merely a back-up measure, like France.

This range of measures designed to reintegrate workers on the labour market may be combined as part of "pilot programmes" either on the employers' initiative, or as part of an approach involving workers and their employers (possibly with public aid), or as part of collaboration between the public authorities and the private sector.

The final additions to the range of instruments examined by McKersie and Sengenberger are redevelopment strategies: public investment here is frequent and is tending to become increasingly targeted and selective, in their view. It may also be combined with incentives to recruit workers who have lost their jobs. Some large companies may take it upon themselves to contribute to the development of regions affected by factory closures. This was the case from 1975 with the British Steel Corporation, which set up a branch responsible for promoting enterprise creation by playing the role of broker (to obtain finance) and of catalyst. The "neighbourhood workshops" scheme enabled it to make premises freed up by business closures available to small companies. However, an evaluation of this type of activities shows that few jobs are generally created by these initiatives compared with the number lost, and the new jobs are often taken by younger and more skilled workers than those who have lost their jobs following restructuring.

Measures by the public employment service

The instruments we have just looked at are all still relevant today. Actors and decision-makers have used them in differing degrees and in very different combinations. It is interesting to note the uneven and fragmented role played, in this picture of the 1980s, by unemployment insurance and public employment policies. The "laissez-faire" option relies on the compensation arrangements provided for all the unemployed, while with the "integration" option, early retirement schemes feature among the adjustments carried out within the company, and employment subsidies among the labour market interventions. Although not intended to be exhaustive, the recent selection presented by Tejada and Swaim (2004), which focuses on public employment policy measures, offers an interesting contrast that condenses most of the innovations seen over the last 20 years.

In their presentation (Part 3, p. 13 et seq., and Table 6 in the annex), they confine themselves to what they call "labour market intervention programmes" designed to reduce the cost of adjustment, and they describe a whole range of active employment policies. These may either have been set up for the exclusive use of workers who are the victims of restructuring, and are therefore "targeted" at that group, or else they may have been developed for all workers (or a subgroup including some or all victims of restructuring). Only one case is mentioned of ambitious, evolving and sustained targeting: the TAA (Trade Adjustment Assistance) in the USA. In the second alternative, programmes may either simply be made available to "displaced" workers, or offered preferentially through privileged, explicitly advertised and organized access. They may also be offered in combination with each other and/or with other incentives.

Tejada and Swaim obviously include subsidies for redeploying a particular category of workers, which we have already discussed and which we will therefore not go into. It should be noted that, in their view, only Japan has introduced (2003) subsidies targeted at the re-employment of workers who have been the victims of restructuring.

The other headings in their list cover, with an emphasis and systematic approach not found in the report on the 1980s, all *active employment policies*: job search assistance, training and retraining, public geographical mobility allowances, grants for starting a small business, and lastly two financial incentives to accept less well-paid jobs than those lost: re-employment bonuses and wage compensation schemes.

Exceptionally, the authors cover job-creation measures in the public sector, and give as an example the policies adopted to cope with restructuring in the new German Länder after reunification in 1991, and the community benefit work introduced in Italy in 1993, which helps "redundant" workers such as the long-term unemployed.

Aid for *job-seekers and for training/retraining measures* all come under the heading of "initiatives combining multiple services", most of which have preferential access. Among the examples given is Australia, which in 2004 and 2005 introduced two supplementary job assistance programmes targeted at workers in two sectors directly threatened by globalization: sugar and textiles. In France, the "retraining leave" schemes are mentioned. These provide training and job-search allowances for six months to workers who have been the victims of collective redundancies. In Germany, the public authorities subsidize measures included in redundancy schemes (on this idea see Section 3). In New Zealand the Work Track programme provides a three-week training course designed to give job-seekers who are at risk of becoming long-term unemployed better job-search skills. The TAA in the USA organizes similar training and job-search services, but only for "dislocated" workers (see below).

Aid for *geographical mobility* is provided in many countries, including Austria, Finland, France, Germany, Portugal, Sweden and the USA, again under the TAA. It includes repayment of travel and removal expenses or straightforward rewards for agreeing to change region or to take a job far away from home.

Most of these same countries provide *enterprise creation benefits*, and are joined in the selection here by Greece and Japan. In this area direct grants, interest-free loans and the provision of guarantees may be combined in vary different ways. Some benefits are linked to the situation of the person setting up the business, while others are dependent on the business surviving for a minimum period.

However, emphasis should be laid on the last two instruments presented, which are designed to compensate for and to persuade people to accept loss of income as a result of taking a new job that is less well-paid than the one they lost. *Re-employment bonuses* give workers all or part of the benefits to which they would have been entitled if they had remained unemployed instead of quickly taking a job that is probably not entirely satisfactory. Two examples are given. The first is the "cooperation agreement" introduced in France in 1995, which allows re-employed workers to receive 65 per cent of the remainder of the unemployment benefits to which they are entitled if they take a job within ten months of going on benefits. The second example is the "early re-employment grant" that was introduced in Japan in March 2003 and which is graduated: if a worker finds a job before the end of the first third of the benefit period, s/he receives 40 per cent of his/her residual benefit entitlements; if s/he finds a job before the end of the final third, s/he receives 30 per cent.

Wage insurance schemes offset part of the wage gap between the old and new jobs. Three examples are given: first, an experimental scheme in Canada dating from the late 1990s, the Earnings Supplement Project. This combines an incentive for a rapid return to work and acceptance of lower wages, providing compensation of 75 per cent of the wage difference for displaced workers who take a job less than 26 weeks after being laid off. Next is a French programme, the "graduated temporary benefits agreement" dating from 1999, which provides a grant of 50-70 per cent of the wage difference between the old and new jobs for workers who have been the victims of collective redundancies. Lastly, in the USA, again under the TAA, an experimental programme provides compensation for loss of earnings for workers aged over 50 who have lost their jobs because of international trade or offshoring.

Tejada and Swaim note that there is a tendency to group together very different measures, either for a group of displaced workers from a single company or on a national scale. Australia provides a very striking example with the Mitsubishi Labour Market Adjustment Package of 2004, designed solely for workers laid off by the company in Australia as part of a plant offshoring. The measures grouped together include supplementary job-seekers' allowances, wage subsidies, geographical mobility aid, enterprise creation grants and training courses specific to the industry. However, the targeted group of measures most commented on by Tejada and Swaim is the TAA mechanism and its many incarnations in the USA (op. cit., Box on p. 29-30). This is an old programme which dates back to the Trade Expansion Act of 1962. At that time, Trade Adjustment Assistance (TAA) provided income assistance and re-employment services for workers directly affected by trade liberalization measures. However, the eligibility criteria for the programme were so strict that no workers were accepted in its first seven years, and very few in the five years after that. Once the criteria were relaxed the programme became a great success, but then during the 1980s its budget was slashed. It has helped two million workers since it was set up. In 1993, when the North American Free Trade Agreement (NAFTA) was signed, a second programme was introduced with the same acronym but a slightly different title, the NAFTA-TAA, where the initials TAA stand for Transitional Adjustment Assistance. This opened up eligibility for workers in supplier or subcontractor companies and to those whose companies had relocated to Canada or Mexico. In 2002, the TAA and the NAFTA-TAA merged, with more flexible eligibility criteria and more generous payment conditions.

Two practical analyses

The works produced by Auer (2001) and Hansen (2002) for the ILO reproduce and reorganize the range of instruments from the point of view of company
bosses or trade union officials having to deal with and manage a restructuring.
They condense the experiences gained and the evaluations made with a view to
"socially responsible workforce adjustment", identifying desirable measures
and presenting suggestions for actors and decision-makers in the form of advice
or decision aids. Auer (2001) presents a broad and "comprehensive" view,
while Hansen (2002) focuses on certain prevention and retraining measures,
describing in a detailed and practical way how to involve the community of
actors concerned. These two contributions therefore complement each other
and summarize, in our view, what might be called the "state of the art" in
this field.

Presented in the form of an imaginary computer programme whose
reader/actor clicks on the menu, P. Auer's report is organized around three
headings: prevention of lay-offs, internal adjustment and external adjustment.

The *prevention of lay-offs* menu lists and comments on the following
headings:

–   Development of advance warning systems beyond the advance notification
    procedures that are sometimes compulsory in certain countries;

–   Training and development of human resources in order to create a flexible
    and transferable workforce

–   Investment in worker employability (which often remains vague, see
    below), with greater emphasis in training on skills that promote mobility

–   Changes in work organization: it is easier to transfer workers used in flexi-
    ble teams than those used to working in a traditional hierarchy

–   Workforce management planning: this practice has been borrowed from
    large firms in France and can act as a synthesis, since it brings together the
    majority of the items listed above in the form of forecasts and a group of
    programmed and concerted measures, while offering the possibility of using
    aid from public employment policies to fund these measures.

The *internal adjustment* menu follows, and the order suggests that it is
always preferable to start with this or to exhaust the options it offers before
resorting to external adjustment.

The menu contains training, not in the form generally practiced as part of
human resources management, but in the form of programmes linked to the
temporary management of surplus labour. These courses are funded by the
company or most often jointly by the company and the public authorities, and
they enable firms to restart (when circumstances permit) with a more highly
skilled workforce.

Leave schemes with right of return to the workplace (variously funded) can
also be envisaged within the same context of temporary adjustment, although
this instrument is limited by the relative unpredictability of economic cycles.

Working-time changes are, in Auer's view, a powerful instrument for coping with temporary and permanent redundancies. The famous example of Volkswagen in the 1990s shows how, in concession bargaining, the company introduced a 28-hour, 4-day week, with only partial wage compensation, in order to save 30,000 jobs or 30 per cent of the workforce employed in Germany. The "solidarity contracts" in France and Italy are further examples. Here, major changes have to be made to work organization, in particular to make shorter working time compatible with extended equipment running time.

The author highlights partial unemployment or short-time work, where the employment contract is maintained, while hours not worked are partially compensated. In 1991, Germany used such schemes on a massive scale: two million workers benefited, with some of them stopping work altogether. The famous Cassa Integrazione Guadagni in Italy was able to keep almost 400,000 workers in employment during the full-scale expansion of the 1990s. For a time the scheme served to compensate workers who were permanently redundant, then it was cut back to temporary redundancies only. The USA has a functional equivalent of this scheme with its "temporary lay-off".

Finally, the *external adjustment* menu lists the adjustments to be considered as a last resort. These include most of the instruments mentioned by McKersie and Sengenberger (1983), and most of the instruments selected by Tejada and Swaim (2004). It starts with methods which allow surplus labour to be shed. Direct dismissal is generally an option that cannot be taken by decision-makers, who are forced by statutory requirements to find alternatives, many publicly funded or co-funded. This is why the first instruments listed are attrition and early retirement. Auer notes that early retirement schemes (and invalidity pensions), despite their many disadvantages, remain among the main tools used in restructuring (see Section 3). He then mentions dismissals leading to redundancy payments, pointing out that these are still widespread, though not very expensive, in the UK, and that they appear to create additional problems for the workers concerned when they try to find another job.

He ends his review with the active employment measures that we have listed elsewhere, and lays particular emphasis on "intermediary organizations". These take different forms, ranging from specific units in large firms through public-private partnerships and temporary work agencies to small, specialized private firms, and their purpose is to bundle all the information and services provided for redundant workers. The benefits of this "one-stop shop" and specialization are offset by the disadvantage that they tend to dilute the responsibility of the firm making the redundancies. Among the successful examples given here the author mentions British Steel Industries, the employment foundations in Austria (see below) and the Beschäftigungsgesellschaften or "employment associations" in Germany.

No country offers all the instruments described, but some offer a wider range than others, particularly those providing strict protection against lay-offs. The author ends by pointing out that the choice of instruments needs to be adapted to different local situations, and that it is not out of the question that political pressure will take the "early retirement" option off the menu altogether (see Section 3).

Hansen's contribution (2002) adds to this practical perspective by taking the point of view of local community leaders (mayors, county, district and regional officials, trade union officials, etc.) facing mass lay-offs. He puts forward a range of advice and suggestions under four main points, based in particular on initiatives in the USA and Hungary in partnership with the US Department of Labor (USDOL).

First of all, local officials must encourage company bosses and workers to adopt proactive lay-off averting strategies. The first "community" measure is to set up an information system enabling companies and sectors under threat to be identified in advance. Next, concerted action initiatives can help companies to involve their staff in cost-cutting measures in order to save jobs. He gives (p. 16) the example of Xerox in the early 1980s, when it had lost a large part of its market share; by introducing a cost-reduction programme in consultation with its staff it managed to save 180 jobs. Another very different option is to encourage workers to take over their own companies in difficulties. The example given (p. 18) is Spain, which since the 1970s has developed cooperative forms of enterprise enabling workers to buy their company if it is threatened with closure. This has saved over 100,000 jobs. Legislation was introduced in 1986 to regulate these forms of enterprise.

Next, the author mentions instruments enabling workers to react very rapidly to announcements of collective redundancies. The desirable reaction time is 48 hours. He recommends setting up ad hoc groups which he calls "Re-employment Assistance Committees" involving representatives of workers, local communities and management. Their task is to decide on the type of services to provide for workers with the help of experts specializing in restructuring, and to represent all those concerned.

A third stage involves setting up on-site local agencies ("Worker Assistance Resource Centers") which combine many different activities: job search assistance, diagnosis, job clubs, advice, online help, etc. A lengthy example given is that of Hungary in 1994, during its transition to a market economy. Confronted with mass lay-offs, experts were brought to five locations with the help of the US Department of Labor (USDOL), and followed the approach recommended here, bringing together workers, managers and representatives of the local authorities in a coordinated structure. By reacting rapidly and setting up services and networks, this tripartite organization succeeded in halving the average time taken by laid-off workers to find another job, in the author's view.

A fourth, longer-term phase involves assessing the local scope for creating and establishing new businesses, again calling in experts, and then drawing up a local redevelopment strategy.

The approaches described by G. Hansen clearly make more sense in contexts where public employment policies are not widely developed, such as in the USA, where the budgets spent on active and passive employment policies remain very low, and in Hungary and the former socialist countries. On the other hand, the measures may become redundant and difficult to coordinate where these policies are highly developed and already offer various instruments which workers and their representatives can turn to directly.

A number of elements can be noted from these lists of practical measures. Whatever the reasons for lay-offs, which may be open to criticism or question, the policies recommended merely note that they have occurred and try to limit their impact by taking a proactive stance involving all the actors concerned. Hence the emphasis on the importance of following the sequence of measures and managing time: anticipation or prevention, rapid or even instant reaction, followed by the identification of pathways; it is also made clear that expert services need to be combined with appropriation by local actors. In both cases, a sequence of measures is laid down to ensure that mass lay-offs are only a last resort.

3. TWO BASIC TRENDS: "PROCEDURALIZATION" AND "ACTIVATION"

The lists of instruments that we have just reviewed provide evidence of a gradual evolution or change in priorities. We can sum up the general direction taken by saying that the approach is becoming increasingly "Schumpeterian", referring to the famous Austrian economist who formulated his analysis of the "creative destruction" of capitalism in the first half of the 20th century. With his approach, there is no point in delaying job losses resulting from capitalism, nor should this be done to protect workers under threat. On the other hand, it is justified to compensate for the consequences and to organize the "offloading" of workers rejected by certain sectors or businesses onto other sectors that are taking workers on.

However, this change is taking place in a context where lay-offs no longer appear to be unfortunate but isolated incidents: they are gradually becoming more widespread and are tending to become permanent. Some authors have even talked about a "genetic mutation" in restructuring (Carabelli and Tronti, 1999), in Tronti and Carabelli (eds.), 1999, p. 9) to refer to the constant need to be flexible and competitive which is making it harder for workers to find and keep jobs. The result has been two major changes in the ways that instruments accompanying restructuring are used. The first, which can be seen behind the growing importance of public employment policies, is the collectivization of restructuring. As we have seen, these have usually triggered public interventions, but now, in the developed countries at least, they tend to be conducted according to permanent rules and schedules drawn up by the public authorities. This trend towards "proceduralization" is coupled with a growing emphasis on "active" approaches that are supposed to be looking to the future of new jobs rather than trying to preserve the past. The result, according to Teyssier and Vicens (2001), is that they are bringing a "new balance of rights" in Europe for economic redundancies. However, these two trends are not without reactions or limits. We will examine each in turn, before showing that their joint impact leads to considerable tension when put alongside the available assessments of the effectiveness of measures accompanying restructuring.

Trend towards "proceduralization" and introduction
of permanent mechanisms

According to Carabelli and Tronti (1999), modern life is likely to become one continuous restructuring process, and as a result the measures accompanying these restructuring need to be closely linked to any changes in the political and legislative mechanisms framing the operation of the labour market and organizing adjustments to it, as greater and greater flexibility is required. They summarize trends in Europe, identifying three fields where flexibility is exercised, which are found in every country but explored to varying degrees in each national situation: the adjustment of labour contracts to provide less protection; the introduction of greater flexibility in managing working time; and the application of flexible pay arrangements.

Within this briefly outlined general framework recourse to the law or the courts becomes a central issue every time a contract is likely to be terminated. There is thus a trend towards the "juridicization" of labour relations, the effects of which are most visible when restructuring occur, because the workers concerned have usually been employed for a long time in sectors where stable, protected labour relations are guaranteed.

In the USA, it is anti-discrimination measures that come to the fore in any mass redundancy procedure, particularly when there are disputes relating to age discrimination (Burrows, 2002). In many countries in Europe, "redundancy programmes" set out the substantive and above all the procedural requirements to be complied with by major companies when carrying out mass lay-offs. As Morin and Vicens (2001) point out, the extent to which employers are made responsible varies enormously from country to country, as does the content of the "redundancy programme" itself. In France, it is a document drawn up by the employer in accordance with the requirements of the Labour Code, and is the result of the employer's obligation to provide both internal and external redeployment, depending on the company's resources. In Germany it is an agreement negotiated between employers and trade unions and mainly contains financial measures. Its less binding nature is counterbalanced by the fact that the staff representatives have a right of veto and are, in law, involved in selecting the workers laid off. In Italy, external redeployment measures for which the company is responsible are required only in exceptional cases, but if a worker brings legal proceedings and wins, the reinstatement order is compulsory (Carabelli and Tronti, op. cit.). In the United Kingdom, the obligations are limited to redundancy payments, which remain modest. In Spain and Denmark, the obligations on the employer are much lighter.

Despite this variety of situations, the authors identify the emergence, in Europe at least, of what they suggest might be called an "economic redundancy system", ranging from the limitation/regulation of redundancies (the administrative authorization introduced in France in 1975 and abolished in 1986 was a special case, but other countries require grounds to be given for redundancies or make them legitimate in only restricted cases) to the obligation to give advance warning or consult the workforce and/or various regional or national public bodies, or to follow a series of predetermined steps. This "system" also has a basis in European legislation (1975 directive amended and expanded in 1992 (for an overall description, see Guéry, 1999). A comparative legal study published by Bernard Bruhnes Consultants in 2002 covering Germany, Belgium, Spain, France, Italy, the United Kingdom and Sweden (Chassard et al., 2002a and b) bears out the fact that most European countries are converging towards bureaucratic, complex procedures accompanying collective redundancies.

The case of France is a good illustration of this proceduralizing trend, and a specialised jargon that is impenetrable to the uninitiated is even emerging: the provisions of the Labour Code distinguish between procedures linked to restructuring plans in Volume III and procedures relating to plans to safeguard jobs in Volume IV, and any criticisms of a completed or impending redundancy programme tend to be referred to (by specialists!) simply as "Volume III" or "Volume IV".

However, because of their changing aspect, these national "systems" are actually more like works in progress, often debated and disputed by employers, than a stable body of rules and institutions. A distinction can be drawn in this field between "hard" and "soft" versions (Villeval, 1993, Sisson, 2001). The first is found in countries where there is strong State involvement and tends to result in a fairly detailed and binding network of laws and regulations, while the "soft" version is merely a statement of principles and general frameworks, and is found in countries which allow the social partners greater room to take action. These differences are something that enterprises making redundancies adapt to, sometimes having to bow to particular national requirements, and sometimes exploiting different levels of permissiveness.

Regardless of the institutional diversity in which these "systems" are rooted, one paradox is typical of all of them: they often serve to protect older, poorly-skilled workers who have been in their jobs for a long time and are therefore less likely to be mobile and are difficult to train, *and* they serve to organize their mobility and increasingly include options or even obligations to undergo training or retraining. This brings us on to the second trend – "activation".

Trend towards "activation" and difficulty in challenging early retirement schemes

We have already mentioned the characteristic instruments of "active employment policies" which have grown in importance over the last 20 years, so there is no need to review them. Return-to-work grants, job placement services, instruction in job search techniques and training are thus increasingly included in redundancy schemes.

The trend towards "activation" is also evident in the increasing criticism of early retirement schemes (see, for example, Kohli et al. (1991), Guillemard (2003), and the series of 20 national reports on "Ageing and Employment Policies" published by the OECD), and it is this point that we would like to focus on. Such schemes continue to be very widely used. As far as we know there are currently no reliable figures on the relative share of the workforce covered by early retirement schemes and other employment policy instruments in the management of collective redundancies globally or even in Europe or the USA. However, an examination of a number of cases suggests that in European countries at least that share is rarely less than 50 per cent of the workers concerned (see, for example, the comparative evaluation monographs by Auer and Speckesser (1998)), nor is it declining. This staying power is one of the main characteristics of policies accompanying restructuring.

A distinction must be drawn between countries where this instrument exists but is limited to economic redundancies, and countries which, like France, Belgium and the Netherlands, use it much more generally or even systematically. It should also be mentioned that some countries use different mechanisms which nevertheless have similar functions, such as programmes for the disabled allowing them to leave the labour market; the Netherlands combines both strands here.

The national trends promoting "active ageing" seen at the end of the 1990s were first and foremost the product of governments anxious about funding pensions and demographic decline. The social partners are generally much more circumspect and want to keep early retirement schemes in use. The employers' organizations sometimes express hostility to early retirement schemes at national level, but are much more in favour at local level.

It might be thought that all the social partners are caught up in the usual mechanism of grading "surplus" workers, picking out the least productive, or supposedly least productive, for rejection. For the sake of the company's future, faced with stronger competition and in the context of work reorganization and intensification, it seems natural to keep the workers regarded as the most adaptable and productive. Older, poorly trained workers then become the main target of redundancies. They are also difficult "clients" for active employment policies. Early retirement schemes then appear to be the only possible solution for most of them, and a counter-concession for the increased effort demanded of other workers under an implicit "social contract". In many countries, access to early retirement is seen as a right by older workers threatened by globalization.

The trend towards "activation" is circumventing the resistance put up by early retirement schemes, first and foremost by making them less advantageous. In France, for example (Courtioux, 2001), early retirement schemes proper are being restricted in favour of "job search exemptions" for older workers who are the victims of economic redundancies and are merely covered by unemployment insurance. These early retirement substitutes are clearly less advantageous for their beneficiaries and clearly less costly for the public authorities. In Belgium, a similar scheme has been dubbed, ironically, "Canada Dry" early retirement. Another sign of the trend towards "activation" is the attempts to introduce part-time early retirement schemes. These exist in France and Germany, but in most cases they were marginalized or diverted from their purpose. The trend here is to "lock in" workers (Courtioux, op. cit.), as compared with the "early-exit-from-activity culture" (Guillemard, 2003).

Downward mobility markers?

If we try to assess the joint effect of the two trends described above, which have not developed unopposed, as we have seen, we come on to the question of the effectiveness of policies designed to *redeploy* workers who are the victims of restructuring. Here again few analyses have been carried out, probably because processing restructuring is primarily about managing a dispersion: a group of workers previously together are dislocated and filtered, with some workers (the most able?) advancing the timetable and changing jobs or regions very quickly, while others (the majority, as we have seen) are sidelined, and others are covered by redeployment measures of varying duration. As a result, the evaluations available have often had to deal with fragmented career paths.

Among the analyses available that genuinely focus on restructuring, the work of Tejada and Swaim (2004; op. cit) for the OECD is probably one of the most comprehensive. It also confirms what we know: that redeployment rates for workers looking for a new job rarely exceed 50 per cent. What we find here, accentuated by the special nature of the circumstances and people involved, is that active employment policies perform relatively poorly or disappointingly (see Auer et al. (2005) for a global assessment, which is that they are useful, but need to be reviewed to improve their organization, monitoring and appropriation by the communities concerned). In particular, there is great scepticism about training as an employment policy tool when dealing with restructuring. It is often deemed to be ineffective if it is too general, but more effective if it is vocational. However, workers made collectively redundant, who are often specialized in a particular trade that is disappearing, often find it very difficult to feel motivated about training or gaining access to it.

The American study by Jacobson L., LaLonde R.J. and Sullivan D. (2003) is interesting here, because it reports fairly good performances. It focuses on public retraining courses for "displaced" older workers in the USA, and shows that this policy is generally effective for those "displaced" workers that have access to it (as much as for other groups of workers). However, the final assessment is pessimistic: the emphasis placed on the shorter perspective of improving new skills limits the social profitability and therefore, in their view, the legitimacy of this instrument. Older "displaced" workers suffer by comparison, even where they do as well as everyone else!

A comparative examination of the choices made by firms to manage restructuring shows that the early retirement option is often chosen even though it is expensive, either for the company itself or for the public authorities, and is sometimes the most expensive option compared with training, redeployment, etc. (see Auer and Speckesser, 1998) for estimated comparative costs in the European automobile industry). What companies are actually doing is buying harmonious industrial relations and greater productive commitment from the remaining workers.

We can therefore conclude that, as firms' career management policies currently stand, the gradual withdrawal of early retirement schemes is leaving most workers who are the victims of restructuring with no other public option apart from help towards finding rarer, poorer quality jobs, with compensation either in the form of a one-off payment by the firm, or through public compensation or grant schemes spread over time. There is a resulting risk that career paths will be downgraded or even marginalised, the best possible scenario being a less skilled and more poorly paid job than before, with the wage gradually re-attaining the previous level over a number of years.

The accompanying measures provided for restructuring are thus gradually tending to force people into downward mobility.

4. NEGOTIATING EMPLOYABILITY

There are, however, many initiatives aimed at rebuilding a future in areas where disruptions caused by restructuring reveal only a desolate past made up of job or income losses. These are based on two findings. The first is the need to take on responsibility not only for jobs that were lost or need to be restored, but also for careers. Most of the studies tracking what happened to workers who became the victims of restructuring underline that the results in terms of redeployment depend very much on the past career of the workers concerned. Looking only at France, this finding applies as from 1988 (Outin et al., 1988). It also applies to "redeployment agreements" (N. Cloarec, 1998). A recent assessment of the retraining of miners in France (Mazade, 2004) highlights how far the career paths pursued by miners depend on their earlier job conditions. This first observation goes hand in hand with a second, regarding the importance of local actors appropriating the tools and procedures that allow them to confront retraining. Active participation by those undergoing retraining is vital to success. This is, however, not so easy to achieve, because involving workers in the management of what they may regard as the consequences of an act of aggression against them cannot be a simple measure and implies a reversal of expectations.

The term employability, in the sense of the ability to obtain and keep a job in a given context, broadly summarizes this change of perspective, because it means addressing the future of a potential that needs to be consolidated or increased and enhanced and taking account of the experience acquired in a career and preparing to modify or redirect it. Yet the use of the term remains uncertain if not controversial, no doubt because of its virtual connotations: in cases of unemployment, to focus on the development of employability seems far less positive than a job offer and to open the door to promises that are not kept. Also, the term is often perceived as holding the individual a priori responsible for the possible failure of redeployment. Some of the wording and some of the priorities contained in the European Employment Strategy first set out at the 1997 Luxembourg summit (see Gazier, 1999) are open to this kind of criticism, in confining themselves to "activating" the assumption of responsibility for the unemployed.

In this final section we would like to show that measures designed to reverse pessimistic expectations are based on various methods of boosting employability, not only individual but also and in particular collective. It is worth presenting two in particular: (a) preventive measures, whether at the initiative of large groups or based on the signature of "employment and competitiveness pacts", and (b) procedures for the negotiated management of "transitions" on and around the job market.

Agreed or negotiated preventive measures

Conscious of the risks of social disruption and damage to image resulting from poorly managed or poorly anticipated retraining measures, large groups that have the necessary resources have sometimes opted for advancing the timetable and taking full or partial responsibility for reindustrializing the labour market areas under threat and for the anticipated retraining of employees. The study by M. F. Raveyre (2001) shows that very varied measures were taken in France with a view to combining expansion, the creation of retraining associations, aid for enterprise creation, and so forth, when a large group was considering medium-term job losses. A similar type of analysis is proposed by M. Campinos-Dubernet (2003), which emphasizes the need for discretion if these initiatives are to succeed. It takes the view, in fact, that this is a matter of "mine-clearing", based on the confidence of the actors and in particular the workers, which cannot be achieved in a climate of dramatization or media attention.

This is a very good indication of the important role of anticipation and the imperative need for careful management. At the same time, the observed and advocated approach is rather paradoxical: it is agreed on, yet it is unilateral and confidential. Perhaps these characteristics, which are only partially compatible, stem from the particular nature of social dialogue in France, which is not based on a tradition of sustained partnership. An example from the Netherlands shows that it is possible to negotiate about employability with the open aim of boosting productivity and cutting staff. The case in point is the Netherlands Railways (see Gazier and Schmid, 2001 and Gazier, 2005b). In this case, an agreement was signed which provides, in exchange for a period of wage restraints, for the organization every three years of an appraisal of skills that establishes the position of all the company's employees on the employment market. This appraisal, carried out by a group of experts selected by common agreement by the management and the unions, is financed by the company. The agreement provides that if extra training is needed to bring some employees up to the market level, given their seniority and pay, a dual obligation applies: the company must finance this training and the employee in question must follow it. This is, therefore, a preventive agreement to facilitate the redeployment of employees in anticipation of the rationalization of the company in the context of European competition.

There is a more general formula that goes beyond this observation: the "competitiveness and employment pacts", which were presented in some detail in 2001 in a special issue of the journal *Transfer*, introduced by A. Martin Artiles (2001). Such pacts have come into being since the early 1990s in many parts of the world, at four different levels: national, regional, sectoral and enterprise. They consist of exchanging employee concessions (generally, wage restraints or the acceptance of organizational changes) for various measures and commitments entered into by the firm that are supposed to protect jobs for a given time. Examples of this kind of "concession bargaining" can be found throughout the world, as shown in the article by Ghellab and Kelly (2001) in that same issue.

One interesting example quoted by the authors is the Ford car company in Argentina, which, against the background of a general downturn in activity, concluded an agreement suspending any lay-offs for 15 months. Over that period, employees do not work and receive compensation. If production has not recovered by the end of that period, employees may be laid off and receive an allowance. This reflects, in a more modest form, the employment guarantees GM agreed in 1996 following negotiations with UAW (ibid.).

Another example is the metal-working industry in South Africa. In 1993, NUMSA, the main union operating in the sector, signed an agreement modernizing the qualification grading scales, reducing the grades from 13 to 5 and organizing the acquisition and enhancement of multiple skills, in order to create qualifications that are valid in very diverse working environments and can be transferred from one sector to another.

Government intervention may aim to prevent redundancies while also promoting social dialogue. For instance, in 1998 Korea introduced an "Employment Maintenance Support Scheme" (EMSS) as a means of coping with a serious economic crisis. This fund, part of the unemployment insurance scheme, helps firms to cut working hours, temporarily suspend their activity or train surplus workers. In order to obtain this aid, however, employers must consult the unions or staff representatives. A total of 4,220 firms received this aid, which is said to have helped keep some 780,000 workers in employment.

At an even more international level, since the famous Wassenaar agreement of 1982, national "pacts" in Europe have involved offering job guarantees in exchange for increased internal flexibility and wage restraints. The Netherlands example that is now operating is no doubt the most typical and the most closely studied pact of this kind. It has been confirmed and modified on several occasions, with a new agreement concluded in 1993 and an "Agenda 2002" concluded in 1997 (Freyssinet and Seifert, 2001).

Going down to company level again, the possibility of concluding "method agreements", as has been done in France since 2003 in the case of announcements of collective redundancies, has paved the way for genuine negotiations relating to redundancy programmes. This makes it possible to go beyond the legal obligations directly linked to the planned dismissals and operate on a wider spectrum of exchanges of information and consultation (Kerbourc'h et al., 2001; Syndex, 2002). This instrument, which remains optional and experimental, is, therefore, a milestone on the road to the negotiated and shared management of restructuring.

Towards the negotiated management of "transitions"?

It is possible to extend these experiments by endeavouring to generalize about them. The most common result of restructuring is that it forces workers to change career, with losses in terms of income but sometimes also dislocation of their living environment and way of life, if not a questioning of their identity. One theoretical and practical approach developed in Europe since 1995, entitled "transitional labour markets", seeks to build up collective bases for career management by those actually involved (Schmid and Gazier (eds.), 2002; Gazier, 2005a). Here, job promotion (not forgetting growth and competitiveness conditions) is based on promoting the chosen form of mobility and may therefore use all the career stages as so many risks, but also as levers for coping with the hazards of job destruction.

A prime concern is how to restore workers' autonomy, by promoting both voluntary participation and solidarity among the workers involved. One highly original feature of the Austrian "employment foundations" (*Voest-Alpine Stahlstiftung*) referred to earlier is that they were based on this principle. These "employment foundations" date back to 1987, to the measures taken by the social partners when the large steel company Voest-Alpine made redundancies. The programme has been carefully studied and evaluated (Winter-Ebmer (2001)). We will show how it operates in the context of the announcement and implementation of collective redundancies.

1. Restructuring is announced at least six months in advance, so as to leave time for collective concerted action and individual initiatives.

2. The retraining programme is run by a foundation, which means it is funded from fixed capital that the firm laying off workers sets aside for that purpose. So the foundation is independent and stable and will remain as long as it is needed. Apart from this capital, it is funded from three sources: public funds for employment policies, a significant share of around one-third of the retraining allowance received by the "leavers" and a very small contribution paid by the remaining workers (about 0.2 per cent of their wages) to pay for the training schemes. This last funding is particularly original. It means that solidarity between the "leaving" and the "remaining" workers is organized deliberately and that the "remaining" workers also have an interest in ensuring that the retraining is rapid and effective.

3. In this context, the "leavers" do so on a voluntary basis and may vary widely in age and qualification (reflecting the average composition of the firm in question) and are identified as dynamic employees seizing the opportunity to advance their career or diversify their experience. As a result, the social climate is far better than in the more frequent cases where the firm separates itself from what it regards as the least productive employees.

4. The approach to "leavers" is to give priority to training schemes, which are regarded as a central component of the redeployment programme.

This approach clearly enables the actors concerned to regain control of their options and timetable. The evaluation by Winter-Ebmer (op. cit.) found that under this programme redeployment outcomes were better than in the case of traditional restructuring.

It is quite clear, however, that there is no job-creating component in this form of organization. Workers are therefore still reliant on the local and global functioning of the job market and the concerted action described above. This is where the "transitional" approach may be generally applicable (Gazier, 2005b). It suggests that a network of job opportunities or paid temporary positions may be identified and managed at regional level if one looks at career intersections; for example, some workers take leave for various reasons (parental leave, training leave) and are replaced by others who use this opportunity to enhance their employability. This could improve the functioning of the job market, by harnessing certain external factors that stem from better coordination (e.g. if workers feel more secure they can take more initiatives and more risks) and by making the job market less segmented, with less of a distinction between "good" and "bad" jobs.

There is not enough space to discuss the contributions, implementing conditions and limits of this systematic approach to improving career security. It suggests that the earlier basis for stabilizing workers, i.e. "internal markets" and adjusted careers, has become too narrow and fragile to achieve this end. It therefore needs to be supplemented by definitions and rights that apply as much outside as within the firm. These are the "transitional" rights that the Supiot report (Supiot, 1999) has set out in legal terms. This would make it possible to construct credible and socially acceptable alternatives to irreversible full-time early retirement, for example by letting employees regarded as surplus work part-time in the firm (which implies public funding of the additional organizational costs) and offering them a second part-time job in the community, co-financed by the association and a municipality. This diversification of career paths, with maintenance or enhancement of employability, could give a boost to strategies to revitalize the industrial and social fabric in areas at risk of mass job cuts.

This ambitious approach, which is still in its early days, combines a proposal to reform employment policies (in the sense of their appropriation by the actors involved) with reform of the employment relationship (in the sense of taking account of all the parties involved in the firm, and not just the shareholders). It presupposes the development of a capacity for consultation that at present exists only in small countries that have developed a strong tradition of social dialogue.

5. CONCLUSION

The challenges of job losses due to globalization have generated a wide variety of attitudes, tools and experiments, of which this paper has endeavoured to give some idea at national level. Between laissez-faire and the attempt to slow down the march of history, an intermediate option has prevailed. It seeks to compensate for job losses and increasingly to redeploy workers. The instruments used to that end often remain rather ineffective, despite their cost and at times their sophistication. An intensive drive towards solidarity is needed to reconcile commercial openness with social justice – as also, no doubt, a very imaginative approach, at both national and international level.

THE INTERNATIONALIZATION OF EMPLOYMENT AND THE DEBATE ABOUT OFFSHORING IN FRANCE: LEGAL PERSPECTIVES

BY MARIE-ANGE MOREAU

1. INTRODUCTION

The report published in February 2004 by the World Commission on the Social Dimension of Globalization provides more than just a useful snapshot of the economic phenomenon known as globalization, with its widely varying effects on different geographical areas and occupational sectors, and the extent of the shockwaves it has generated across the planet – impacting on jobs and the nature of employment, exacerbating many forms of inequality, increasing purchasing power and affecting efforts to combat poverty.

It has, in addition, two particular merits. On the one hand it demonstrates that we cannot regard economic globalization as a black-and-white issue and take a stand for or against; we cannot fail to recognize it as a complex and unprecedented phenomenon which assumes many forms and thus demands many different types of response at different levels.

On the other hand, the report highlights the need for consistency in the relevant institutional and legislative choices. The importance of consistency implies in turn a need to examine different regulatory approaches[1] and to select the levels at which responses are possible.[2]

The debate about offshoring is particularly interesting here inasmuch as it is the most obvious "symptom" of the internationalization of employment in the industrialized countries – offshoring being the clearest proof of companies' capacity to use the options presented by economic globalization for constructing their strategies at global level.

---

[1] Because responses to globalization are multi-disciplinary, it makes sense to use the term "regulatory approaches" implying something more than mere sets of rules. The social regulation of globalization entails, however, new levels of complexity (Murray and Trudeau, 2004). It is impossible in the context of this paper to consider all potential regulatory approaches, although the trend in labour law towards a highly interesting combination of traditional "hard law" responses and new "soft law" regulatory techniques is worth noting.

[2] At a European University Institute conference in October 2004, Giuliano Amato, a member of the World Commission, placed great emphasis on the need for coordination both of measures taken at different policy-making (and regulatory) levels and among the international institutions whose activities affect employment issues (the ILO, WTO, IMF, World Bank and UN). Another aspect that we will not attempt to consider here concerns the roles of the different international institutions in regulating the impact of globalization on workers.

It is clear from the debate about offshoring in France, as reported in the media particularly since September 2004, that, for political reasons, the consequences of the internationalization of employment are seen only in terms of restructuring and its impact in the form of redundancy programmes and net job losses at local and national levels.[3] The problem of offshoring is thus addressed solely as a matter of job losses in France, ignoring its European and international dimensions and without any attempt to understand the offshoring in question as part of a movement towards the internationalization of employment beyond French borders. The only aspect highlighted[4] has been the negative impact on employment.[5]

The questions that have been asked reflect national and corporatist thinking – justified by the need to explain at national level the loss of jobs and the lack of a satisfactory political response – and fail to take proper account of the European dimension in issues concerning companies' freedom of movement in Europe.

This very French analysis of the situation at least has the merit of demonstrating the importance of the national level when addressing the territorial consequences of work redistribution and the radical changes wrought on employment by economic globalization.

The response to job losses at national level cannot be "delegated" to a higher level of regulation, given that national political choices are the determining factor in attracting international investment. Yet to see the issue in purely national terms is to ignore the economic choices open to companies which define themselves globally, and in such choices lies the potential for more sophisticated responses at European and transnational level.

In considering offshoring within the European Union we need to set about identifying company strategies, which constitute the framework for economic competitiveness on the international market. What criteria determine these strategies and companies' choices when setting up or moving inside the European market? What factors impel companies to locate where they do, or to award contracts outside the European market? What type of statutory measures might offer a response to the new strategies?[6]

---

[3] While this is, of course, justifiable, we should bear in mind that the debate comes on the heels of existing discussions between the social partners about a legislative response to restructuring, in the light of the attempt by the "Fillon Act" (2003) to suspend measures taken under the Social Modernization Act of 2002 which had considerably extended the powers of works councils, giving them the option of submitting alternatives to management proposals. The Borloo Act of 18 January 2005 has had the effect of terminating the discussions because inter-sectoral negotiations were unsuccessful.

[4] It is no surprise that members of the public in the new EU member States should have reacted with particular indignation to the stances taken in France.

[5] While the figures on offshoring reported in the press were highly exaggerated, estimating their impact in quantitative terms is nonetheless a tricky matter, as indicated in the Lorenzi and Fontagné report (2004) quoted below.

[6] Studies show that social considerations have to be seen in combination with other factors (tax arrangements, transport, infrastructure and the rules of corporate law, for example).

We therefore need to look beyond the simplistic perception of offshoring as transfer of production units from one place to another[7] or movements of capital (in the form of foreign direct investment) or of manufacturing activities. Instead we need to see them as one aspect of corporate strategies for responding to the attractions of different territories within a given market.

2. THE SEARCH FOR NEW AVENUES

The search for new avenues of approach depends heavily on the theoretical groundwork done in research on globalization, the strategies of multinational companies, the international division of labour, and the switch to a new paradigm for corporate organization as a result of globalization.

In our view, the most significant contributions to a rethinking of legislative and regulatory responses stem not only from economic analysis but also from ideas developed in the sociology of employment and the law, which are summarized below.[8]

1) It is important to see globalization as a system characterized by the *interdependence* of different factors associated with a specific stage in a process: it involves not only the development of international trade and international exchanges, as institutionalized by the WTO, for example, but also the development of multinational companies and constant changes in their methods of organization and in market financing arrangements (C.A. Michalet 2000, 2002; Aglietta and Rebérioux, 2004).

2) The reorganization of companies on a global basis entails not only the introduction of new structures but also "global networking" and "global switching" as well as the concentration of certain functions (R&D, finance, etc.) and the selections of locations in the world economy ("global focusing").

These new strategies are justified in the name of "efficiency seeking" and the quest for profitability in absolute terms at a global (as opposed to a national or indeed a regional) level (Mucchielli, 1998; C.A. Michalet, 2000, 2002; J.H Lorenzi and L. Fontagné, 2004).

---

[7] Defining offshoring is not easy when it comes to analysing its economic impact and statistically evaluating it as a phenomenon. See, in the report entitled *Désindustrialisations, délocalisations* by J.H. Lorenzi and L. Fontagné, November 2004, the highly pertinent analyses by L. de Gimel, p. 163. Offshoring is defined here as "the closure of a production unit in France followed by its reopening abroad with a view to re-importing into the national territory at reduced cost, or continuing to supply the export market, from the new facility" (p. 12). J. Fayolle (ibid., p. 144) writes that offshoring "may be regarded as a particular form of FDI foreign direct investment] covering a wide range of activities from the creation *ex nihilo* of a new production unit abroad to the offshoring by transfer of pre-existing activity, and including corporate buy-outs". Neither definition offers a comprehensive understanding of the question because corporate strategies involve not only mobility in terms of capital, the siting of economic activity and installations, but also choices with regard to the way that production is organized, notably through international subcontracting.

[8] Clearly we lack the space here to explore in depth the ideas of the authors quoted and to situate them in the overall spectrum of thinking about globalization, characterized as it is by a great diversity of opinions, ideas, disciplinary approaches and methodologies.

The quest for economic efficiency thus leads to a global-scale reorganization of processes, with profound implications in terms of changed employment patterns. It is driven by pressure of competition in the various sectors.

3) This reorganization of processes entails a new international division of work
    according to complex plans, which aim not only to minimize costs but also
    to achieve market penetration. Companies justify their choices not only in
    terms of seeking to minimize costs but also according to a whole range of
    factors,[9] utilizing any geographical advantages they may possess (Pottier,
    2003). This international division of work is based on the organization of
    companies as networks, both in a vertical sense...

4) (from parent company through subsidiaries to branch level) and horizon-
    tally (through an international web of subcontractors) (Markusen, 1995;
    Barba Navaretti, 2004; Hanson et al., 2003).

5) We have seen the emergence of a new model for production, leading in turn
    to a new style of production management based on flexibility and process
    standardization; systems of organizing work that prioritize the mobilization
    of skills and qualifications; and new employment relationships based, in
    some cases, on the paradoxical search for flexibility on working conditions
    coupled with employee participation and commitment to corporate goals.
    We are thus able to identify radical changes in the post-Fordist model of
    production and to focus on the tensions and contradictions inherent in the
    new model, requiring, as it does, fresh criteria for reviewing both public
    policies and systems of representation (Murray, Belanger, Giles and
    Lapointe, 2004; F. De Coninck, 2004).

Statutory responses must therefore adapt to address the specificities of the
economic structure erected as a result of globalization and must reflect both new
employer configurations (by nature transnational) (Moreau and Trudeau, 1995,
1998; I. Daugareilh, 2001), and new network-based corporate structures (also
transnational).

This means that, if the intention is to provide legal coverage for companies'
activities, legal standards can no longer be applied solely within national

---

[9] Studies also show that strategies are increasingly complex (Lorenzi and Fontagné report),
covering:
–   the specific features of competition in particular sectors;
–   the type of corporate organization selected (according to the degree of internationalization);
–   group structure (notably networked companies);
–   constraints on the financing of economic activities (Aglietta and Rebérioux);
–   capital structure (insider/outsider, see the work of Tony Edwards on "Corporate
    Governance, Industrial Relations and Trends in Company-Level Restructuring ...]
    in Europe", 2004)
At the same time, companies' needs are increasingly diverse, concerning as they do:
–   national infrastructure;
–   flexibility in the way that production is organized;
–   distribution costs;
–   levels of qualification and of State-provided education;
–   workforces' levels of qualification.

borders. The same holds true with regard to corporate offshoring, which increasingly affects groups of countries.

From studies of multinational companies' strategies, we see that these are no longer confined to national territories and that they function within a context of decision-making at global level and at an accordingly accelerated pace. **Spatial and temporal aspects of law-making therefore need to be adjusted** (Moreau and Trudeau, 2000).

It is thus clear that statutory responses to questions concerning the internationalization of employment must be tailored to **the scale of multinational companies' activities**, in other words there must be a fit:

– in terms of territory (a transnational arena),
– in terms of pace (permitting rapid reaction), and
– with regard to the nature of activity (ongoing renewal of strategies at global level, and stability in the institutional machinery designed to address them).

Such an approach requires us to reconsider the underlying concepts of labour law, which are rooted in the dualistic model of employers/workers or capital/labour (Supiot, 2002), and spatially and temporally conditioned by the Fordist corporate approach, ignoring completely the transnational, web-type systems of organization favoured by the "network economy" (Mückenberger, 2004).

With regard to offshoring, Lorenzi and Fontagné, in *Désindustrialisations, délocalisations* (2004), demonstrate well not only how hard it is to assess precisely the shifts that cause companies to relocate across national borders but also the importance of the trend towards "reshuffles" on the European or international game board.[10] The sectors most concerned here (already identified in 1992 in the Arthuis Report) are the clothing and leather industries, information and communications, household goods, electrical and electronic equipment, textiles, and the steel industry. Those most affected by restructuring are telecommunications (20 per cent) financial services (15 per cent) transport (12 per cent) and, in manufacturing, steel, leather, chemicals, engineering and food processing.

Specialization strategies, however, affect not only manufacturing but also those services, which, for technological or practical reasons, need not be located close to their clients or users.

The report indicates[11] that the companies performing best are those which have adopted a global strategy – thus justifying certain offshoring choices designed to boost international competitiveness, ensure survival ("defensive offshoring") or increase employment ("offensive offshoring").

Whatever the nature of the offshoring or – more generally – of companies' strategic decisions on business location, such shifts are permissible as a result of choices made in the regulation of international trade (by the WTO) that have

---

[10] See comments by P. Arthuis (on the Lorenzi and Fontagné report), and his estimates pointing to a recent acceleration in the pace of corporate reorganization (ibid., p. 70)

[11] ibid., p. 64

tended to eliminate protectionist-type barriers, and at European level in relation to the establishment of multinational companies on European territory (since 1961 multinationals have been able to enjoy the economic freedoms recognized within Europe).

Because the changes resulting from companies' strategic choices in a global marketplace – including the European market – are irrevocable, they require statutory responses that reflect what are permanent transformations in employment.

The proposals contained in the Lorenzi and Fontagné report are in line with the conclusions reached by Bob Hepple in the UK (2005): he explains that statutory responses to the internationalization of employment need to be mindful of the comparative advantages existing in each country, including social advantages. It is, indeed, highly unlikely that, whatever the measures taken to reduce social costs in France, French wage bills could ever compete with those of China or India. It is also highly unlikely – even if permitted overtime is increased and the laws on the 35-hour working week reviewed – that working-time flexibility in France could compete with the British goal of complete freedom in the use of overtime (the right to work a 48-hour week being regarded as a social achievement).

Research into comparative advantage in social terms suggests that we should encourage those policy choices that enable a country to be distinctive by combining its social and economic strengths.

Statutory responses may thus be based on the need for solutions that:

– integrate a given territory's **comparative economic advantages** with comparative social advantages (in France, for example, a high level of technology and a highly qualified workforce and, at EU level, the safeguards offered by the European economic model);

– reflect the **ongoing** nature of corporate strategies for location/establishment and offshoring of capital and activity in the global market by ensuring that employment protection can be sustained in ways that will match the pace of changing employment strategies.[12]

– can adapt to the transnational nature of companies' activities at both European and global level.

---

[12] We do not intend to consider the time factor here although it is important, particularly if procedures for anticipating restructuring, and for expediting measures in relation to redundancy programmes, are to be effective (Aubert and Beaujolin, 2004). The fact that the French Court of Cassation admits urgent applications for judicial review of redundancy programmes indicates the importance of having emergency procedures that enable social response measures to keep pace with employers' decision making.

2. DERIVING MAXIMUM VALUE FROM COMPARATIVE SOCIAL ADVANTAGES AT NATIONAL AND EUROPEAN LEVELS

In considering how to derive maximum value from existing comparative advantages in the social sphere[13] we need to look at three levels because companies face pressure of competition simultaneously in the local (or regional), national and European arenas. Naturally this raises the question of the appropriate regulatory level, given that corporate strategies take account – among other factors – of social advantages or social costs that make particular territories more or less attractive.

Clearly, therefore, we need to begin by addressing the question of regulatory levels before going on to consider the consequences of an approach based on maximizing comparative social advantages at European level.

Levels of regulation

There is no doubt that all three levels are currently extremely important in addressing the impact of the internationalization of employment.

– *The local level* is important in terms of ensuring consistency in the responses of locally based institutions[14] and the ability of communities to adapt when job catchment areas and industrial districts are constructed or reconstructed. Job catchment areas and industrial districts may be characterized by having a recognized specialization (Silicon Valley, Sophia Antipolis, and industrial districts of Italy are examples) and thus a key economic advantage on which to build in the world marketplace (see Lorenzi and Fontagné report on development poles and "clusters", C.A. Michalet, 2002).

– The job catchment area [*bassin d'emploi*] or economic pole is therefore a physical reference that extends beyond the legal framework of the company, can embrace both independent companies and self-employed workers and therefore allows us to see the pattern of economic dependence among workers who find themselves almost beyond the pale of labour law, and also among companies (however large or small) that form part of international subcontracting networks.

– Job catchment areas began to be referred to in a tentative way in France in 2003 and again in 2005 as areas that merited targeting with specific information about the territorial impact of redundancies and to be the object of measures for dealing with them.

The job catchment area is not currently an entity recognized in labour law (P. Waquet et al., 2003). Nor is it a territory designated at institutional level for

---

[13] It is feasible to assume that comparative social advantages existing in particular countries or regions can impact in different ways on different sectors: for example, the skills of leather workers in the Prato region (in Italy) allowed a luxury leather industry to develop there (subcontracting for Gucci).

[14] Catherine Stone's research (at Columbia University) indicates that local community development in the USA has resulted from globalization (2003).

the encouragement of measures to anticipate restructuring, or the coordination of industrial policy measures or steps to tackle unemployment.

It is thus feasible to ask how job catchment areas might be developed into poles of attraction in economic and social terms.

The Lorenzi and Fontagné report suggests that such poles should be built around innovation. Their comparative economic advantage in social terms would lie in better occupational training and in retraining schemes that could also become a focus of social promotion (helping people to obtain high-level qualifications, fostering mobility, hiving off various functions and creating specific types of enterprise), reflecting the demand for retraining and redeployment that is created by offshoring and restructuring.

At the social level, this implies that it would be important to establish territorial social dialogue in job catchment areas that would provide the opportunity for local decision-makers in the fields of regional/sectoral/industrial policy, education policy, occupational training, and social partners, to come together.

Linking the main players in job catchment areas in the framework of social territorial dialogue could help develop not only rules for anticipating and managing restructuring but also help develop efficient measures for ensuring the supply of a local labour force that was qualified and geared to conditions in the job catchment area.

It appears that currently negotiated agreements on methods tend towards the setting up of territorial measures based on commitment by the firm shedding jobs that are outside of the obligations which are part of the job protection plan, in order to organize with exterior partners a linkage between action to promote local firms in the framework of a "territorial social charter".[15]

The national level continues to be prioritized in France[16] but in the context of globalization we have to question the impact of government intervention in the area of social protection. On this point the World Commission report reasserts the importance of positive and negative decisions taken in the face of organized pressure to deregulate employment protection. Obviously a territory can make itself attractive by engaging in a "race to the bottom",[17] going so far as to create "free zones" in which workers enjoy no social protection, and the mobility of capital acts as a brake on government attempts to control corporate behaviour and strategies on the world market. Nonetheless, the choice to retain a social model is, in one respect, a clear political choice as well as a factor for competitiveness at global level. The promotion of basic social rights is generally

---

[15] See the agreement signed on 21 December 20004 by the Arc International group, Liaisons Sociales 17, March 2005, no 330. The idea of a territorial social charter has also been proposed by the Economic and Social Council in the report on externalization (30 March 2005, op.cit.).

[16] We shall not devote further attention here to developments in France. On practices involved in restructuring and the interactions among those affected, see Aubert and Beaujolin (2004); on the Borloo Act of 18 January 2005, see the April issue of *Droit social*, in publication at the time of writing; and on the progress of restructuring, see M. Campinos-Dubernet (2004).

[17] The term emphasizes that the process of deregulation is actually a downward spiral driven by efforts to be as attractive as possible to investors.

accepted as a factor contributing to economic efficiency (OECD reports 1996 and 2000).

A growing number of authors see the development of innovative social policy as a key factor where economic performance depends on stable employer-employee relations, the legal certainty necessary for assessing location options, and a well trained, specialized and professional workforce (report by the Director-General of the World Commission, Kevin Banks, 2004).

It is thus particularly important in France to be able to identify and build on the comparative social advantages that contribute to attracting investment. It is clear when we contrast the French policy with that of other countries in Europe and worldwide, that it is neither about increased flexibility in labour relations, achieved through greater insecurity at work, nor about reducing the social costs of unskilled labour to achieve the type of comparative advantages enjoyed by countries like China and India or, closer to home, the UK and Ireland.

In effect, creating career security by enabling people to develop their occupational skills and acquire new qualifications along a personal career path independent of any corporate setting would introduce a genuinely new basis for social innovation.[18]

Analysing the situation in terms of comparative social advantage does not provide miracle recipes, or to bring the current debate to a conclusion, but does have the advantage of allowing targets to be set. But these objectives, whatever the parity agreed between the social partners or political actors, will take account of the choices which will attract jobs in France: job stability and therefore stability in the relationship of unlimited-term work, conflict resolution and social peace, hence more mechanisms that favour action of staff representatives and collective agreement negotiation, high levels of education and skills, skills adapted to technological change, in short measures which require a link between economic, social and education policies both at national and regional level.

The European level, within the EU, inevitably remains the framework of reference in efforts to be competitive with non-EU countries.

Statutory responses to offshoring must thus be directed towards ensuring that economic activity remains within the EU, which implies building economic and social cohesion across the Union.

Comparative social advantages at European level

It is difficult to defend the proposition that the European Union should organize employment protection measures at national level. The conception of responses to globalization at European level reflects not only the principles of economic freedom that have been in force since 1958 but also the principle of social and economic cohesion within the Union.

EU enlargement has not changed those principles, but its consequences have helped to exacerbate the risks of social competition, making it easier for companies to opt to locate in the new member States. EU policies thus need to

---

[18] See II below.

take account of the resulting "reshuffle" effects. Policies under the Structural Funds have not so far been used to make the connections between employment shifts among the countries of the Union, although the Commission's social agenda set out in February 2005 paves the way for Social Fund financing of retraining measures in competitive sectors when low-skilled jobs are transferred into the new member States.

The next question is how to build or rebuild the principle of social cohesion within the EU to reflect the context created by globalization.

The European Commission proposals in its release dated 31 March 2005[19] are a move in this direction, aimed as they are at ensuring that employment requirements are taken into account in all European political areas. To this end, a task force will be created to provide for coordination between managements which adopt the standards that have an incidence on the area around restructuring or on restructuring itself domestic market, competition, regional policy, etc.). It proposes a modification to structural funds in the framework of the ESF so that the Fund can help "put in place partnerships and agreements on employment thanks to the networking of actors involved at the national, regional and local level".

It also proposes that an "anti-shock" fund be used to finance measures required movement of activities, firms and jobs between the different areas of the Union (European funding of the sharing out of jobs on European territory). Modification of State aid programmes is also under way.

The choice of the open method of coordination as the preferred form of governance has not to date been much directed to the social consequences of the objectives of competition. The accent has just been put back on the necessary status of social cohesion in the Lisbon strategy (European Council of 22-23 March 2005), with special stress on active labour market policies.

Even though the MOC's attitude has little changed and the accent is still on competition and employability, there seems to be a change in European policy as witnessed by the will to develop policies that place social dialogue at their heart.

There is nothing to prove that the Commission's proposals will be followed and implemented, but they do provide a new stimulus for action to the social partners and hold out the hope that a turning point has been reached in the redrafting of the principle of economic and social cohesion.

The recent clashes between the EU Social Affairs Commissioner and the French Government on the question of offshoring demonstrate the problem of finding the right balance between the necessary protection of jobs at workplace level (a national concern) and the development of employment across the Union as a whole. The European market continues to function as a generator of intense

---

[19] Restructuring and Employment, Anticipating and accompanying restructuring in order to develop employment: the role of the European Union, COM (2005) 120 final, Liaisons socials Eutope, 13 April 2005, no 125, p.2.

social competition between different regions,[20] thus giving companies a very wide choice in the location of their activities.

The competition is curbed, however, on the one hand by general observance of the *acquis communautaire* (in principle it will eventually be observed in full throughout the Union[21]), and on the other by respect, in measures taken by Community bodies, for a core set of fundamental rights.

Notwithstanding this internal, interregional competition, the EU member States also have to organize competition with other non-EU countries.

At EU level the preferred policy must be to facilitate change within the Union in order, wherever possible, to prevent activity being shifted *outside* it: in other words, it is wrong to be systematically opposed to shifts of activity from one EU country to another where there is a risk of activities being transferred away from the Union altogether to China, India or Brazil.

From this perspective, the stances taken in France on the issue of offshoring have so far entirely failed to take account of the dual dimension of international competition (i.e. competition both outside and inside the Union).

The Lorenzi and Fontaigné report makes it quite clear that, in future, the focus needs to shift to the comparative advantages of the "European national company" (albeit a somewhat ill-chosen label from a legal standpoint[22]). The merit of this proposal is to highlight the fact that, against a backdrop of globalized strategic thinking, the Union is the framework within which competitiveness needs to be redeveloped. It is also the framework within which social solutions need to be found, despite the highly national orientation in systems of workers' rights as well as trade union activity and employment policies (Moreau and Trudeau, 2000, and see below).

Attention thus needs to be focused on two areas.

– A European policy must be developed to require systematic linkage of Community policies for attracting industry (through State aid, tax incentives, etc.) with the question of employment, so that a sharing of social costs can emerge at EU level, enabling retraining and re-skilling measures to be financed.[23]

---

[20] Another factor restricting competition has been the harmonization of social standards in various important fields (P. Rodière, 2002). The development of a "social Europe" remains patchy and incomplete, however.

[21] The new member States have undertaken to transpose into their national laws all the social provisions adopted by means of directives or regulations since the signing of the Treaty of Rome (the *acquis communautaire*). Obviously transposition is not in itself a guarantee that the rules will be applied (and this was the position in the 15 member States pre-enlargement). The new member States will have to develop, or indeed create from scratch, systems of industrial relations – and this will take time, although extensive support programmes have been put in place to help them.

[22] The label is ill-chosen because the question of corporate nationality has long been controversial and the solution finally arrived at in the Treaty is a pragmatic one whereby the location of a company's decision-making is not the sole determining factor. Corporate nationality thus continues to depend on the place where the company is registered or on where it is incorporated if it operates in other countries. In the 30 years of efforts to develop European corporate articles of association, the question of creating a European nationality was avoided, there being a general recognition that anything affecting nationality affected national sovereignty.

[23] The development of a "social mainstream" will be a research theme in 2006.

– An active policy is required for building on the body of basic social rights in Europe to make them not just a bulwark against deregulation within the Union (Moreau, 2005) but also a genuine social comparative advantage on the European Union market (Hepple, 2005). This will require that practical implementation of the basic social rights proclaimed in the European Charter of Fundamental Rights becomes both

– a positive duty for the member States and

– a factor in the method of open coordination (MOC) (see network reports on fundamental rights, 2003); and

– that the *acquis communautaire* – permitting real expression of the Charter's principles in the area of workers' rights, notably with regard to information and consultation, health and safety and equal treatment – is respected, particularly in the new member States.

3. CREATING A PERMANENT STRUCTURE FOR EMPLOYMENT ADAPTATION BY PROVIDING CAREER SECURITY

In 1999, the Supiot report highlighted the radical transformations affecting employment and the need to look beyond the traditional framework of labour law to provide primary security of employment in the "grey areas" inhabited by economically dependent workers. The same conclusion emerged from the Silvana Sciarra report on the evolution of labour law in the then 15 EU member States (2005), part of the problem being changes in the nature of employment, with an extremely worrying slide towards self-employment coupled with new forms of insecurity and poverty. Growing inequality is directly related to ongoing change in the way that companies are organized and is exacerbated by networked forms of organization.

The idea of creating a mechanism to link security with flexibility was promoted in the context of disseminating "best practices" in the field of European employment strategy – one such being the "flexi-curity" policy practiced in the Netherlands and Denmark.

There are various definitions of flexi-curity, some very general and others quite specific. It has been defined as "social protection for a workforce with flexible working conditions" (Klammer and Tillman, 2001, and Ferrara, 2001)[24] and also in much greater detail, as, for example, "Flexi-curity can be defined as a distinct policy and strategy used by industrial relations actors to enhance the flexibility of labour markets, work organization and employment relations, while improving security of work and protection of workers and, in particular, to weak groups in and outside the firm or labour market." (Report of the high level group, 1/2002, p. 18). A further, more sophisticated, definition proposes that flexi-curity "is a policy strategy that attempts, synchronically and in a deliberate way to enhance the flexibility of the labour markets and the labour relation on the one

---

[24] Quoted by T. Wilthagen and F. Tros, 2003.

hand and to enhance security – employment security and social security – notably for weaker groups in and outside the labour market on the other hand" (Wilthagen and Rogowski, 2002).

The key elements in the definition are the concepts of *deliberation*, based on participation by industrial relations actors, and *synchronicity*, of the process introduced (in order to respond to lasting changes affecting employment), as well as the need to make appropriate arrangements for those groups of workers rendered vulnerable (in terms of increased insecurity, the demands of flexibility and new forms of poverty) by the internationalization of employment (see Wilthagen and Tros, 2004).

Clearly, the introduction of career-security mechanisms that did not depend on workers' belonging to a specific company, but by being attached instead to the individual rather than the workplace, would be a means of addressing not only the pressing demand among employers for flexibility (echoed in the European Employment Strategy), but also the workers' need for occupational security, the permanently evolving nature of companies, and constantly changing requirements in terms of qualifications and skills. Such a system could also potentially reduce those gender-based inequalities that are exacerbated by flexible practices and new forms of insecurity. Constructing a flexi-curity system can thus contribute to the development of a labour market appropriate to a time of transition (Gazier and Schmid, 2002, and Gazier, 2003).

In other words, "flexi-curity" is proposed as a means of reconciling the irreconcilable in the current context.

Two questions need to be asked before considering the possible impact of "flexi-curity" in France: can we really base our approach on the experience of other countries, or can we extract from that experience building blocks for our own "flexi-curity" system?

Lessons to be learned from European countries' experiences with "flexi-curity"

Considerable caution is required here because the machinery introduced under other European countries' social policies not only reflects very different systems of labour relations, and systems of social and unemployment protection whose theoretical bases are quite unlike that of the French system (and in many cases more protection-orientated), but also has to function in labour markets that are quite differently organized.

– Research into "flexi-curity" has focused on the Netherlands and Denmark which, with their systems of standards based on a strong tradition of collective bargaining, have managed to strike a compromise between demands for greater labour-market flexibility and the safeguards negotiated by trade unions.

– In Denmark – with 80 per cent trade union membership and a system of controlled decentralization of labour relations (Vissher, 2001) – the most interesting measure is probably "job rotation", whereby workers taking time out for training are replaced by people from the unemployment register. The scheme has been used by 10 per cent of the working population and has given fresh impetus to a policy of enhancing skills and qualifications and combating unemployment.

- The "Polder model" in the Netherlands also relies on regulated and coordinated decentralization whereby days and weeks of holiday entitlement can be combined during periods of reduced production and/or demand, thus allowing work to be organized in an extremely flexible manner based on changeable working hours. [25]

- Detailed analysis of the compromises reached in different countries suggests a number of conclusions. Comparative research into the Belgian, German, Danish and Dutch systems (Wilthagen et al., 2003), revealed that the combinations of flexibility and security arrived at reflected compromises in relation to the national systems of labour law and industrial relations, but that in all the countries concerned there had been controversy about striking the right balance – and in some cases major reforms had resulted.

The Silvana Sciarra report on the evolution of labour law produced a similar conclusion: the balances and compromises amounted to a general tendency towards greater flexibility in individual employer-employee relationships but the nature of the balance differed under the different national legal systems. This was particularly apparent in the regulatory choices made with regard to contracts for part-time and agency work and fixed-term contracts.

- The more "Fordist" the national model (as in Belgium and Germany) the harder it was to reach a compromise on "flexi-curity" because the search for flexibility focused more on internal corporate organization than on the wider labour market.

- Ultimately, the introduction of a "flexi-curity" system requires the controlled or coordinated decentralization of labour relations based both on the strength of the social partners and on a tradition of negotiation under the auspices of the political authorities, for example through a system of tripartite relations.

What constitutes "flexi-curity"

By definition, "flexi-curity" implies that flexibility can be combined with security and thus that the two concepts need not (or no longer) be mutually contradictory.

This idea is rooted in neo-liberal thinking directed at finding a balance between greater flexibility in individual working relationships and stronger employment safeguards provided by social institutions – a notion clearly invested with ideological implications (Zachert, 2004).

---

[25] Developments in the two countries need to be considered in detail, which is beyond the scope of this paper. For more information, see the periodical *Transfer*, which published a series of very comprehensive studies in 2004, analysing how the two systems evolved; and the studies by Wilthagen and Tros and Wilthagen et al.. quoted above.

Moreover, the relevant research – including, here too, comparative studies – suggests that a high degree of caution is in order in considering what happens when labour markets are made more flexible. Osaki, for example, concluded in 1999 that greater labour-market flexibility had eroded workers' rights with regard to employment, wage security and stable living conditions.

The conclusions of the Silvana Sciarra report (2004) are more ambivalent, for employment rights in Europe have clearly not undergone radical deregulation. The core set of basic social rights has clearly developed both nationally and at European level. Greater flexibility therefore depends on changes in individual working relationships and thus on contracts of employment, and this is a subject of considerable concern.

Nonetheless, studies of the developments and reforms introduced over the last ten years, in response to pressure from the European Employment Strategy for various forms of flexibility, do not highlight any real convergence but rather, using different technical approaches, suggest there has been an increase in "new" forms of poverty and insecurity. In Spain, for example, 30 per cent of employment contracts were found to be fixed-term rather than permanent. What was observed was not a system of "flexi-curity", because the policy being implemented was one of flexibility coupled with deregulation (F. Valdes Del Ré, 2004).[26]

Studies based on comparative analyses show that the component elements of flexibility and security around which compromises can be reached are as follows (Wilthagen et al., 2002, 2003, 2004):

–   external flexibility (on conditions of recruitment and contract termination);
–   internal flexibility (on working hours, overtime and part-time working);
–   organizational flexibility (including the possibility of multiple employers);
–   wage flexibility (with individual rates of pay and payment by objective);
–   job security within a given company and the (relative) certainty of remaining with a particular employer;
–   employment security, i.e. the assurance of having work, albeit with a different employer;
–   wage security with protection against the risk of loss of income;
–   the combination of entitlement to substitute income with other forms of security.

The end result of the compromises and combinations must be to facilitate adaptation to the new changes in the nature of employment: i.e. adapting workers' qualifications and skills, effecting a transition from insecure to more secure forms of employment status, and permitting both functional and geographical job mobility to cope with ongoing changes.

---

[26] Hence the importance of strengthening basic social rights in Europe and the need, as part of the method of open coordination (MOC), not only to impose quantitative targets but also to reconsider the implications of job quality in terms of workers' rights. The Sciarra report proposes that the MOC should take a more legalistic approach.

The comparative studies underscore certain prerequisites with regard to the nature of the players involved and their commitment to a process of "controlled decentralization" that will facilitate the introduction of flexibility at the most decentralized level possible, while at the same time enabling the authorities to put transitional safeguards in place (in the areas of substitute income and the training and retraining of workers).

With regard to employment law, a number of aspects need to be highlighted (Zachert, 2004).

- In terms of striking a balance on flexibility in the external regulatory environment, models of protection against redundancy clearly vary – from those that provide little protection (as in the UK and Denmark) to highly detailed systems of regulation (as in Spain, France and Portugal) which have been the subject of reforms designed to remove or limit the protection provided by the administration and to encourage forms of "moderate liberalization" (as in France, Spain, Portugal and the Netherlands).

- In all the countries studied there would nonetheless seem to be certain core provisions.

  1) Redundancy payments can be linked with possibilities for extended employment, re-employment or periods of transition.

  2) Forms of protection against redundancy, and indeed procedural "rigidities" – such as the requirement (in Austria) that works councils be consulted, or the duty to observe specific procedural time lapses (as in France, Portugal, Spain and Germany) – have a preventive function, and indeed may allow developments to be anticipated (as in the case of restructuring operations in France, or the administrative authorization system in Spain). This preventive function is another element that merits assessment in the implementation of a "flexi-curity" system.

  3) In order to establish a comprehensive system, arrangements should be introduced to make redundancies "traceable" – an element directly related to Article 30 of the European Charter of Fundamental Rights,[27] which provides for the assurance of a basic level of protection against unfair dismissal. The traceability aspect will allow a correlation to be established between companies' responsibilities and the safeguards offered by the system of transition.

- In the area of access to the labour market, any linkage between flexibility and security must necessarily include the creation of a springboard or bridge between insecure, flexible contracts and access to stable employment. The periods that workers spend between jobs varies widely from one European country to another (Zachert 2004, OECD, *Employment Outlook 2002*). In the Netherlands, for example, the transition can take less than year.

---

[27] "Every worker has the right to protection against unjustified dismissal, in accordance with Community law and national laws and practices."

- Introduction of a springboard mechanism is particularly justified in the case of under-qualified, marginalized workers in the twilight zones of labour law (see Sciarra report, 2004, on self-employment).[28]

In conclusion, the comparative studies show that systems for combining flexibility and security must be constructed within national frameworks, reflecting the characteristics of national labour relations and social protection systems, while at the same time introducing transitional arrangements that justify the necessary compromises.

Is there a future for "flexi-curity" in France?

In France today, the prerequisites in terms of a "multi-level" system of governance or "controlled decentralization" are not in place, neither with regard to arrangements for intersectoral negotiations (which demonstrated their limitations and capacity for deadlock in 2004 on the issue of restructuring) nor in relation to the system of provision for unemployment, which is the product of negotiation between the social partners.

Obviously one can work from the premise that career-security provisions will aim to produce not a system of "flexi-curity" but an original French construct that will offer a new way out of the current impasses.

Many questions need to be asked, however.

- Could the development of career-security provisions entail tripartite participation or negotiation?
- Is it possible to design a transition period that will be not merely the extension of an employment contract (through some type of intermediary contract) but will offer people who are already marginalized, excluded or economically dependent the possibility of integration into the career-security system?
- Is it possible to prevent the introduction of a career-security system from being no more than a form of deregulation in disguise, at odds with the legal security implied by the basic right to protection against unfair dismissal?
- How can the transition period be associated with the improvement of vocational qualifications leading to real skills development, and with requirements identified (by sector or employment catchment area) on the labour market?
- What sort of package can be designed for financing the transition, which will include periods out of work (and thus on unemployment benefit), periods of vocational training (financed in different ways) and redundancy (covered by redundancy payments), with the focus on conversion and mobility so as to create employment security based on a structured succession of jobs?

---

[28] The situation in the new EU member States in this regard is alarming: see the analysis of employment conditions in chapter 6 of the report on *Industrial Relations in Europe* published by the Commission in 2004, www. Europa/com/employment and social affairs/.

–   What sort of career-security system can accommodate "springboard" arrangements for the most disadvantaged groups of workers?

The questions themselves suggest some possible answers.

It is probably ill-advised, today, to call into question the contractual machinery for recruitment or for termination of employment contracts, particularly open-ended contracts, given the need to maintain the bases and values of labour law.

The same conclusion applies from the point of view of comparative social advantage because the fact of having a stable, well qualified workforce is an obvious advantage of the French social system. Finally, it is important to bear in mind that investors need legal certainty and this is another reason for avoiding overly frequent reforms (the rules on redundancies were changed in 2002, 2003 and again in 2005) and/or reforms likely to generate social conflict.

With regard to provisions for internal flexibility in the workplace, these have already called into question the 35-hour working week.

One possible and original avenue of approach, however, might be an optional system based on insurance (see Supiot, 1999, on special drawing rights) whereby the parties involved determined the nature of the contract subject to a legally fixed minimum period, with a short period of notice. Such arrangements would provide the basis for a system of cover allowing workers extended transitional periods for retraining in new types of work, and focusing on access to employment.

The disadvantages presented by this type of optional system would be fewer than those of doing away with open-ended employment contracts, increasing the length of temporary contracts or permitting an increase in the number of appeals, particularly if the conditions of access to the system of career protection were negotiated.

While the aim is to resolve the questions raised by the internationalization of employment, it is also important that the system should be linked to the development of employment catchment areas and centres of excellence, which represent economic responses to the problems posed by corporate restructuring.

As in other countries, these are inevitably extremely controversial issues. A high level of political commitment will be needed if avenues of compromise and efficiency are to be found in cooperation with the social partners.

4. TOWARDS A NEW SYSTEM OF TRANSNATIONAL LABOUR RELATIONS?

Studies show that change in the way companies are organized – horizontally and vertically into transnational networks – and in the organization of production based on an international division of work, is exposing the inadequacy of nationally-structured labour relations and pointing up the need for a radical shift to place them on a transnational footing.

It is interesting to observe that the 15-year experience with transnational workers' representation is gradually producing an original form of transnational negotiation.

The contribution of transnational workers' representation

It is important to emphasize that nationally based systems of labour law are incapable of giving workers a voice in transnational relations (Mückenberger, 2005). The distance and dissociation between the centres of decision making and the various scattered communities of workers impose separation which impedes the machinery of worker's representation, traditionally organized as it is at national level (Supiot, 2002; Mückenberger, 2005). Since 1994, however, the European Union has appreciated the need to help build a new system of collective representation at transnational level.

Conclusions on ten years of experience with European works councils are mixed. Legally recognized transnational representation is developing strongly in quantitative terms (with 700 European works councils) and fostering the emergence of a new type of negotiation (E. Bethoux, 2002 and 2004; M.-A. Moreau, 2005). Currently, agreements are signed at the rate of one a week on such very different questions as training in transnational groups,[29] health and safety, trade-union rights and, indeed, restructuring.

This emerging movement demonstrates the clear need in Community-scale groups to find appropriately tailored (i.e. *transnational*) modes of representation and negotiation. It also confirms that the logical extension of necessary group-level negotiation, which has developed to a considerable extent in France, leading to the legalization of group agreements,[30] is international negotiation.

Sociologists are currently assessing the impact of all this (J. Waddington, 2004). The wide-ranging nature of the constituting agreements for European works councils means that few assessments of their activity have been carried out. Those available show that, although a European social culture is taking shape, the position of European works councils in the industrial relations system is not strong enough to effect the shift towards a transnational model.

In fact, it is clear that both trade union representation and legal provisions for collective bargaining are structured on an exclusively national basis. The shift towards European-level activity is proving difficult, including within European representative organizations (such as the ETUC, UNICE and CEEP), which are structured as confederations with national bases. The national level of reference for all this machinery – including the mechanisms for European industrial-relations dialogue – constitutes an obstacle to the emergence of transnational trade union activity. Apart from the action undertaken when Vilvoorde closed and that within the Arcilor group, there are few examples of trade union coordination in Community-scale groups undergoing restructuring. Nonetheless there

---

[29] Most of these agreements are analysed in *Liaisons sociales Europe*. The importance of the negotiations is also explored in the University of Warwick's special bulletin on European works councils.

[30] Decision of the Court of Cassation of 30 April 2003 and Act of 18 May 2004.

is evidence that the situation is evolving in this respect, especially in industries with European trade union representation at sector level (the EMF in the steel industry is an example). This evolution is based on the negotiation of agreements with European works councils because they are the bodies that provide representation tailored to the Community-scale structure of the industrial groups in question.

The emergence of transnational negotiations

This new type of negotiation, geared to addressing the challenges posed by the internationalization of employment, is also emerging at a wider international level. The fact that international trade union confederations are concluding worldwide agreements through the International Professional Secretariats is very clear evidence of new relationships between groups of international dimension and bodies providing representation at international level.

Recent studies (I. Daugareilh, 2005 and R. Bourke, 2004) highlight a new linkage between the international confederations, supported by the European trade unions and European works councils, and the existence of a negotiating arena that can be useful in promoting groups and their development at international level. The Renault agreement on Employees' Fundamental Rights (2004), the Rhodia agreement on Global Corporate Social Responsibility and the EDF agreement (2005) are cited as examples of the trend.

This movement, based on the emergence of bodies with a mandate for representation at transnational group level (whether the scale of the group is that of the European Community or wider), shows that one consequence of the internationalization of employment is – despite the obstacles – to promote increased awareness of the transnational dimension of industrial relations, reflecting the structure of the employers. Clearly it is a slow and difficult shift.

At European level, change in this direction is taking place because a model for representation has come to the fore since the adoption of Directive 94/45 of 22 September 1994 on European works councils. It goes without saying that the transnational representation currently fostering development of a "European social culture"[31] has its origins both in agreements concluded by Community-scale groups as long ago as 1986 and in the adoption of a directive based on the concept of collective autonomy for the social partners in transnational groups (as identified in the directive).

In effect, the shift to a transnational model will depend on two pre-conditions: the existence of signed accords (some of which are already in place) and the development of a legal framework for transnational collective agreements.

In its agenda for 2006-2010, the European Commission proposes introducing a legal framework for European collective agreements.

---

[31] All the interviews conducted with members of European works councils confirm that the cultural dimension is the most significant because trade unionists with experience of a specific national culture (French, for example) find themselves having to deal with totally different approaches and procedures among their British, German and Swedish counterparts. A new kind of learning is thus developing from this clash of trade union cultures.

There have been immediate negative reactions from the UNICE, which systematically opposes European-level negotiation; from trade unions which believe that collective action must continue to be organized at national level and which have to cope with the existing competition for jobs inside Europe; and from industrial relations experts unconvinced that laws and regulations can promote a movement of change in industrial relations in Europe.

Clearly there are many obstacles to the creation of a legal framework for transnational negotiation in the European Union. Questions about how workers and employers are to be represented may be resolved with reference to the model offered by the transnational directives providing for workers' representation within transnational groups, namely the Directive on European works councils (1994), the Directive on employee involvement in European companies (2001), and the Directive supplementing the Statute for a European Cooperative Society (2003) (see Moreau (a), 2005), as well as the experience of Community-scale groups with collective agreements. Questions about the content of transnational agreements can also fall within the scope of collective autonomy as it emerges in practice.

Two issues are particularly problematic: how will national and Community-level negotiations be linked, and what will be the effect of the new agreements within different legal systems?

–   With regard to levels of negotiation, practice within the European Union varies widely, although there is a marked tendency towards decentralization of collective bargaining. Company-level negotiation remains an option even though, in certain countries, it has little function. Group-level negotiation has yet to be generally recognized.

    There is scope, however, for recognition of agreements concluded by Community-scale companies, particularly as such agreements already exist through the intermediary of those national laws that lend them force. Sector-based or inter-occupational agreements, meanwhile, are underpinned by arrangements deriving from Articles 138 and 139 of the EC Treaty.

–   Collective bargaining models differ widely with regard to the effect of collective agreements, which may or may not be binding in different EU countries. It has to be asked whether developments at the level of the European social partners will open the possibility of moving beyond the national standard-setting model – as was done in 1991[32] – in order to create a transnational, European framework.

Nor is there any shortage of obstacles in the area of industrial relations: the major one concerns negotiating mechanisms, which, in every country, reflect the

---

[32] Before the signing of the Maastricht Treaty the European social partners were not involved in the legislative process. The agreement signed on 31 October 1991 between the UNICE, ETUC and CEEP was a historic step in the development of a social Europe for it showed that European employers were prepared to participate in the preparation of legislation, and this represented an important shift. The agreement was incorporated in its entirety into the Social Protocol appended to the Maastricht Treaty, which is still the basis for the sharing of social responsibilities.

respective interests of the parties. There is currently a lack of solidarity among workers at European level. Employment issues continue to be dealt with via collective bargaining and collective action at national level. The French debate on offshoring demonstrates that we cannot realistically expect an approach that addresses the impact of corporate mobility on jobs at EU level. Why should French trade unions negotiating about the impact of restructuring in France concern themselves with the skills needs of Polish workers who are benefiting from the creation of new jobs? Trade union activity at European level is moving very slowly towards acknowledgement of European-level situations (Moreau, 2001) although examples of mobilization affecting more than one country remain few.

The transnational negotiating framework can evolve to address the changes brought about by corporate mobility in Europe only if the parties involved in the different countries, and particularly the trade unions, are motivated to engage in transnational negotiation. It seems obvious that the EU will have to develop forms of incentive to draw trade unions that are "losing jobs" into transnational negotiation in situations where workers employed by the same group in another country are "gaining jobs".

The introduction of coordinated, logical incentives may provide the impetus for putting in place a system to negotiate change at European level.

The development of transnational workers' representation, followed by a transnational legal framework for collective bargaining, has potential to help resolve issues raised by the internationalization of employment at European level, all the more when linked with the coordination of European policies (see I above) and the building (or rebuilding) of social cohesion within the EU.

All this lies very much in the future but it is important to note that the three areas outlined do represent possible avenues of change if those involved – and particularly the trade unions – can get the measure of globalization's impact on the structure of labour law regimes. While there are questions to be addressed about the linkage between levels of law-making in the traditional national-regional-international pyramid structure, an even greater shift is required with regard to recognition of the "networked" transnational level. This has to go hand-in-hand with equally radical change in regulatory techniques, using a new type of architecture based on the inter-meshing of "soft law" and "hard law".

Offshoring must thus be seen very much as a symptom – both of companies' strategies for mobility and of the need for change in existing systems of labour law.

SOCIAL ACCOMPANIMENT MEASURES FOR GLOBALIZATION: SOP OR SILVER LINING?

BY RAYMOND TORRES[1]

1. INTRODUCTION

Beyond all the controversy about the impact of globalization on employment and working conditions, governments are gradually coming to realize that they themselves can take steps to improve the benefits of globalization and reduce adjustment costs. Market openness, and the technological and organizational changes that go with it, seem to have the effect of increasing instability on the labour market (Rodrik, 1998). Some authors have claimed that comparative advantages have become 'kaleidoscopic': a country's strong points, which give it its comparative advantage, are no longer as stable as they used to be. Globalization is bringing rapid changes in the relative prices of goods and services, leading to job losses in some sectors and opportunities to create jobs in others. With the new technologies any company can outsource some of its activities, generating a fundamental reorganization of work (Arnal et al., 2002). These changes have also tended to go hand in hand with greater inequality of income.However, globalization is not necessarily a zero-sum game. On the contrary, it is a process of creative destruction that can improve the well-being of the countries involved because of the benefits of having the comparative advantage, the resulting economies of scale, and the greater choice offered to consumers (see, for example, the study on trade liberalization in 63 countries by Frankel and Romer, 1999, and the study by Bhagwati et al, 2004, on outsourcing). We can see in particular that the countries that are most open to the outside have a higher growth rate over the long term than countries that are less open, which would also explain why most countries – including the developing countries – do not want globalization to pass them by.

But the benefits of globalization are not automatic, and entail adjustment costs. Table 1 shows that, on average, 2-3 per cent of jobs are lost to redundancy in the EU and the USA every year. The rate is more than double this in the manufacturing industry, where the process of globalization and the adoption of new technologies is more intense. Public measures are therefore needed if the benefits of globalization are to be felt in practice. This article will focus more

---

[1] The views expressed in this article do not necessarily reflect those of the OECD or its member countries.

specifically on two reasons for taking public measures: to try to achieve greater efficiency, and for redistribution purposes. Our analysis will mainly concentrate on the developed countries and will draw heavily on the results of research soon to be published in the *OECD Employment Outlook*.

2. HOW CAN EMPLOYMENT POLICIES IMPROVE THE BENEFITS OF GLOBALIZATION?

The first task of any employment policy is to redeploy workers who are the victims of restructuring. Job losses are often an inevitable consequence of trade liberalization and the technological and organizational changes that this brings. Redeployment policies are designed not only to provide financial support for those affected, but also to ensure that new opportunities for growth emerge. While these may be less visible than the job losses, they have to be taken into account if globalization is to succeed. For example, if the developed countries relocate certain activities to the emerging and developing countries, those countries will then import other goods and services. Furthermore, purchasing power gains linked to the drop in the prices of imported products (such as textile and clothing products, for example) may be used to meet other needs provided for by domestic producers (such as leisure spending). New employment pools eventually emerge, and it is the task of the employment policies to smooth the transition here, otherwise the new growth potential will not be achieved.

One way of promoting the transition to new jobs is to **reduce benefits or keep them at a low level**. Those who have been made redundant obviously have no option but to find a new job very quickly. However, apart from the fact that such a policy runs counter to social objectives, another approach – active labour market policies – appears to be possible.

Under certain conditions, **active labour market policies** form a vital part of a successful response to globalization. Schemes to provide individual support for the unemployed, appropriate, job-related training or assisted employment can prove particularly effective. However, these schemes need to be well designed, since this field is littered with glaring failures and huge disappointments. The following are examples of ones that work (for more details, see OECD, 2005):

–   Individual job-search advice schemes and individual support schemes for the unemployed often prove cost-effective.

–   Training, assisted employment and other employment aid can be a useful addition, provided that they are targeted, job-related and, if necessary, compulsory.

–   The public employment services running these schemes must have adequate means, in particular sufficient competent advisers capable of communicating with at-risk groups.

–   It is vital that all these schemes should be based on reciprocal obligation. The job-seeker receives a benefit and good-quality services, and in return undertakes to look actively for a job.

The Nordic countries, the Netherlands, Ireland and the UK have all placed the emphasis on 'activation' policies. In some cases, of course, the impact on the national budgets has been considerable, as we can see from Graph 1 (particularly for the Nordic countries, where benefits are fairly generous). But the results in terms of employment are undeniable, and studies have shown that the efficiency of the public employment services in these countries has been a major factor in this success.

Advance notification of lay-offs can also help with redeployment, particularly where it is accompanied by job-search assistance. According to some studies focusing on the USA, workers with advance notification of redundancy spend less time unemployed than those laid off without advance warning (Addison et al, 1997). Similarly, research has shown that the notification period reduces the time spent job-seeking by manual workers in Sweden (Storrie, 1992).

The benefit of advance notification as a way of reducing adjustment costs would appear to be even greater if the workers concerned are also offered job-search assistance or training during the notice period, even though no rigorous assessment has been made of this. A number of OECD countries have introduced rapid intervention systems which are triggered by the announcement of collective redundancies and are designed to reduce the potential effects (by steering workers towards job vacancies even before they are laid off). Some of the Nordic countries offer the widest possible range of proactive services for workers threatened by an announced collective redundancy. In such countries, action on the ground is highly developed, with staff from employment offices dispatched to firms where lay-offs have been announced. In Finland, a public employment service is often created on the premises of the dismissing firm, allowing the workers affected to have access to all the services it provides, including training, during the advance notification period. The costs of this are often partly paid by the company. The question now is how to enable small firms to benefit from these arrangements. Decentralizing the employment services, although it may help, is perhaps not enough here.

3. HOW TO COMPENSATE THE VICTIMS OF DISPLACEMENT?

Providing financial compensation for the victims of displacement is something that economists have to accept, since it results from a collective decision. Because market openness is not a zero-sum game, it can be shown to improve efficiency, as Pareto defines it, in that the "winners" compensate the "losers". However, this theory does not say *how* they should be compensated. Clearly, if displaced workers were compensated for their total loss of income on a permanent basis, they would have little incentive to find another job. The question also arises whether groups that previously benefited from monopoly profits should be compensated, as compared with workers facing loss of income because, say, their skills were specific to the sector where they worked.

Unemployment benefit for trade-displaced workers risks reducing efficiency because there are fewer incentives to go back to work, although well-designed deduction/transfer and activation schemes can reduce these disincentives, as we saw earlier. However, there are social insurance reasons why a certain level of compensation might be regarded as improving efficiency. These reasons are often mentioned in the context of unemployment insurance, which offers workers a guarantee against loss of income resulting from unemployment, and may have certain advantages, in terms of efficiency, over private insurance schemes (Blanchard and Tirole, 2003).

As a compensation mechanism for job losses resulting from international competition, **severance pay** has the considerable disadvantage that it does not reflect the actual amount of income lost, depending on the length of time spent unemployed after displacement or the reduction in pay (if any) between the old and new jobs. On the other hand, severance pay has the advantage that it usually varies according to the income lost as a result of being unemployed, but at the same time it creates distortions in the labour supply which may be particularly pronounced in the case of trade-displaced workers. Severance pay also does not compensate for loss of wages associated with a new job. This is why wage insurance was put forward.

Wage insurance schemes enable displaced workers who take new, lower-paid jobs within a specified period to claim compensation making up part of the difference between the old and new wages. Some American researchers support the idea that wage insurance should be reserved only for workers who have lost their jobs as a result of globalization (see Brainard and Litan, 2004), while others take the opposite view (Kletzer and Rosen, 2005). The idea of paying wage insurance to trade-displaced workers was put forward for three reasons. First, it would help provide a more equitable distribution of the gains from globalization by reducing the adjustment costs faced by those who are hurt by trade and investment liberalization. Second, wage insurance would serve as an incentive to speedy re-employment, as remaining on unemployment benefits becomes less attractive relative to accepting a new job, perhaps in expanding sectors. In their new jobs the workers would have more chance of receiving the sort of training needed to make progress in their new firm or sector.

France, Germany and the USA have recently introduced wage insurance schemes for certain displaced workers. A pilot wage insurance programme introduced in Canada provides some insight into the potential of these programmes to speed re-employment and better reconcile efficiency and equity objectives (Bloom et al., 1999). The programme increased the percentage of displaced workers who found jobs by 4.4 percentage points, reflecting both a shift from part-time to full-time work, as well as an increase in overall employment. However, these initiatives are too recent to draw any firm conclusions about the potential of wage insurance to speed up a return to employment and better reconcile efficiency and equity objectives.

4. SHOULD SCHEMES BE TARGETED AT THOSE LOSING THEIR JOBS BECAUSE OF MARKET OPENNESS?

One fundamental question is whether special schemes are needed to help those who are the victims of restructuring resulting from international trade or investment. Most OECD countries have set up general schemes for everyone requiring redeployment, whether trade-displaced or for other reasons. There are a number of factors in favour of this. Granting aid only to the victims of globalization – rather than to everyone needing redeployment – may be seen as unjust. It is also often difficult to identify the causes of collective redundancies in practice.

What are the characteristics of workers who lose their jobs because of globalization?
Having said that, targeted mechanisms can often be justified, particularly where workers laid off as a result of globalization have clearly different characteristics from other displaced workers. An analysis of the situation in the EU and the USA leads to the following conclusions (Tables 2A and 2B):

– Generally speaking, workers who have lost jobs in high-import-competing manufacturing industries have very similar characteristics in terms of age, level of education, seniority in the job and previous wage to those of workers who have lost jobs in other manufacturing sectors.

– There is a much more marked contrast, however, between workers who lose their jobs in the manufacturing sector and those displaced in the services sector, who tend to be much younger, have a higher level of education, are more often women, and more generally have office jobs; their previous wages and seniority in the job also tend to be lower.

– International competition has less effect on particular types of workers than on jobs in particular sectors, and so the adjustment assistance provided has to take account of the different needs of a very heterogeneous group of displaced workers. A more detailed analysis of the situation in the USA shows that workers laid off in various high-import-competing sectors have widely varying characteristics (Kletzer, 2001). For example, workers in the textiles, clothing and footwear sector tend to have less seniority in the job than those in many other vulnerable sectors, but more seniority than in most service activities; there also tends to be a larger proportion of women and wages tend to be below-average for the manufacturing industries (Rosen, 2002). Steelworkers, on the other hand, are more often men and better paid than workers in the other manufacturing industries. They also have greater seniority, and their firms are usually larger and concentrated in regions rich in iron ore or coal, which means that declining employment in steel firms can have a major negative impact on the local demand for labour. Employment in shipyards has similar characteristics.

Another approach is to quantify the consequences of globalization-related job losses for the workers affected. In the USA, displaced workers in high-import-competing manufacturing industries have slightly poorer chances of having found a new job when surveyed (63 per cent) than workers who have lost jobs in other manufacturing sectors (67 per cent in low-import-competing manufacturing sectors), and the re-employment differential is greater than for workers in the services sector (69 per cent re-employed). The re-employment rates appear much lower in Europe than in the USA, with an average of 57 per cent for all manufacturing industries, and barely 52 per cent for high-import-competing industries in this sector. This suggests that the workers concerned generally face greater difficulty in finding a new job and/or are more inclined to withdraw from the active population in Europe than in the USA.

In the USA, displaced workers in high-import-competing sectors have to take an average pay cut of 13 per cent when they find a new job, with a quarter of them taking a cut of 30 per cent or more. In other manufacturing sectors the pay cuts are slightly smaller, and in the services sector they are considerably smaller: the average is barely 4 per cent, although one in five displaced workers report having taken a drop in wages of more than 30 per cent. In Europe, on the other hand, those returning to work after losing jobs in the manufacturing sector earn the same pay, on average, while workers displaced in the services sector earn, on average, 7 per cent more in their new jobs. The proportion of European workers reporting pay cuts of at least 30 per cent is much lower than in the USA (8 per cent compared with 22 per cent for all displaced workers), which shows that the difference in wages between the old and new jobs is smaller in Europe. To sum up, it appears that trade-displaced workers are more likely to face a pay cut when they return to work than other workers made redundant, both in Europe and in the USA, but the average size of the pay cuts and their variability are much higher in the USA.

Do trade-displaced workers find new jobs in the dynamic sectors of the economy? In the USA and in Europe, half or more of all workers losing their jobs in the manufacturing industry find new jobs in the same sector, despite the downward trend in manufacturing employment in most of these countries. Most of the other workers move to the services sector, mainly sectors such as the retail trade, where the skills required tend to be relatively low-level and general. Lastly, it is important to note that wages in the new jobs compare more favourably with those in the old if workers stay in the same sector, particularly in the USA (Table 3).

These re-employment profiles highlight a major distinction between the macro and micro levels when it comes to the adjustment of the labour market to trade liberalization. At the macro level, the idea is to make it easier for labour to flow from sectors in decline to sectors that are expanding, so that the maximum benefit can be obtained from new sources of comparative advantages. At the micro level, however, the situation is more complex, since it is often more appro-priate for workers who have lost jobs in declining sectors to look for a new job in the same sector. The scale of the gross flows in the labour markets shows that even in declining sectors there is considerable hiring. Staying in the same sector is probably particularly advisable for older workers who are very senior and whose skills and experience are likely to be very specific to the sector or occupation in which they have worked to date. This does not necessarily compromise redeployment requirements at the macro level, since the expanding sectors can probably meet their recruitment needs by attracting new arrivals on the labour market and workers changing jobs voluntarily.

All in all, the adjustment costs would be much less high if steps could be taken to ensure that, wherever possible, job cuts linked to trade liberalization do not result in long-term unemployment, an early departure from the labour market or persistent underemployment (in other words re-employment for much lower wages). In order to do so, policies must tackle the main obstacles to re-employment in posts that make the best use of the productive skills of displaced workers. In addition, trade-displaced workers are a heterogeneous group whose adjustment problems can be very minor or very serious; the oldest, most senior and least well-trained workers, particularly those who cannot find a new job in the same sector, are those that face the greatest difficulties. The problem of bringing down adjustment costs is therefore closely linked to lifelong learning, which aims to maintain workers' employability as they grow older and as the level of skills required increases (OECD, 2004, Chapter 4).

What role might targeted programmes play?
Despite these difficulties, targeted programmes can play a positive though limited role. There are three cases where a targeted approach is justified.

First of all, special programmes could be designed for cases where workers displaced because of globalization-related restructuring are concentrated geographically. Having said that, very few assessments have been carried out in this field, and there is very little information on what works and what does not. Second, job losses may sometimes be concentrated in certain badly-hit sectors, which could be another reason to have targeted programmes. Lastly, and above all, it is important to note that, unlike other displacements, those related to trade liberalization are directly attributable to government policy. Opening up a sector to international competition is a deliberate decision, often with predictable consequences. This was one of the reasons why the USA introduced the Trade Adjustment Act (TAA).

The TAA, which has been in force since the 1960s under various names, offers trade-displaced workers unemployment benefits for 78 weeks (three times longer than other unemployed workers), together with greater opportunities for retraining and special help with medical expenses (the Health Care Tax Credit). The many assessments that have been carried out have not proved conclusively that the TAA is effective. The main drawback is a practical one: it is not easy to verify whether displacement is indeed linked to trade liberalization, which has sometimes led to long delays in applying the programme and has limited the number of people with access to it. Nevertheless, the TAA has strengthened public support for trade liberalization in the USA.

Other countries too have special schemes for certain trade-displaced workers. In Australia, for example, schemes exist for workers in the textiles and clothing sectors, the sugar industry and the automobile parts sector. The authorities justify the schemes on the grounds that trade liberalization has a serious impact on entire sectors and that job losses are concentrated in declining regions, thus considerably restricting the scope for redeploying the workers concerned. Compared with the TAA, targeting specific sectors or regions makes it easier to implement the programmes. Nevertheless, some countries have found that these aid schemes can hinder change, which is why it has proved essential to place them in the context of active labour market policies (discussed earlier) and to combine them with efforts to revitalize local economies.

5. CONCLUSION

Overall, the application of effective employment policies means that help can be given to those displaced as a result of globalization (the sop), while at the same time giving them greater mobility towards new growth areas (the silver lining). Measures specifically targeting those affected by trade liberalization can be useful in certain circumstances, particularly where job losses are concentrated in declining regions and/or if they affect an entire sector. Such measures can also provide social back-up for the policy of trade liberalization itself: those displaced because of liberalization are, to a certain extent, the victims of a deliberate political decision. However, experience shows that such specific measures have their limits and sometimes actually hinder adjustment. This is why general policies are needed, particularly activation schemes, effective public employment services and a sufficiently lengthy redundancy notification period, together with adequate levels of benefits.

One question yet to be answered, however, is how these measures should be funded. Some observers note that globalization brings with it the risk of fiscal competition, and in particular reductions in income tax for high-earners. If this risk materializes, it would compromise implementation of the employment policies recommended here.

BETTER GOVERNANCE OF THE INTERNATIONALIZATION OF EMPLOYMENT

BY BRIAN A. LANGILLE

1. INTRODUCTION – BASIC NATIONAL AND INTERNATIONAL GOALS

The questions which our title suggests are many and complex. Although these questions are important to all economies and societies, they present a distinct set of political and policy puzzles for "developed" and successful OECD economies, including France and Canada. While I am a Canadian and not an expert on the French labour market, I do believe that there is a common set of issues facing the successful economies and societies of the world as the project of globalization continues. These are issues about which national policy has a great deal to say. One of my main points will be that what we require to address this set of issues is not only sound analysis and policy, but policy consistency and coherence across a number of policy domains, and at both the national, regional, and international levels.

But our title may also mislead and confuse us in some ways. What does "governance" as opposed to government really mean? Is "governance" an unwanted and watered-down idea of "government" forced upon us by globalization? And what do we mean, exactly, by "the internationalization of employment"? Not that the jobs of many people will take them abroad – although this is true for more and more people, and for example presents issues within WTO Services negotiations – this is not our central problem. But if not that, then is it the idea of the "job" going elsewhere while the former holder of it remains at home and unemployed? Or is it that even the jobs which remain at home are increasingly part of larger, global, networks of production and consumption?

We shall return to these and other questions, but I wish to begin with the most basic question which our title prompts, i.e. "what do we mean by 'better'?" I take "better" to mean neither smaller nor larger government or governance (which can have no intrinsic merit of their own), but rather smarter governance – that is, governance which better achieves our true goals. But what are our true goals? This is a question which is seldom asked or answered explicitly, but I think it is the correct place to start. My view is that we, that is the developed countries such as Canada and France, 1) have both domestic and international

---

[1] See Sen: *Development As Freedom*, 1999.

goals, 2) that these goals are fundamentally the same, but 3) that the difficult task of "governance" lies in managing (coherently) the two spheres so that one does not become the enemy of the other.

But what are these common goals? At the most basic and philosophical level our goal is to construct durable and just societies and economies both at home and also abroad. The Nobel Laureate Amartya Sen[66] is right, in my view, that the key to just societies is what he calls "human freedom" – which is not a formal, empty idea of freedom, but a substantive vision of freedom as "the real capacity to lead lives we have reason to value" – that is, the capacity to live longer, happier, healthier, and freer lives. Increasing GDP per capita or drafting comprehensive labour codes are not our gaols – they are ways there – i.e. "means" not "ends". For our purposes there are two other vital ideas in Sen's writings – first, that human freedom is both our destination and one of the most important ways there. Second, that there exist deep connections between different aspects or dimensions of human freedom, including social, economic, and political freedoms:

> Political freedoms (in the form of free speech and elections) help to promote economic security. Social opportunities (in the form of education and health facilities) facilitate economic participation. Economic facilities (in the form of opportunities for participation in trade and production) can help to generate personal abundance as well as public resources for social facilities. Freedoms of different kinds can strengthen one another.[2]

This is the sort of understanding we require to underwrite, from an intellectual point of view, any possible "post-Washington consensus". This is because the "Washington consensus" is, or was, a view which insisted upon the segregation and sequencing of the economic as prior to the social and the political – getting economic fundamentals right, getting prices right, and so on, comes first. Social justice is seen as a kind of after-thought. This is not sensible in Sen's opinion because, first, it misses the whole point of development and, second, it overlooks the mutually reinforcing "package deal" characteristic of economic opportunities, political liberties, and social powers. Sen's views should not come as a surprise, if we think about it, for this package is exactly what characterizes all successful and just societies – the large majority of OECD countries. Sound social policy is not the enemy of economic progress but one mutually supporting element of the overall structure of various sorts of human freedoms.

Sen's understanding is our best account of how just societies operate, what they stand for, and how to construct them (i.e. the process of development). But if we share this set of ideals then we also hold them for others and for other societies. That is, these ideals also underlie our international and development commitments. One of the most striking aspects of Jim Wolfensohn's presidency of the World Bank was that he began almost every one of his many speeches with the same first paragraph – noting, essentially, that there are (roughly) six billion

---

[2] ibid.

human beings on our planet, that three billion of them live on less than two dollars a day, and that 1.2 billion live in absolute poverty of less than one dollar a day. That is the problem beside which all else pales. The global project, to which countries such as ours are committed, is to do something about it – to move these societies toward real human freedom, in which there is real capacity to lead lives people have reason to value.

Employment is in this respect a very interesting idea because it is also both an important **means** to a life of real human freedom, and also an **end** in itself, that is, an element of freedom in and of itself. To be excluded from the labour market is not just to be excluded from a means to other important aspects of life (food and shelter) it is also to be excluded from an important realm and dimension of freedom itself which is expressed in the self-respect which flows from being a contributing member of society.[3] A world without jobs is a world from which a significant dimension of real human capacity is lost.

At the same time, the labour market is changing. It is very useful to recall that there was a time when labour was not organized through contracts of employment negotiated in the labour market. The ideas of "employment", "employee", and "employer" came to dominate our thinking quite recently in legal history.[4] Employment is one mode or way of organizing productive activity. It turns out that now our very familiar category of long-term (life-long) employment with a single employer is less and less common, as Alain Supiot and others have noted.[5] But employment, whether classical or "atypical", remains for our societies the central legal concept and organizing mechanism for mobilizing what we now often call "human capital". And, as we have noted, a job is not only an end in itself, but the means to much more. This is true in domestic policy and in our thinking about how to assist developing countries. Creating jobs not only helps people, it helps them help themselves. And given Jim Wolfensohn's reminders it is critical that we push hard on the solutions to our global problem. This is the key idea behind the ILO's efforts to make decent work a global goal.

2. ARE THESE NATIONAL AND INTERNATIONAL GOALS ACTUALLY COMPATIBLE?

Thus, if there is such similarity between our domestic and international goals, where is the difficulty in governing employment in an era of internationalization? One difficulty, obviously, is that there is a view that our domestic and international goals, while seemingly in harmony, are actually in tension. The most familiar expression of this point of view is found in the very popular notion that creating jobs abroad reduces employment at home, as current debates

---

[3] Beatty: "Labour is not a Commodity" in Reiter and Swinton (eds), *Studies in Contract Law*.

[4] Deakin and Wilkinson, forthcoming.

[5] Supiot: *Transformation of Labour and the Future of labour Law in Europe*, (European Commission,1999).

(not least of all in France) about offshoring and outsourcing reveal. I shall return to this issue, and the role of international labour law in dealing with it, but the issues of governance of employment are actually much more complex than that argument suggests. This is so for a number of reasons, but the most basic reason is that pointed out by Sen – important aspects of human freedom are interconnected, and, given both the centrality of employment in our society/economy and its own "double aspect" as both means and end in itself, it follows that in thinking about how to increase productive employment, "just about everything matters".[6]

In my view the most helpful way to think about employment is to begin with some basic reminders. For a long time the ILO has reminded us that economic growth, for all of its complexities, can be understood in terms of the following equation:

(A) GDP growth = (B) Employment growth x (C) Labour productivity growth[7]

Conceptually, there is a limit to employment growth – i.e. "full employment", however defined. A society can "only" put 100 per cent of its citizens to work. But there is no *a priori* limit to the other factor in the equation – productivity growth. So, as Paul Krugman so aptly put it, "in the long run" the only way "in which sustained, long-term growth and increased living standards can be achieved is by raising productivity".[8] Krugman is also correct that this is as true and as important for countries which engage in no international trade as it is to open economies such as France or Canada. International competition is not the issue per se. The issue is simply productivity growth. As he puts it – "productivity isn't everything, but in the long run it is almost everything" adding:

> In the long run, barring some catastrophe, the rate of growth of living standards in a country is almost exactly equal to the annual increase in the amount an average worker can produce in an hour.[9]

Ultimately, it has to be the case, as Krugman puts it, that the bottom line in productivity is the "education of the children of the nation."[10] But as the ILO noted:

> The benefits of improving productivity seem straightforward, but a thorough understanding would fill (and has filled) many volumes as, rather unhelpfully, just about "everything" matters. ...For example, the prime source of productivity growth is technological change. Technological change, in turn, relies on innovation, which itself is influenced by an array of institutions, the quality of the supply of human capital, competitive market dynamics, spending of research and development, and investment in general. These in turn depend upon strength and stability of aggregate demand, and thus on the macroeconomic framework.

---

[6] ILO: *World Employment Report 2004*, p2.

[7] ILO: *World Employment Report, 1995*, p.189

[8] Krugman, *Peddling Prosperity*, p56.

[9] ibid.

[10] ibid.

> Investment is a catalyst for innovation, but the reverse is also true: innovation spurs investment. ... [P]roductivity growth also depends on ...regulatory factors...[c]hanges in the organization of work and production... [c]ommercial regulations...basic infrastructure...[11]

In spite of the basic truths about the central importance of productivity growth and about its complex connections to so much else, we are now witnessing a vigorous dispute about that very idea. The claim is that productivity increases are dangerous to, and can be achieved by reducing, employment. This is simple to see in terms of our basic equation. If we maintain A (output) while decreasing B (employment) we must have an increase in C (productivity per worker). There is much debate, in North America for example, about a single-minded focus on productivity as an end in itself.[12] From the perspective of the individual firm there may well be an incentive to "producing more with less" – i.e. fewer people. And indeed it is critical that this be the case. But firms, driven by a short-term/shareholder value imperative, may lay off workers in ways which amount to underinvestment in long-term productivity gains – in R&D, for example. But this is a problem of short-termism, not the idea of productivity per se. As the ILO put it – "in the long term there is no necessary trade-off between the growth of productivity and that of employment".[13] From a societal, rather than a business, perspective however productivity is never an end in itself and the real issue is maximizing growth as a vehicle (means) to enhancing human freedom – and employment is both a means to, and part of, that goal itself. This is not to say that there is not a requirement to address often large "transitions" and transitional costs – i.e. job losses born by individual workers in declining industries. But this is a problem in a world without internationalization. And the labour market policies, that is, active labour market policies required to address this reality would be necessary with or without globalization. Globalization may make such policies more relevant – but also while providing the resources to provide them. To be sure much remains to be done to adapt our labour laws and institutions – portability of pensions, pro-rating of benefits, training, relocation assistance, and so on – to enable workers to make these transitions. This is part of what is required in a coherent approach to managing the internationalization of employment. Productivity matters, but the obtainable policy objective is high productivity AND high employment, as our formula makes so plain. The policy issue for nations such as Canada and France is therefore "what are the conditions under which employment and productivity growth can advance in tandem, creating an expanding "virtuous circle" of decent and productive employment opportunities"?[14]

---

[11] ILO: op.cit., 2004, p.2.

[12] See for example, Henry Minsky: "Productivity is a Time Bomb", The Globe and Mail (Toronto), 13 June 2002, p.A17.

[13] ILO: op.cit., 2004, p.6.

[14] ILO: op.cit., 2004, p.9.

From this perspective human capital policy, of which labour law is a key part, lies at the heart of sound national strategies, not at the margins.

It is important to recall that not only does globalization increase the pressure on domestic policy coherence to foster transitions but that Wolfensohn's numbers remind us that this is indeed the point. The developing world needs investment, jobs, and market access. The ILO is committed to development through what it calls decent work, i.e. good jobs. This fits well with Sen's basic theory. The developed world, nations such as France and Canada included, has become accustomed to these truths and has taken on international commitments (not complete – see agriculture for example) at the WTO and elsewhere to help accomplish this internationalization of production and consumption often expressly with a view to achieving development goals. This has often been "sold" politically in domestic debates through the idea that the adjustment in the international division of labour which this entails is easily absorbed because it involves the loss of jobs in low paying/low skill/low productivity sectors to countries where an abundant supply of unskilled labour provides a comparative advantage. The road to the high skilled/ high value added/high productivity end of the production chain is necessary and available. In this respect, job losses, whether caused by loss of market share due to foreign competition, plant relocation to take advantage of lower costs elsewhere, or outsourcing, are manageable and even a necessary spur to productivity growth. This is not to deny that this set of policy prescriptions is a difficult enough political task to manage. It requires a coherent set of well articulated domestic and international policies and a thorough understanding of the dynamics of outsourcing and other phenomena. But there are three developments, two domestic and one international, which we are now witnessing which will put even greater stress upon the need for smart and coherent policies concerning our mobilization and utilization of human capital, i.e. which will put even greater pressure on our need to produce coherent and smart policies regarding employment and productivity.

1. The ageing population. Countries like Canada and France need to face up to a compelling set of demographic facts. In a recent OECD study[15] it was pointed out that by 2050 the over-65 population of France could rise to 58 per cent of the 20 to 64 age group population – double the current percentage. Furthermore, France's labour force will begin to shrink and age significantly from 2010. This coming demographic reality is combined with the existing fact that, comparatively, France already employs few older workers.

2. The structure of the labour market is changing. "Traditional" long term employment is declining and "atypical" employment is increasing and as explored in the Supiot report, this generates the need for new labour market policies, laws, and approaches that take account of these realities and which enhance the utilization of human capital, rather than obstruct it.

---

[15] OECD 2005, *Aging and Employment Policies – France.*

3. The doubling of the global work force with the entry of India and China into the world economy. In 1985 the "global economic world" consisted of 2.5 billion people. With the "collapse of communism, China's shift to market capitalism, and India's turn from autarky" this grew to six billion people. This doubled the global labour force. As Richard Freeman makes clear the "challenge" that India and China pose is not simply in the unskilled sectors. Rapid growth in higher education, in research and development capabilities, and so on, puts real pressure on the familiar account of the global re-division of labour set out above.[16] This point has been given very recent emphasis by India's decision to reverse its policies regarding intellectual property protection – in essence joining the consensus of the developed countries.[17]

Each of these changes puts increasing pressure on the need for coherent policies, domestically and internationally, to manage these phenomena so that we might be able to adhere to our basic goals concerning human freedom, just societies, and not have our international goals "canabalize" our national goals, or vice versa.

3. A NOTE ABOUT LAW

The approach taken here is to address the issue of "the internationalization of employment", and the role of law in addressing it seriously. This requires a broad framework of basic thinking within which we can place all of the details of our law and legal institutions, which bear on this phenomenon. Without such a broad policy overview sensible analysis is not possible and reform will very likely be partial and unhelpful. Moreover, there is a common view that the legal dimension of the internationalization of employment is about specific and limited interventions to deal with job losses (whether to international competition, offshoring, etc.) – for example, whether we should have specific laws to compensate those who lose their jobs. But the role of law is much more important than that view allows. Labour law is critical in creating and recreating jobs in the first place. As we have noted, changes in the nature of much domestic employment require that we reshape much of our normal day to day labour law (labour standards, collective bargaining, and so on) in order to achieve our goals. This kind of approach forces us back to basic principles. But this is not "un-legal" – it is the necessary precondition to any detailed legal reform. Of course it is not a sufficient condition for sensible reform or reconsideration, but it is a necessary one. And detailed prescriptions are beyond the scope of this paper. This approach has the added advantage of reaffirming that the law is not autonomous from the real world of the economy – but both answerable to, and a shaper of, it. From this perspective much of labour law is seen as having a more central and critical

---

[16] Freeman: "Doubling the Global Workforce" (notes for an unpublished talk, available at www.cgdev.org)

[17] Financial Times, 23 March 2005, p.1.

role in our pursuit of our most basic goals both internationally and domestically. It is not an afterthought and its role not to simply pick up the pieces after internationalization has done its work. Our labour law is much more important than that.

4. FOUR LEVELS OF POLICY COHERENCE

The position I am advocating is that productive employment is central to our most basic goals, both as a means to our basic goals and as an end in itself, both domestically and internationally. We would face our real domestic problems about maximizing employment and productivity even in the absence of globalization. But "internationalization" has and will increasingly put pressure on us to forge policies which enable us to pursue both our domestic and development goals without one becoming the enemy of the other. This requires an overall strategy of policy coherence. There are four levels or "meanings" of "coherence" which need to be noted here. *First*, we require coherent and systemic domestic policies to promote both employment and productivity growth "in tandem" and in a mutually supportive way. This is especially true given an ageing population and changes in the structure of the labour market. Greater coherence across a greater range of issues is required. *Second*, we require coherency at the international level. It is not adequate to have policies regarding aid, finance, trade, international labour standards and other ILO projects, and regional integration – if they are not part of an overall plan geared to our goals. To use an example I will return to, there is something wrong with an international policy which worries about ILO fundamental rights, but sees no connection between them and, for example, China's WTO accession negotiations. *Third*, we require not only (1) horizontal coherence at the domestic level and (2) horizontal coherence at the international level, but (3) "vertical" coherence between the domestic and international levels. For example, it is incoherent to worry about China's impact upon domestic employment without seeing the connection to China's exchange rate policy – and again seeing no connection between those two and WTO accession, to stick to our one example. But the *fourth* level of policy coherence is the most critical – and it informs the content of a coherent policy which would satisfy the first three coherence requirements. This is the deep policy coherence about which Sen instructs us – between economic, political and social rights – the integrated and interactive account of what were separate policy realms. It is only with a deep and integrated account of the relationship between market/economic freedoms on the one hand, and social and political freedoms on the other that we will find the way to maximizing productivity and employment. It is in this light that many of our policy agendas can be seen as complementary and mutually reinforcing, and not in contradiction.

I will touch, briefly, upon each of these four dimensions.

Domestic policy coherence.

As the 2004 ILO World Employment Report makes plain, almost "everything matters" in generating productive employment. Generating productive

employment is the most fundamental of government policies. We are committed internationally to a rules-based open trading system, and have benefited from
the growth trade liberalization has made possible. But "job churning" occurs
even in non-traded sectors and our concern for those out of a job is not limited
to those who have lost their job to foreign competition. Our goals and international commitments instruct us to secure the advantages of global markets and
production and to pursue "active" rather than passive labour market policies –
of which Denmark is now regarded as the model[18] – to provide the kind of flexible security required. This is also required by the evolution in the structure of the
domestic labour market with its tendency away from lifelong employment with
a single employer. These changes have, as Supiot has written, forced us to reconsider large parts of our labour law – which have been based upon the assumption of the long-term employment relationship. Simply put, if our paradigm of
employment has changed then we need to rethink our traditional "platform" for
delivery of entitlements, rights, negotiation, risk sharing, etc.[19] So too the coming
demographic realties force a re-evaluation of not only, for example, pension
systems, retirement age policies, and so on – but of immigration policies as well.
But the key to policy coherence domestically will be to realize that "human
capital" **formation** (education and training) and **deployment** (structured by
labour law which maximizes its potential rather that blocks it – pension portability for example) is a most vital, if not the most vital of, domestic policies for
developed nations. This reality is only heightened by the facts we have noted
about the impact of India and China upon the world system.

Then, as we have noted, it will be argued that it is precisely globalization,
which, while making necessary sound domestic labour policy, also makes it
impossible. This is the "regulatory competition/social dumping/race to the
bottom" argument which is very prevalent. My view is that the evidence does
not support this sort of claim – and that Sen explains at the conceptual level why
this should be so. The race to the bottom view really depends upon the
"Washington consensus" being correct. That is, contrary to Sen, that the
economic realm is separate from and prior to social and political rights and the
latter, rather than being part of the mutually reinforcing complex of freedoms
necessary to successful economies, is a drag upon growth – i.e. a tax which
mobile capital would rather not pay. It is only, according to this view, that it can
be in the dominant self-interest of nations to lower labour standards to attract
investment. But if Sen is right this is nonsense – and the evidence bears him out.
Sound social and labour policies are not a brake upon the construction of durable
economies but one of the necessary parts of the package deal which all such
societies have constructed. Here I leave that issue mainly to the paper by Werner
Sengenberger, one of the world's experts in taking on the "labour standards are
a cost" line of thought. But a few words about the "race to the bottom" argument

---

[18] OECD, ILO.

[19] Langille: "Labour Policy in Canada- New Platform/New Paradigm" (2002), 28 Canadian
Public Policy 133.

are in order; this argument that in essence says that governments should view sound labour policy as a cost or a tax which they are now powerless to impose is, in my view, almost entirely wrong. I cite below some of the well known data undermining that thesis. But the key is (as we would expect from Sen's view) that governments are not acting rationally and in their self-interest by entering this race and responding to corporate pressures to do so. Any gains are in the long run suboptimal individually and in the short run collectively. A government is not a company. Its role is to provide the public goods which individual firms may undersupply, or seek to avoid paying for, but still require. From this point of view, the role of international labour law is not so much to constrain nations from pursuing their self-interest, but rather to help them secure it in the first place. This leaves aside however the really problematic reality of non-democratic States which systematically forbid the expression of public self-interest through the suppression of basic democratic and labour rights – Burma/Myanmar being poster child for this phenomenon, and China being the really important case. This is a dramatic reality which requires (coherent) and urgent attention. But our argument is not "merely" that this results in "unfair competition" and that this is a playing field which needs to be levelled. Rather, our arguments are much more powerful than that. The best arguments are simply our concerns about denial of human freedom. Beyond that we are not "merely" concerned about unfair competition but about suboptimal development with many global consequences – on exchange rates, employment, restriction of market access, trade, global consumption, security, and so on. To see the problem as one of "unfair competition" is to underestimate, if not mis-state, our concerns which are really about the need for "good" globalization.

But leaving aside the issue of non-democratic States still leaves us with plenty to worry about domestically which our current debates about "outsourcing" and "offshoring" only confirm. This is because even if we leave behind the regulatory competition argument (which is an argument about the **indirect** impact of internationalization) we still have arguments about the **direct** labour market impact upon jobs and employment. And as I have noted the familiar story about only low valued added jobs being vulnerable is increasingly difficult to believe, so one can expect this argument to become re-heated, not cool down. What is it about outsourcing and offshoring which causes such problems? We have by now absorbed many of the lessons of global production of goods, and their employment impacts, which seem directly parallel. Canada used to produce televisions, suits, cheap wine, but we see that we are all immensely better off now that we no longer do so. The policy task was to address the costs which were visited upon the group of Canadians who bore the cost of that transition by providing employment elsewhere through active labour market policies.[20] And we are clearly at home with the idea of "our" firms, Airbus for example, securing greater market share, with clear negative labour market effects elsewhere.

---

[20] Trebilcock, Chandler, Howse: *Trade and Transitions*, (Routledge, 1994). ILO: *Active Labour Market Policies Around the World: Coping With the consequences of Globalization.*

What is it about outsourcing which seems to strike a different nerve? First, that the jobs are often not in manufacturing and not lower skilled ones perhaps increasing the level of perceived vulnerability. This is one of those new realities we listed above. But are there reasons to think that this calls for a different set of domestic policy responses? In my view no, at least if we pursue a policy coherent with the dimensions set out above. It is true that outsourcing affects different categories of workers but this also means that they are occupied by persons with skills and levels of education such that they are more generally able to make successful transition. Moreover, I do not know how we could defend, consistent with our core values, the idea that we are happy to be members of an open world economy but only if we (and others in the OECD) retain all of the high end jobs. But it also appears that there are many misconceptions about the realities of outsourcing and its impact upon domestic labour markets and firms. A number of studies have sought to put the outsourcing idea into context. One of the key findings is that outsourcing actually generates positive – including employment – results for domestic firms. In my view Theodore Moran's study *Beyond Sweatshops: Foreign Direct Investment and Globalization in Developing Countries*[21] usefully summarizes these lessons as follows:

> The long-standing concern that outward investment could siphon off productive activity – and hence, jobs – from the home country has been most memorably encapsulated in Ross Perot's reference to a "giant sucking sound." A series of studies conducted over many years has found, however, that in developed countries, firms that engage in outward investment have higher export levels than otherwise similar firms that do not invest abroad. Moreover... this positive relationship holds not only for components shipped for assembly overseas but for final products sold in the host economy. In fact, the pull of exports from the home country to the host country is high enough to offset any displacement of exports from the host country to third markets. The same study findings also reveal what would happen if outward investment from the home country were inhibited or prevented altogether: exports would drop – and both union and non-union jobs would drop with them.

> The findings ... are consistent with the observations made about specific industries ... The advent of global sourcing on the part of multinational corporations in the automotive and computer and electronics sectors reversed the decline of the parent firms and reinforced their competitive positions in the home market and around the world. The creation of supply chains, via foreign direct investment in developing countries, fortified the high wages and productive jobs available to workers in developed countries. Companies with less successful strategies for the globalization of production faltered and shrank, both at home and abroad.

> Outward investment improves the composition of jobs in the home market by raising the number of export-related jobs, which pay between 5 and 18 percent more than non-export-related jobs. The presence of "globally engaged" firms may also generate productivity spill-overs and other externalities in the communities in which they are located. The globalization of industry, via foreign direct investment, thus turns out to be, like trade, a win-win phenomenon for workers and the overall economy in home and host countries alike. Like trade, however, the globalization

---

[21] Brookings, 2002, p. 164-65.

of industry also produces dislocations for less competitive firms, workers, and plants in the home economy. ... [E]mployees need to be cushioned from the effects of displacement; in the long term, strong and effective measures along these lines will be much more effective, both for displaced workers and for the larger economy, than ineffective and counterproductive efforts to slow down or try to halt the process of globalization itself.

These findings, and those contained in other studies, provide the intellectual ammunition needed to address the outsourcing issue. But, politically, it may be that it will be the (coherent) appeal to our development goals, and Wolfensohn's numbers – that are a claim to fairness, as well as self-interest – which will be required.

International policy coherence

It is often assumed that our international commitments are at war with our domestic goals regarding employment – as we have noted in our discussion of popular views about outsourcing. As seen, this does not have to be the case – and from the formal legal point of view of our international commitment this is not at all the case. In fact, quite the opposite. Here are words from the constitutions of two critical international organizations involved with our issues:

> "The Parties to this Agreement,
>
> Recognizing that their relations in the field of trade and economic endeavour should be conducted with a view to raising standards of living, **ensuring full employment and a large and steadily growing volume of real income and effective demand**, and expanding the production of and trade in goods and services, while allowing for the optimal use of the world's resources in accordance with the objective of sustainable development, seeking both to protect and preserve the environment and to enhance the means for doing so in a manner consistent with their respective needs and concerns at different levels of economic development..."

And the second institutional constitution reads:

> "Confident that the fuller and broader utilization of the world's productive resources necessary for the achievement of the objectives set forth in this Declaration can be secured by effective international and national action, including measures to expand production and consumption, to avoid severe economic fluctuations to promote the economic and social advancement of the less developed regions of the world, to assure greater stability in world prices of primary products, and to **promote a high and steady volume of international trade**, the Conference pledges the full cooperation ...with such international bodies as may be entrusted with a share of the responsibility for this great task and for the promotion of the health, education and well-being of all peoples."

The surprising point is that the former words are from the 1994 Agreement establishing the WTO, and the latter words are from the ILO Constitution. But while there is formal coherence expressed here, I would say it is very clear that nations such as France and Canada have failed to pursue these institutional mandates in an integrated and coherent manner. This is a matter explored at some length in a new essay by long-time WTO/ILO observer Steve Charnowitz, entitled, tellingly, "The (Neglected) Employment Dimension of the World Trade Organization".[22] We can start with the symbolic point that WTO/ILO members, far from pursuing their dual and complementary constitutional mandates, have not even extended observer status from the WTO to the ILO. The recent "wise persons" report on the future on the WTO offers little hope on this score.[23] As Charnowitz puts it, the WTO proceeds as if goods to be traded "were immaculately produced".[24] This is in part driven by the WTO's fear of international labour standards which it sees only through a protectionist lens and about which Werner Sengenberger has much to say. But this is simply to say that it has been unable to move beyond the Washington consensus view which is so antithetical to the integrated approach (as explained by Sen) – and expressed in the two Constitutions set out above. In fact that view has become a barrier to the WTO fulfilling its constitutional mandate and acting according to its own constitution. The obvious question is why WTO members, such as Canada and France, have permitted this to occur. The result is that there is, as Charnowitz points out, a completely unhelpful attitude pervading the WTO – those wishing to discuss labour issues are viewed as mere rent seekers motivated by protectionist interests rather than sensible people with a sound view of the point and potential of international trade to improve the lives of the world's citizens. At the very least the WTO should be a leading collaborator with the ILO on issues such as labour market adjustment programmes. (This would have the added advantage of providing some positive political and public relations coverage for that institution.) It is difficult enough for nations to pursue the benefits of an open and rules based trading system, providing the kind of active labour market and adjustment policies required, without the additional burden of having to defend a WTO which adheres to the view that any discussion of the impact of trade upon peoples' lives and employment is a threat to the system, rather than the point of it.

There are many other questions that could be asked which would reinforce our key point about a lack of policy coherence at the international level – the non-use of the Trade Policy Review Mechanism regarding employment agendas, to note merely one.

One area in which the WTO cannot totally ignore labour market issues is in the GATS (General Agreement on Trade in Services) negotiations where two of the four "modes" directly concern the movement of persons to either consume or provide services. Yet even here the WTO has not established contacts with either the ILO or the International Organization for Migration.[25]

---

[22] Forthcoming in Leary and Warner (eds) *Social Issues, Globalization, and International Institutions* (2005).

[23] *The Future of the WTO.* 2005.

[24] Charnowitz, op.cit., p.7.

[25] Charnowitz, p.10.

We have already mentioned the looming issue of India/China and the doubling of the world's workforce. The negotiations leading to China's accession the WTO should have but did not provide an opportunity, structured with clear incentives, for improving governance of the internationalization of employment. But by concentrating on the WTO as the locus of our complaints about international policy coherence is to largely underestimate our problem. If we stay with the China example for a moment, it is quite clear that much more "matters" and bears upon our issue. It is not an insight of startling originality to point out that a core aspect of governance of the employment issue lies in basic global macroeconomic governance issues – particularly the management of the global financial system. It is a common view that a better alignment of world currencies, especially a de-linking of the yuan from the dollar and resulting appreciation, is required to redress current imbalances, reduce American external debt, take some of the upward pressure off the Euro, reduce protectionist pressures there, and so on.[26] This precise and very common view may or may not be mistaken, but the general idea that there is a link here to employment that requires a coherent approach is not. The whole world, including China, has enormous stakes in managing its extraordinary entry into the world system.

But our search and demand for coherent governance of employment does not end there. As we have noted above at the same time we need to attend to China's "obscure", to use the very soft term, relationship with the ILO's core labour rights – the procedural or process rights, most critically freedom of association, which are essential to the legitimate and fair expression of labour policy (and the construction of just societies based upon and advanced by human freedom which as Sen points out, is the point of it all) – yet which seem to be ignored in the rush to invest in, or sell military hardware to, that nation. A recent but somewhat chilling example – China abruptly cancelled (by withdrawing visas at the last minute) a global meeting organized by the OECD to discuss worker rights. Another sign of the state of affairs is that WalMart recently agreed to let its Chinese workers join the official State union. This may tell us more about the state of Chinese unions than about WalMart.[27] But these are mere anecdotal examples – a full account of China's policies on core labour rights has just been published[28] which makes the case for a coherent international approach even more compelling and suggests that a number of the new elements of governance we see emerging – see below – will need to be harnessed to this task.

This appeal for policy coherence is not meant to be or even to sound "Utopian", as that term is normally understood. In fact, I think Utopias have been given a rather a bad name recently as something hopelessly out of touch with reality. But consider the following claim by a distinguished thinker:

---

[26] Jeffrey Garten: "Dealing With a Declining Dollar", *Yale Global online*, 7 February 2005.

[27] "China Blocks International Meeting Focusing on Worker Rights", New York Times, 9 December, 2004, p.A-21.

[28] "Justice for All – The Struggle for Worker Rights in China – A Report by the Solidarity Centre' available at www.solidaritycentre.org.

Every person with any function in society at all will have some kind of ideal vision of that society in the light of which he operates. One can hardly imagine a social worker going out to do case work without thinking of her as having, somewhere in her mind, a vision of the better, cleaner, healthier, more emotionally balanced city, as a kind of mental model inspiring the work she does. One can hardly imagine in fact, any professional person not having such a social model – a world of health for the doctor or justice for the judge – nor would such a social vision be confined to the professions.

It seems to me in fact that a Utopia should be conceived, not as an impossible dream of an impossible ideal, but as the kind of working model of society that exists somewhere in the mind of every sane person who has any social function at all.[29]

The plea regarding policy coherence, even if "utopian" should be understood as utopian in just this sense – as a working model of our approach to governance of the internationalization of employment. And there is at least some international legal support for the coherence approach as a basic methodology. Among the international instruments in existence which directly address our issue is ILO Convention No. 122 on Employment Policy (1964). That Convention has only two substantive articles. Article 1 states that each member State which ratifies (Convention No. 122 has 95 ratifications) "shall declare and pursue as a major goal an active policy designed to promote full, productive, and freely chosen employment" – not a difficult constraint for nations such as France or Canada, given our goals and basic formula. Article 2 holds that each State should "decide upon and keep under review…the measures to be adopted" to achieve article 1's ambitions. This is in itself not terribly informative as to where national interest lies – or how to achieve it. It may help explain the relatively large number of ratifications. But from our "coherence" perspective the 1944 Declaration of Philadelphia is of more assistance and in fact might more usefully be viewed as the draft of a possible "coherence convention" on employment in itself. The Declaration reads, in its relevant part:

Believing that experience has fully demonstrated the truth of the statement in the Constitution of the International Labour Organization that lasting peace can be established only if it is based on social justice, the Conference affirms that-

(a) all human beings, irrespective of race, creed or sex, have the right to pursue both their material well-being and their spiritual development in conditions of freedom and dignity, of economic security and equal opportunity;

(b) the attainment of the conditions in which this shall be possible must constitute the central aim of national and international policy;

(c) all national and international policies and measures, in particular those of an economic and financial character, should be judged in this light and accepted only in so far as they may be held to promote and not to hinder the achievement of this fundamental objective;

(d) it is a responsibility of the International Labour Organization to examine and

---

[29] Northrop Frye: *On Education* (1988), p.70.

consider all international economic and financial policies and measures in the light of this fundamental objective;

(e) in discharging the tasks entrusted to it the International Labour Organization, having considered all relevant economic and financial factors, may include in its decisions and recommendations any provisions which it considers appropriate.

This is, particularly in paragraph (c), a much more concrete and useful instruction to member States as to how they might usefully conduct a coherent approach to the internationalization of employment in our integrated world. This should not seem utopian in the "impossible dream" sense. Rather it looks mundanely common-sensical and merely required for rational engagement with our issue.

Vertical coherence

It is often the case that not only do we have policy inconsistency at either the domestic level or international level, but that we also lack coherence between the two levels. Our international policies can conflict with our domestic employment agenda. This is so not only at the level of detail but, it seems, at a philosophical level. As we have noted we have a WTO operating on a very dis-integrated, "Washington consensus" view of the world – while much of our domestic policy is organized around a more integrated and organic view of the interaction of the social and economic dimensions of modern societies. But, given, 1 and 2 above, this point does not require much further elaboration. The essential point is that it is through a failure of policy consistency or coherence that our domestic and international goals can come increasingly into conflict and be at odds with one another. Policy coherence is the only path to avoiding this doubly unsatisfactory situation.

Deep coherence

Any effort to achieve any coherence must be underwritten by a coherent account of our basic goals and how they interact with the real world. As I have stated, I believe that the integrated, post-Washington consensus, view is our best account of our goals and of the world – as such it offers the basic structure of thinking necessary to achieve overall coherence. A chief virtue of this view is precisely that it is itself a view which sees a complex, positive, and mutually supporting interaction between aspects of policy where other theories see tension, trade-offs, and zero-sum games. Because it is a comprehensive view which sees deep complementarities between economic and social and political freedoms, it is a view which permits and requires a degree of possible policy coherence which we could not see as either possible or desirable on our prior and more partial perspectives. This of course raises the question of how viable the integrated view actually is. The data on deep compatibility of, for example, respect for labour rights and better trade and FDI performance, is crude, but consistently positive in this regard. Beginning with the OECD study in 1996[30]

---

[30] OECD: *Trade Employment and Labour Standards.*

(and the 2000 follow-up study[31]) the flow of research has continued to affirm the same findings. The only possible explanation for this and other clear observables must be found in a post-Washington consensus, Sen-inspired theory of complex interaction of human freedoms. Given that productivity is the key, and that human capital policy is at the core of increasing productivity, it seems entirely plausible that the central policy dimension for States such as Canada and France is precisely in adapting our labour policies to attend to the three pressing dynamics identified – ageing populations, changing labour market structure, and the doubling of the world's workforce. The future of our societies and economies lies in governing these precise issues from a coherence perspective. But there is also a pressing need to explore further the actual mechanisms of interaction between various elements both to identify best practices and to expose counterproductive ones. That is, there is a great need to strengthen the case for the coherence approach and to further expand its potential insights.

But, as we have noted, the coherence approach is one that rests upon an appeal available essentially to national democratic governments. In other cases, the appeal to human freedom and national self-interest of citizens is not available. Here we will as we have stated need to deploy as many of the credible elements of "governance" of our issues as are or can be made available.

5. A NOTE ABOUT "GOVERNANCE"

At the outset I posed some questions about "governance" as opposed to "government". In my view governance is not a weak substitute for government but best seen as a new dimension of, or set of possibilities for, government. It is government law and policy which will either lead and help structure useful "governance", i.e. new techniques, sometimes involving new actors, etc., or, failing to do so, will either intentionally, but more probably by default, add to the heady mixture of incentives to policy incoherence as narrow minded, unrepresentative, inexpert, interest groups dominate the space of governance. Governance which deploys and utilizes actors with expertise, knowledge, resources, and critically, broad political legitimacy, is simply potentially useful. Government should be keen to support actors and processes with these characteristics. This is particularly true in the area of human capital policy where the social actors are often exemplars of the qualities we seek. It is even more critical in a world of the coherence approach in which the appeal is less and less to centralized "command and control" legal structures and more and more to the self-interest of capital and labour in productive human capital creation and deployment.

The idea that human capital is critical and that it is via sound human capital policies that productivity is increased, will lead to an increased effort at "self-regulation" by firms and "certification" by industry organizations seeking to promote their own self-interest. These are not a threat to our basic goals but an

---

[31] OECD: International Trade and Core Labour Standards.

adaptation to a new positive dynamic. This requires leadership and coherence at the domestic and international levels. Nor would it be surprising for organizations such as the ISO (the International Organization for Standardization) to see a role in labour matters as it has in environmental issues. If it is the case that there is a large degree of self-interest in sound labour/ human capital policy, then the old "command and control" model of labour law will be less useful (because it aims at constraining self-interest which is not the problem). It will be in the self-interest of those, especially in global production sectors, to certify their human capital quality. Sophisticated pools of capital will be guided by both corporate and national characteristics in this regard. Sophisticated consumer and human rights "watchdogs" will assist in creating incentives. We will see and need more "Global Compacts". So too other forms of CSR – corporate social responsibility – will be a growth industry. Many of these are private initiatives – but many are mixed – and all good forms of such undertakings can nourished by government support in domestic and international fora, such as the ILO, OECD, etc. Here globalization becomes a "driver", rather than the enemy, of respect for core labour rights and the advancement of other labour standards. But it is important to realize the limitations. As the report on workers rights in China details, transnational corporations operating in China are clearly not observing codes which call for respect for the fundamental rights of freedom of association. The positive view is that such codes do provide another pressure point for change.

In industries characterized by non-traditional forms of employment we may expect to see unions and other "human capital organizations" take on new functions and structures. How else will we deal with, for example, employees who do not have a single long-term employer? Laws and systems of representation must evolve not simply to keep up – but to avoid being part of the problem. Simple examples abound – such as not tying pensions to single employers (which made sense in a different and earlier world). Here the law blocks employees and thus our domestic goals regarding employment in an internationalized world. New technologies make possible new platforms for such delivery of labour law – by both the State and the social partners.

It is therefore not surprising that the maritime sector has undertaken a broad reform of its labour policies for it is the ultimate example of the internationalization of employment. Its reality is, as we noted at the outset, vastly different from what we normally think of as the problem of the internationalization of employment. But the idea of thinking radically about how best to achieve our goals in the modern world is a very relevant model in the more common circumstance.

Social dialogue will also develop as a vehicle for regulation. Open methods of coordination, framework agreements, and other initiatives by the social partners, and other newer intermediaries, will be required to respond to our new workplace realities and needs – for training, provision of non-employment contract based platforms for social protection, for new levels of negotiation, for dealing with global firms, and so on. Some of these techniques are particularly useful in addressing the issues which are faced in non-democratic regimes.

Framework agreements, CSR, Global Compact, etc. all have the benefit of "flying beneath the radar" of national policy. This is one of the great advantages of globalization – precisely that it offers non-State actors, most critically the social partners, the space to affect change where international, State-to-State relations have been less productive in meaningful change. But, again, it will require governments guided by a coherent approach, to nurture these initiatives at the ILO and elsewhere.

And perhaps finally we will have to, and we will be able to, as Robert Reich has recently put it "stop blaming WalMart",[32] or China for that matter. The ultimate governance tool is human freedom, including market freedoms. Our choices as consumers and shareholders have the best chance of influencing behaviour, so we should take responsibility for them and engage in some personal, individual level "coherence". From this perspective the methodologies of new modes of governance, which rely more on national and personal freedom and choice, represent a new world of instruments for pursuing our goals and not abandonment of them. There is of course a risk here that this kind of effort can be captured by purely protectionist interests – but the answer to that is, first, that we run greater risks by ignoring the effects of our decisions and, second, that with broad based legitimate actors with credible information

But firms, social partners, and individuals are not countries and there is an increased role for governments as they solve the public policy dilemmas created by new employment relationships – "atypical" working arrangements – by providing what individual firms are increasingly less able to do – provide the long-term stable platforms for the delivery of social protection, insurances, pensions, etc. This involves thinking about which labour standards are appropriately attached to individual or collective contracts, which to the worker and not the contractual relationship with any particular firm, and which to the status of citizen. These are serious and difficult questions – but the point is, again, that we are answering them now, and we will always be answering them – so we should attempt to ensure that we are providing the correct answer. So, for example, it turns out that among the other good reasons for public health care – i.e. attaching that social entitlement to citizenship and not to employment contracts (as is the case in the United States) – is that it assists in labour market mobility and is a positive competitive advantage in an internationalized economy. It should not surprise or disappoint us, but it does in an age still under the influence of the Washington consensus, that doing the right thing is also in our self-interest. At the international level the positive approach to labour rights will lead to increased use of "carrots" rather than "sticks" – preferences in trade, and promotion (rather than sanctions) at the ILO, and so on.

Finally, to focus on a point which I have mentioned but largely left to others to discuss, let me point out the wider implications of the view set out here. It is a commonplace to view labour law as a cost or a tax upon economic progress and to see globalization as a threat to labour law. The account just offered rests

---

[32] New York Times, 28 Feb. 2005, p. A 19

upon a completely different understanding of our true state of affairs. Labour law is more important than ever. It is now more than ever at the heart of the enterprise of constructing successful and just societies. As a result, the traditional view of internationalization as a threat is unhelpful – and very dangerous for our basic global goals. A coherent approach is required however to achieve the benefits of these insights.

6. CONCLUSION

The central political challenge facing the successful nations of the world is, in a few words, to make the successful transition from a view of the world which sees globalization bearing upon existing just societies in a purely negative and threatening way. The truth of the matter is that globalization (G) is both a "driver of" and is "driven by" just (and successful) societies (JS). Globalization both requires and is made possible by just societies. And vice-versa. The causal arrow does simply not run G => JS, but rather G <=> JS. This is as true of the governance of employment as it is of most of our pressing policy issues. This insight does not solve all of our policy dilemmas – but gives us a framework for thinking about them clearly. Our national and international policies can and should be in harmony – but they will be in danger of undermining each other without a "coherence agenda" in place.

THE ROLE OF INTERNATIONAL LABOUR STANDARDS FOR GOVERNING THE INTERNATIONALIZATION OF EMPLOYMENT

BY WERNER SENGENBERGER

1. INTRODUCTION

There are two distinct meanings of the term *labour standard* which tend to be used interchangeably. The first refers to actual conditions of employment, work and welfare of workers in a particular location and point in time, normally using statistics that indicate the national, subnational or sectoral average level of education and vocational skills, labour force participation, employment, wages, hours of work, occupational health and safety, social security, and so on. The second connotation of the term is normative or prescriptive. Labour standards stipulate "what should be" the terms and conditions of work according to national or international agreement. They specify norms embodied in national labour law or the instruments of international labour law, including ILO Conventions and Recommendations, relevant norms in the UN Covenants on Civil and Political, and Economic, Social and Cultural Rights, and regional agreements such as the Social Charter and employment focused directives of the European Union.

The ILO instruments cover core standards, or basic worker rights, of freedom of association, collective bargaining, freedom from forced and compulsory labour, freedom from child labour, and freedom from discrimination in employment and occupation. They also stipulate substantive rules, often called economic and social rights, such as the norms on employment, vocational training, social security, occupational safety and health, minimum wages, maximum hours per day or week; minimum rest periods, paid holidays, maternity leave, protection of vulnerable workers and those with special needs, such as migrant workers and home workers, social security, and rules for conflict resolution.

The most pertinent normative ILO instruments on employment are the Employment Policy Convention (No. 122) and its accompanying Employment Policy Recommendation (No. 122), of 1964, aiming at full, productive and freely chosen employment. Other relevant ILO standards concern the Human Resources Development Convention (No. 142) and accompanying Recommendation (No. 150) of 1975, aimed at vocational guidance and vocational training; and various conventions on employment services and employment agencies, rehabilitation of disabled persons, employment security, and specific forms of work (e.g. home work, part-time work, night work). In addition, a large number of ILO Conventions, including all core Conventions and those for the protection of vulnerable workers and workers in particular occupations, bear directly or indirectly on the quantity or quality of employment. Virtually all relevant employment standards provide for bipartite or tripartite social dialogue. They request the consultation of representatives of the persons affected by the measures to be taken, and in particular representatives of employers and workers.

This paper addresses the following issues: are normative labour standards at the international (ILS) level needed, and are they useful, for the improvement of national employment and working conditions? Do they produce adverse or unintended economic effects? Under what conditions are labour standards effective? How favourable is the global political context for the observance of standards today?

2. THE TRADITIONAL RATIONALE FOR ILS: REGULATION OF LABOUR MARKET COMPETITION

Setting and applying ILS involves direct interference in labour markets with the objective of intercepting destructive, downward directed competition, reducing vulnerability, and allowing workers to exercise countervailing power to upgrade labour conditions and share in the fruits of higher productivity. From the days of Albert Thomas, the first Director-General of the ILO, the Organization maintained that the improvement of labour conditions would not simply come about in the wake of economic progress, but required a proactive approach on legal rights and international agreement. Unregulated competition in the labour market could depress labour conditions. Low wages, i.e. wages not commensurate with productivity, the absence of social protection and the denial of basic worker rights can be used to gain economic advantages vis-à-vis countries that respect international labour standards. If a country fails to live up to international agreements, the effect could be to force other trading nations to follow suit and to reduce their achieved, often hard-won standards. The remedy to this situation is a common rule or minimum floor – or ceiling – for wages and other terms of employment, which is applied to all actual or potential competitors on the demand and supply side of the labour market. If there is foreign competition, then the normative regulation has to be international. It has to be co-extensive with the labour, product and capital market to prevent undercutting of the standard, and the spill-over of sub-standard labour conditions from one country to another. This functional requirement is recognized by economists when they refer to "moral hazard", "negative externalities", or "free riders". It is found in the ILO Constitution which says that "fair and humane conditions of labour should be applied, both at home and in individual countries to which their commercial and industrial relations extend" and "the failure of any nation to adopt humane conditions of labour is an obstacle in the way of other countries which desire to improve the conditions in their own countries".

There is a long history to the view that the setting of binding rules and regulations is needed in order prevent destructive competition, and to be able to improve employment conditions. As early as the 18th century, Jacques Necker, the Finance Minister of Louis XVI, argued that the practice of work on Sundays could not be unilaterally abolished in France, but required parallel action of other European trading countries. The first wave of economic globalization in modern history in the 19th century, during which the volume of international commerce increased from US$4 billion in 1850 to about US$40 billion in 1913, sharpened the awareness of the potential harm that liberalized trade could inflict on workers, and led to the foundation of the ILO in 1919. Prior to World War I, there had been a number of cases in Europe where poisonous substances harmful to worker health (e.g. white phosphorus for match making) allowed competitors to have lower production costs and gain market shares at the expense of countries where toxic substances were not permitted. To prevent such "unfair" competitive advantages competing countries needed to agree to rule out the use of such materials. The first ILO Convention adopted in 1919, provided the 8-hour workday and the 48-hour workweek. For participants in the first session of the International Labour Conference, it was clear that this standard could only be observed if all trading countries ratified and applied it. If competitors failed to do so, then countries respecting the standard would be handicapped by higher relative labour costs.

The potential scope for social dumping, and a "race to the bottom" as trade unionists like to call it, escalated during the second wave of globalization starting in the 1970s. International competition has intensified. First, many more countries became competitors in the international economy, representing an extremely large dispersion of income levels, wages and labour costs, and working conditions, and resulting in fierce cost competition. With easy access to modern technology, countries increasingly compete in the same product areas, throwing workers in high-wage industrialized countries, newly industrializing countries, and transition countries in Central and Eastern Europe into competition with each other. Second, in addition to the expansion of trade, capital and financial markets were liberalized engendering a surge of foreign direct investment and cross-border financial transactions, including a wave of currency speculation. Notably emerging economies in Asia and Latin America vied with each other to relax labour standards to increase exports and attract foreign capital; some countries deliberately kept trade unions out of their export processing zones assuming that this would please foreign transnational companies; according to UNDP, more than 100 countries provide tax holidays to investors in order to win a larger share of FDI (Hansen, 2001). China has kept the exchange value of its currency low to stimulate exports and woo foreign investors. Industrialized countries responded to such action in the emerging economies by warning against further improvements in labour standards in their economies, or even calling for reducing social protection standards, arguing that they were forced to do so to counteract cost competition from countries in the South, and increasingly also from countries in Central and Eastern Europe.

According to one observer, there is a permanent danger of "global bidding wars". A "race to the bottom" does not depend on investors being truly attracted to countries with lower labour standards. This perception, true or false, will suffice to entice governments to scale down domestic standards or refrain from improving them (Oman, 2000). Thirdly, international competition tends to be more and more focused on the labour market targeted to wages and conditions of work. This holds true especially in the EU where the monetary union has ruled out the possibility of using the exchange rate for making adjustments to national productivity and other differences.

In view of large international wage and labour cost differentials the threat posed by international competition for employment is threefold: products made by cheap labour penetrate the markets of the high-wage countries; low wages and poor standards undermine efforts by trade unions in high-wage countries to improve terms and conditions of work; and low standards provide an incentive for enterprises in the high-wage countries to relocate production. In the face of these challenges resulting from market liberalization, the need to apply and enforce universal international labour standards becomes even more compelling. Presently in Europe, new threats of a "race to the bottom" arise from the draft directive of the EU Commission on free contracting of services. If, in accordance with the principle of "country of origin", statutory or contractual terms of employment of the low-wage countries can be applied in the high-wage countries, the spectre arises not only of massive worker displacement, but also work standards converging at the level of the countries with the lowest standards.

The view, according to which downward destructive international competition among workers and employers had to be suppressed by international law or collective agreement, has been contested by orthodox free market economists. For them, interference in the labour market by "artificial" rules strikes against the "economic law". International labour standards would be ineffective and futile, or worse, they would do harm to economic progress. They will generate suboptimal outcomes. "The greatest damage to growth is in across-the-board labour standards that dictate either minimum standards or minimum conditions for higher and fairer wages" (e.g. Sachs, 1996). The improvement of wages, employment opportunities and working conditions would be endogenously determined by the pace of economic growth. Increases in wages, increases in labour force participation and employment rates, the reduction of child labour, and the reduction of hours would not be consequences of legislation, but at higher national income. According to contemporary free trade economists, constraining a liberal trade regime would make it more difficult for poverty-stricken developing countries to catch up with the economically advanced nations; it would only be fair for developing countries to court foreign direct investment by eschewing binding international labour standards (e.g. Baghwati, 1994).

The orthodox economic wisdom asserts, furthermore, that the best conditions for economic growth, and hence for employment and wage improvement, would be unrestricted competition, unfettered market forces, and a purely market-determined income distribution. For Alfred Marshall, one of the gurus of neo-classical economics, the free market establishes "true standardization" of work and wages (Marshall, 1982, p. 558). Competition forces firms to be "good" employers, paying full attention to the efficiency aspects of the workplace. Not leaving things to perfect liberty, however, produces "false standardization" of work and wages. Trade unions, collective bargaining, minimum wage fixing, welfare state provisions, etc., are seen as representing monopolies, cartels or other restrictions, thereby creating distortions in the labour market, and institutional sclerosis in the economy as a whole. They add to production costs by raising the level of wages above the market clearing equilibrium wage, impede efficiency and restrict flexibility for adjustment to changing demand, squeeze firms out of the market, seek rent from advantaged insider positions, crowd out the less unfortunate outsiders, thereby creating inequalities; moreover labour market distortions deter investment, constrain economic growth, and as a consequence lower the rate of employment and cause unemployment.

Another popular argument leveled against binding international labour standards holds that their applicability is limited to developed countries where the bulk of employment is in the formal sector of the economy. They are inappropriate in countries with large informal economies (see Papola, 1995; Ghose 2003). Other critics went farther and suggested that labour standards could be the root cause of informal activities.

The controversy of the protagonists and opponents of international labour standards is not a purely academic affair. Neo-classical economic theory and neo-liberal policies have exerted great influence in recent decades. They have guided much of the policies and action of the international financial institutions. These remained critical of many substantive standards, and reserved even on the subject of core international labour standards. They have made labour market deregulation a condition for providing credit and technical assistance for developing and transition countries. The neo-liberal doctrine has also gained currency among politicians in the Third World. The natural competitive advantage of developing countries would be the supply of abundant, unprotected labour at low cost, and this should not be taken away by forcing on them the standards of developed countries. Until they reach a higher level of economic development, it would be premature for them to adhere to international labour standards. But, one could ask, will economic growth really bring improved working and living conditions of workers? Should Pakistan, Egypt, or Guatemala really wait until they reach the income level of France or Canada, before they can comply with ILO standards on freedom of association, freedom from discrimination, minimum wages, child labour and minimum social protection?

How sound is the case made by the economic orthodoxy against international labour standards? Their arguments fail on several counts. To some extent they are based on a misunderstanding of ILO norms and ILO policies. The ILO proclaims universality, but not uniformity in the application of its normative instruments. While indeed it insists that core international labour standards can be applied regardless of a country's development, it emphasized early on that substantive standards would have to respect the special economic, climatic and other circumstances of the member country (Article 19 of the ILO Constitution), and practiced flexibility in its policies of implementing ILS. For instance, the ILO does not, as is often alleged, call for the same minimum wage across all countries. Rather, it proposes that each country engages in minimum wage fixing, be it by statute, decree or collective agreement, fully acknowledging that the level of the minimum wage will have to respond to a country's economic development. The level field to be established by international labour standards is to be a relative one, not an absolute one. Pakistan cannot set the same minimum wage as France, but it can have a minimum wage. It needs to have one for the sake of higher productivity. There are, though, examples of national labour standards that may be viewed as "excessive", by being out of proportion with local economic or financial capacity. For instance, the "Termination of Employment Act" in Sri Lanka provided workers with more than 20 years of service a compensation of 60 months' salary in case of dismissal. However, this rule cannot be laid at the door of the ILO; Convention No. 158 on Termination of Employment does not prescribe such a level of compensation, but stresses the principle of feasibility in the application of standards. Frequently, excessive national standards occur because other relevant standards are missing. For example, overly strict employment protection legislation, including long periods of notice and high severance pay, can be found (e.g. in Latin America and South East Europe) where income protection (e.g. unemployment benefits) is weak or severely insufficient. The point is made not to defend excessive employment protection. Rather, it suggests that income protection has to be strengthened in order to create space for social agreement on the alleviation of the rules of employment protection, ending up with a more balanced package of social protection. In fact, ILO Convention No. 158 makes the connection to unemployment insurance.

The economic orthodoxy has to be challenged on its assumption that international labour standards inevitably engender higher labour cost, thereby reducing competitiveness and dislocating jobs. The argument is partly wrong and partly exaggerated. Improved labour standards very often lead to higher productivity which means that unit labour costs, which are the decisive parameter for international competitiveness, need not rise, or may even decline. Employers that avoid excessively long working hours, abide by a minimum weekly rest period and an occupational health and safety work standard, have found that they are not handicapped vis-à-vis competitors who do not observe such rules. The reason is that observing the standards entails higher worker motivation, less fatigue, less mistakes, fewer accidents, and other economic and social benefits. Discrimination in employment can be costly; avoiding it can foster development. Discrimination amounts to the exclusion of workers from employment in general or from particular activities, thereby reducing human resource capacity. It implies the waste or under-utilization of talent and labour market skills. A study by the World Bank concluded that equal education and vocational training for women and men and the absence of discrimination in the labour market would have yielded a 50 per cent higher rate of economic growth in South Asia from the 1960s, and a 100 per cent higher rate in Sub-Saharan Africa (World Bank, 2000).

Minimum wage fixing has been found to improve economic performance. It changes the ways and means by which enterprises compete. In the absence of a minimum floor to wages, innovation by creative entrepreneurs is discouraged. These find it difficult to expand their market share because they cannot dislodge the inefficient firms which can remain profitable because they employ low-wage labour. On the contrary, if the option to compete through sub-standard wages is closed, efforts have to be made to compete in other, more constructive ways. Firms have to attain a level of productivity sufficient to meet the prescribed floor to pay. In effect, minimum wages provide a spur to employers to improve management, technology, products, processes, work organization, and worker skills and competence. Firms that are unable to reach the standard will be squeezed out of the market, and more efficient firms will take over their market share. In this way, minimum wages give rise to "dynamic efficiency", which is much superior to the "static efficiency" of minimizing the cost of productive inputs.

Another important dividend of international labour standards is the promotion of social peace by way of greater justice in the setting of wages and other terms of employment. Based on freedom of association, worker participation through collective bargaining and social dialogue are ways of fostering cooperation and mutual trust, which in turn enhance economic performance at the micro and macro level of the economy. The effects are brought about in various ways: workers contribute knowledge and experience to improve managerial decision-making; conflicting interests can be accommodated peacefully through consultation and negotiation; collective agreements make business conditions predictable and accountable, allowing investment decisions to be taken on firm cognitive grounds; collective bargaining makes wage setting more transparent, thus avoiding discontent and the perception of injustices; it can reconcile aspirations to social progress with the productive potential of enterprises and economic sectors; strong collective organization in the labour market and coordinated collective bargaining tend to contain, rather than cause, inflationary pressures, or accomplish this better than decentralized patterns of bargaining; tripartite social dialogue at the national level facilitates stabilizing of macroeconomic conditions, which is an essential prerequisite for high levels of employment; social dialogue has also facilitated the transition from centrally planned to market economies.

Employment and income security can have various positive impacts: Secure workers are more willing to take risks, and also pass their expertise on to other workers and to management; they are more prepared to cooperate in technological and organizational change. Worker security and labour market flexibility are not conflicting, but mutually supporting objectives. Protecting workers from job and income loss assumes even greater importance in open economies, which are susceptible to greater competitive pressure, faster and more volatile structural change, and contagious external crises. In this situation, protecting workers from social risks and contingencies is the positive alternative to protectionism in the product market by way of import restrictions and subsidies to shield particular jobs or sectors. The elimination of forced labour and child labour is not exclusively a moral imperative. It provides net economic advantages. Forced labour retards development because it keeps capital and labour in pre-modern activities that could not survive without it. Child labour may be a short-term expedient to secure the survival of families, but it does so at the very high price of reducing life expectancy and years of working life. It prevents education and skill formation, thus lowering labour productivity and hampering development in the long run. In addition, child labour increases labour supply and drives wage levels down.

Policies to promote full, productive and freely chosen employment are central to any development effort. They are also essential for making globalization socially acceptable. Workers displaced from technological change, job relocation, or outsourcing, will only be re-employed if new, productive jobs are available. The quantity of employment should not be pitted against the quality of employment. To quote Amartya Sen: "Fighting unemployment should not be used as an excuse for doing away with reasonable conditions of work for those already employed" (Sen, 2000).

Furthermore, it should not be assumed that the costs of applying labour standards are inevitably borne by the employer. The cost of many mandated benefits is shifted to workers in the form of lower wages or higher tax shares. Finally, failure to observe international labour standards may prove very costly, or more costly than compliance with them. For example, in the absence of employment protection, employers may face excessive litigation costs arising from worker dismissals. While the costs of applying standards are mostly direct, easily visible and measurable, immediate and localized, the benefits of applying labour standards tend to be indirect, intangible, and resist easy metrics. It is only when the negative effects of lacking international labour standards cumulate, e.g. in the form of poverty, crime and social disintegration, that people become fully aware of the economic and social utility of standards.

To conclude, international labour standards can both deter destructive competition in the labour market by setting a minimum floor to wages and other terms of employment, and promote constructive competition by providing incentives to firms to improving productivity and fostering social peace and social cohesion. international labour standards are both an end and a means to economic development. In this perspective, the argument of economic orthodoxy and certain politicians that countries have to first develop before they can apply international labour standards is unfounded (for a comprehensive account of the positive effects of international labour standards, see Sengenberger, 2002).

Empirical studies by OECD and the ILO have shown that countries complying with core international labour standards experience better export performance, and that foreign direct investment tends to avoid countries with very low worker rights. This is not true, however, in each and every case. China has been charged with grave disrespect for suppressing free trade unions and using forced labour. Nevertheless, it has become a major exporter and the biggest beneficiary of FDI inflows in recent years. Two factors may explain this anomaly: the size and growth of China's commodity market which makes the country attractive for investors; and the fact that China, as other countries in South East Asia, has made comparatively big investments in technical and social infrastructure, including education and labour market skills. Restricting freedom of association and holding wages down may well curb China's future prospects for growth, as indicated by mounting signs of social tension and political unrest. To judge the impact of labour standards, attention must be given to all types of standards, including norms on participation, protection and promotion. Economic performance is best and most sustainable in countries that apply all three kinds of standards (e.g. the Nordic countries in Europe).

3. A WIDER VIEW OF THE ROLE OF INTERNATIONAL LABOUR STANDARDS: PROMOTING INTERNATIONAL SOCIAL DIALOGUE AND COOPERATION

Preventing sub-standard terms of employment and working conditions through regulation may be seen as the "classic" justification of international labour standards. There is, however, a wider rationale for them. It is revealed by looking at the genesis of standards. ILO Conventions and Recommendations are enacted when a significant number of member countries are simultaneously confronted with the same labour issue or problem, and at the same time some countries have already crafted policies and measures that can successfully accommodate the problem. If an ILO instrument is adopted by a two-thirds majority of the International Labour Conference, it is then relayed to the national legislative authorities for ratification. Subsequent application in the member countries, and the monitoring of this application through ILO committees of experts, usually further improve understanding of the issue and how best to deal with it. If a country fails to live up to an ILO Convention, its practices will be subject to a review, which normally produces recommendations on ways to remedy the problems underlying non-conformity.

Information gathering and consultation across countries prior to setting the ILO norm, its subsequent probing in the country context, and the feedback to the ILO provide a repository of international knowledge about how best to treat labour issues. They embody the accumulated international wisdom on the use of labour, and avoid or resolve labour conflicts by incorporating experience gained from both good and bad practices of employment and work. The tripartite composition (employers, workers and governments) of the ILO legislature and monitoring bodies ensures that in designing the standards due consideration is given to practicability, manageability and cost effectiveness. Through representation in these organs from all over the world attention is paid to the diversity of local situations, institutions and needs. Hence, international labour standards are the product of international dialogue and cooperation. They can be regarded as *international public goods* that can be consumed free of charge by anybody and do harm to nobody. They add value to national employment and labour policy. They are "a source of inspiration for national action" (Valticos, 1979). In this perspective, international labour standards are a service to enterprises and whole economies, and a far cry from being a normative straightjacket for firms and governments they are made to be by economic neo-liberals.

A few examples may illustrate the promotional nature of international labour standards: a salient impact of economic globalization is the acceleration of structural change in countries opening up to international trade and capital flows. To avoid the risks and to maximize gains from trade, employers and employees need to adapt quickly and effectively, by shifting to new products and processes, respectively acquiring new skills and competencies. Governments have to provide knowledge and services to promote trade adjustment through labour market information systems and active labour market policies. Based on the relevant Conventions on human resources development and employment services, the ILO operates a system of advisory services for countries that wish to benefit from the globally most advanced, experienced and effective policies and practices. This service is accessible even to countries that have not ratified the relevant Conventions. China, for example, was eager to profit from ILO experience when it started to face increasing unemployment, mounting frictions in the labour market and social unrest in the course of opening up and privatizing its economy.

Cambodia provides a pertinent case of international assistance to countries whose employment is troubled by trade. In view of the phasing out of the Multi-Fibre Arrangement in the textiles and clothing industry in 2004, and the enormous expansion of Chinese production capacity, countries like Cambodia, Thailand, Bangladesh, Sri Lanka, Morocco and Mexico have felt threatened by intensified competition and fear the loss of jobs. In 2001, the ILO launched a unique multi-donor partnership project – including the Groupe Agence Française de Développement – in Cambodia's garment industry which employs more than 270, 000 mostly female workers and makes up 80 per cent of all exports. The project, called "Better Factories Cambodia", created a team of independent labour monitors to make unannounced visits to garment factories, checking on conditions as diverse as freedom of association, wages, working hours, sanitary facilities, machine safety and noise control. The monitors' checklist, based on Cambodian labour law and ILO standards, contains more than 500 items. The monitoring arrangements provide a source of independent and transparent information that can be used by garment-buying companies to make sourcing and investment decisions. Consumers and workers' organizations can also access this information. In addition, the ILO offers the factories direct remedial assistance, e.g. by providing vocational training opportunities, and capacity building for trade unions, employer representatives and the Government. The project demonstrates that the interests of consumers who seek affordable products, the interests of buyers in making profits, and the interests of young rural women who need to find decent jobs, can be accommodated (see ILO, 2004).

Another example of transnational institutional learning in the ILO context is the fight against child labour, and the elimination of the worst forms of child labour aimed at in ILO Convention Nos. 138 of 1973 and 182 of 1999. The collection, documentation and dissemination of information and experience, and the technical cooperation provided as part of the ILO International Programme for the Elimination of Child Labour, extends and enriches the readiness, means, and capabilities of local actors to address the problem. It makes it more likely that the problem will be recognized instead of concealed, it furthers the conviction that something can be done, while providing advice and model practices to combat child labour.

Dialogue and cooperation are also practiced in the European Union for promoting standards of the European Employment Strategy. These include commonly agreed targets such as the attainment of an aggregate employment rate of 70 per cent by 2010, a rate of 60 per cent for women, and a rate of 50 per cent for workers aged 55-64; another guideline specifies that unemployed youth should be given a job or a training slot no later than six months, and adult workers no later than 12 months, of being out of work. The method of 'open coordination' has been used for achieving the goals. Next to the joint formulation of benchmarks and performance measures (statistical indicators), it includes the conduct of 'peer reviews' between member States as a process of exchanging experience and mutual learning. The method allows to identify what measures and practices are best suited to meet the common objectives in each member State and in the Union as a whole.

To sum up, international dialogue and cooperation are instrumental to bringing employment and working conditions "up to standard", not to make them uniform across all nations but to bring them in line with the internationally available best practice, knowledge and experience.

4. IMPEDIMENTS TO COMPLIANCE WITH INTERNATIONAL LABOUR STANDARDS

In spite of the undeniable economic and social benefits accruing to countries that apply international labour standards, we witness hesitation and even opposition to vigorously enforcing standards. Violation of international labour standards, even of core Conventions, is widespread in developing countries and in some transition countries. But even in the wealthy developed countries significant deficits in applying standards can be found.

The reasons are multifarious and complex, including parochial and ideological objections to international labour standards ("globalization does not permit labour conditions to be improved"), micro-centred business economics favouring an individual rather than a collective economic logic; complacency and inertia ("it requires extra efforts on the part of employers to apply international labour standards"), rejections on cultural grounds ("international labour standards are not compatible with Islam"), questioning the universality of international labour standards; problems perceived by authoritarian and dictatorial governments (fearing trade union power and influence), vested interests (e.g. men who fear declining job prospects and losing privileges if gender discrimination were eradicated).

While these reasons have existed for a long time, there are two salient developments in the global and political and economic environment during recent decades which have generated major obstacles to advancing international labour standards: they concern shifts in the power equation in favour of capital, and at the expense of labour; and a large surplus of labour resources resulting from insufficient efforts to combat unemployment and underemployment through macroeconomic policy.

i) Trade unions are the most important stakeholder of both national and international labour standards and a crucial partner when it comes to social dialogue. In the large majority of countries trade union density and influence have declined. Economic globalization has exerted a negative impact on union strength and bargaining power. Increased international capital mobility has opened new strategic options for employers, such as relocation of plant, and new information, communications and transport technologies have made it easier and cheaper to outsource production and services. The mere threat of moving production from existing locations is sufficient to weaken the bargaining position of workers, and to induce them to make concessions on wages and other terms of employment. There are striking examples of recent concessions in wages, benefits and working hours made in the German automobile and electrical industries following pressure by companies, even by highly profitable ones. A study in the US found that threats by companies of closing or removing plants have been very effective in undermining trade union organizing efforts. In industries most affected by capital flight, such as textiles and garments, electronic components, food processing and metal fabrication, plant closure threats averaged more than 70 per cent in the late 1990s (Bronfenbrenner, 2000). It is obvious that the power shift in industrial relations is detrimental to the enforcement of labour standards, the maintenance of mutual trust in industrial relations, and the pursuit of social dialogue. The asymmetry in the protection of the rights of labour and the rights of capital cannot be overlooked. For example, the WTO has already allowed a linkage of trade sanctions with intellectual property rights. This begs the question why the WTO should be using sanctions to protect intellectual property from theft, expropriation, and imitation – something that is in the interest of multinational companies – while it cannot protect core labour standards by the same means (barring sanctions on forced labour)? Furthermore, why is it that although the Ministers of Trade declare that the ILO is the principal and competent agency for monitoring standards, the ILO is not empowered with greater authority to enforce its Conventions?

To regain strength and bargaining power in the global economy, trade unions will have to seek increasing international organization and conclude international collective agreements. Overtures in this direction have been made. Examples include inter-union cooperation in multinational companies, and framework agreements between multinational companies and global trade union organizations. To date, there are over 30 such agreements (including for the French companies Danone, Accor, Carrefour, Renault, Electricité de France, and Rhodia). In these agreements, the companies commit themselves to obeying core labour standards and joint monitoring with the unions.

Partly as a result of offshoring of jobs from the industrialized countries and an increasing number of emerging and transition economies, and the concomitant decline of worker bargaining power, real wage improvement has been very moderate to nil, and has lagged behind productivity improvement, resulting in a vicious circle of poor employment performance, diminished consumption power and low aggregate demand. According to earlier estimates, the loss of jobs in labour-intensive manufacturing in industrialized countries resulting from North-South trade varies from 3.5 million (Kucera and Milberg, 2003), to 7 million (Wood, 1995). But these figures do not tell the whole story. In addition to relocating production abroad, there is substantial worker displacement as a result of contracting out work to low-price/low-wage foreign firms (viz. the current draft of the EU directive on services widens the scope for low-wage contracting). Even more serious than direct job loss may be the implication of job transfers and subcontracting for perceived job insecurity that leads to consumption restraint and higher saving rates. Furthermore, savings may not, as one might expect, entail higher investment, but instead lower investment because firms expect reduced sales. Obviously, there is a problem of deficient domestic demand. At the same time, the effects of offshoring and subcontracting for the low-wage countries may not be as favourable as predicted by the mainstream economists. Incoming investment may be more labour saving than domestic investment, hence limiting the job generation capacity of FDI. Multinational companies often cream off the most skilled labour workers from the local labour market, creating negative spill-over for domestic enterprises. Investment inflows tend to be highly selective, reaching mainly the most advanced regions with the best infrastructure and bypassing the disadvantaged and rural regions where employment gains are most urgently needed. Evidently, wage and income inequality in poor countries – including China and India – is rising even faster than in the rich nations.

ii) The greatest obstacle to raising labour standards is the huge global "reserve army" of labour. Roughly speaking, one-third of the world's labour force is unemployed or underemployed. It tilts the power relationship in the labour market drastically in favour of employers. Labour tends to be more pliable, and easy to exploit. As long as excess labour of this magnitude is available, and in the widespread absence of social security, it will be difficult to raise wage levels and improve the quality of jobs. Moreover, there is little incentive for employers to invest in human resources to make them more productive. Making jobs more productive is essential for reducing poverty. Massive joblessness, not overregulation, is the main reason for the expansion of the informal economy with low productivity firms and workers. All this ends up in a mutually reinforcing trap of low productivity, low wages, poverty and high population growth in poor countries.

To a large extent the global poor employment performance can be attributed to restrictive monetary and fiscal policies. Fiscal austerity has been imposed on developing countries by the international financial institutions as a condition for providing credit. However, fiscal and monetary restraint has also been practiced in the industrialized countries, particularly in the European Union. Both short-term and long-term interest rates have risen since the 1970s. In the G-7 countries, real interest rates increased from average -3 per cent in the period 1959-81 to 2 per cent thereafter. With rising capital costs, investment becomes more risky. Real investment falls, or is crowded out by financial investments. The resulting gap is not filled by public sector investment, because under the present regime of the European Stability and Growth Pact, the public sector is under strong pressure to consolidate. More expansionary macroeconomic policies, and also countercyclical instead of pro-cyclical public spending, will be needed to attain not merely macroeconomic stability, but higher growth and employment as well. It is difficult to comprehend why the European Union is not ready to commit the European Central Bank to place economic growth and employment explicitly on an equal footing with price stability as goals of monetary policy.

There is lack of a social dimension in the governance of the globalization process. Trade, economic and financial policy-making is largely separated from labour and social policies. The first are put in the driver's seat, while the latter are placed on the back seat. In the employment policy field, "sectorialism" dominates, meaning that competencies are split between the IMF, the World Bank, WTO, and the ILO. Frequently, these organizations give incoherent, even conflicting policy advice to national governments (events where they join forces, as for example in the Cambodia project mentioned above, are rare). At the same time, the competencies are blurred, or overlap. Through its lending policies, the IMF interferes with labour market policies even though this is not within its mandate and although it has no technical competence in this field. There is a parallel lack of policy integration and policy coherence at the national level. Ministers of Labour and Social Affairs and Ministers of Finance often pursue different, if not inconsistent policies, and carry these inconsistencies to the international policy making organizations. Policy coordination will inter alia be required to prevent grossly unequal corporate taxes across competing countries from inviting tax evasion and economically unfounded capital shifts.

5. CONCLUSION

National labour market regulation in conformity with international labour standards is needed to prevent destructive competition and at the same time further constructive competition through better and more efficient use of human resources and higher labour and capital productivity. In addition, international labour standards serve as a basis for international dialogue and cooperation resulting in the dissemination of good labour policies and practices. The pertinent ILO Conventions that are targeted to achieve full, productive and freely chosen employment are frequently hampered by insufficient willingness to standard enforcement. The main obstacles cannot be attributed to lack of economic feasibility or lack of economic returns to the application of standards. Rather, in the main the impediments have political origins. They concern shifts in the power equation at the expense of labour and its organizations as the main stakeholders of labour standards; and insufficient policy coherence and policy coordination, both at the national and international level, resulting in the divorce of economic and social policies and inadequate macroeconomic policies for employment. In the midst of the second wave of globalization, the governance problem is akin to the one experienced at the end of the first wave of globalization in the beginning 20th century. It is time to recall the basic premise on which the ILO was established in 1919: that there is an unequivocal link between the effective mediation of conflict among the social groups *within* nations, and the accommodation of conflict *between* nations. Political failure on one level will entail failure on the other. There is much room for a fuller comprehension of the role of ILS for economic efficiency, social cohesion and political stability.

THE ROLE OF LABOUR LAW FOR INDUSTRIAL RESTRUCTURING

BY PHILIPPE WAQUET

1. INTRODUCTION

The subject of the "internationalization of employment" is an extremely topical one, and the expertise of the participants and their many different backgrounds and fields have given us a broad and detailed insight into its many problems. Particularly interesting has been the all-too-rare confrontation between the views of economists and lawyers.

A priori, of course, we are starting from very different positions. For the economists, as they reminded us, globalization is an irreversible, long-standing phenomenon. The Austrian economist Joseph Schumpeter's theory, which argues that there is no point in delaying job cuts resulting from the evolution of capitalism, was mentioned; such "creative destruction" should simply be offset by organizational measures. The economists, while acknowledging that economic change and restructuring have a human dimension, and sometimes a tragic one, tend to regard the lawyers' efforts to curb the phenomenon as a point-less 'spoiling' measure. Some would even go so far as to argue that labour legis-lation, in regulating redundancies and making them difficult and costly, is actually harmful to employment.

If our meeting had not been so open and cordial, we might have parted in a state of profound disagreement. More than ever, our discussions showed that dialogue is needed between economists and lawyers if we are to gain a better understanding of all aspects of a development that is not necessarily negative, but that requires the rights and interests of workers to be taken into account alongside economic imperatives. Labour law should not be dismissed as a proce-dural system designed to hamper the 'normal' development of a market organi-zation process, nor should it be reduced to a second-rate financial compensation scheme designed to paper over the cracks resulting from the internationalization of employment and offshoring.

Labour law has a higher vocation: it aims to enable workers to participate in the life and future of undertakings which are in operation thanks to their labour; it aims to ensure, without undermining management authority (which is actually more a responsibility), that workers have genuine guarantees that they will keep their jobs and that they will earn enough to live in dignity.

Labour law goes beyond the level of "industrial legislation" as it was still studied at the start of the 20th century, and it relates to more than just employees: it is a constituent element of the advanced democracies that Europe hopes to bring together and lead.

It is essential that economists, regardless of the school to which they belong, realize the importance and contribution of labour law, which merely translates human rights, now recognized globally, into practical rules.

What is now the clearly recognizable phenomenon of globalization and the effects described at length in the media in alarmist and unscientific terms are generating collective anxieties and tempting people to turn inwards and reject the outside world. Relevant, multidisciplinary information, also involving historians and sociologists, is urgently needed to give the public a better understanding of the opportunities and progress from which everyone can benefit if we open up our borders and allow people and goods to circulate freely, but without ignoring the dangers and excesses that come with any evolution, and therefore the efforts that need to be made to prevent countries from losing their own culture and the dismantling of the structures on which our societies are based.

2. ACCOMPANIMENT OF RESTRUCTING

Getting back to the more practical matter of the restructuring of the modern economy, we know that this is now accompanied by a major trend towards offshoring. One of the first cases of offshoring from France, when the Hoover company moved its workshops from France to Scotland, caused considerable outrage in French public opinion some 15 years ago. Since then, France has witnessed many more offshoring operations, to the Maghreb countries (Morocco and Tunisia), Eastern Europe (Slovenia, Poland, Hungary, etc.) and now Asia.

On each occasion, factories or workshops in France close and workers lose their jobs in huge collective redundancies.

These closures do not just affect the workers, who lose jobs that they have often held for ten or 20 years or more and have little hope of finding another.

They also cause serious crises in the region where the companies concerned were based: local shopkeepers and services are themselves affected when these jobs disappear.

Often entire regions and local labour markets are badly hit: as their economic life disappears, their cultural life fades away – only the retired and the elderly are left.

These rather pessimistic observations do not mean that there should be legislation banning all mobility and that firms cannot adapt to remain competitive. But they call for the law to react. The law needs to reconcile the freedoms and rights that everyone enjoys in order to enable others to subsist and exist. There are no absolute freedoms, apart perhaps for freedom of thought. Freedom of enterprise, a constitutional principle, needs to be reconciled with the right to employment set out in the 1946 Preamble to the French Constitution. This was what the Constitutional Council had to say:

"Whereas the Preamble to the Constitution reaffirms the principles set out both in the 1789 Declaration of the Rights of Man and of the Citizen and in the 1946 Preamble to the Constitution;

Whereas those principles should include freedom of enterprise as provided for in Article 4 of the 1789 Declaration and the economic and social principles listed in the 1946 Preamble, which include, in Section 5, the universal right to obtain employment and, in Section 8, the right of every worker to participate, through his representatives, in the collective determination of working conditions and in the management of undertakings;

Whereas it is the responsibility of the legislature, under the powers it derives from Article 34 of the Constitution, to determine the fundamental principles of labour law, and to ensure that the economic and social principles set out in the 1946 Preamble to the Constitution are implemented, while at the same time reconciling them with the freedoms guaranteed under the Constitution;

"Whereas, in order to lay down rules guaranteeing, as far as possible, the universal right to obtain employment, in accordance with Section 5 of the 1946 Preamble to the Constitution, the legislature may impose on freedom of enterprise limits relating to that constitutional requirement, provided that this does not produce an adverse effect which is disproportionate to the objective pursued." (*Decision No 2001-455 DC of 12 January 2002, Law on social modernization*).

Better than any lengthy treatise, this decision by the highest judicial authority in France shows that the limits imposed on the right to make workers redundant are not the result of some whim of the courts,[1] but are the application of constitutional rules (it should be pointed out here that Article 1 of the Constitution of 4 October 1958 describes France as "an indivisible, secular, democratic *and social* Republic"). Although there is no disputing that, in belonging to the European Union, France is wedded to the market economy, the economic mechanisms of competition must give way to the rules established by both the French and the Community legislatures[2] in order to protect the rights of workers.

That being said, let us now take a closer look at the impact of restructurings and offshoring in particular.

A distinction needs to be drawn here between two different situations: the host country, where jobs will be offered to people who were previously often living in insecurity, and the country of origin, where jobs will disappear and industrial resources will be diminished.

3. PROBLEMS OF THE HOST COUNTRY

We will not dwell here on the benefits of offshoring for the host country. Offshoring generates not just work for people living in underdeveloped conditions, but also resources and facilities for the country to which the company relocates.

---

[1] The members of the Social Chamber of the Court of Cassation were recently described by a government minister as "ulemas" of labour law!

[2] And also, of course, by the ILO.

All of this is important, of course.

But the reality can be less rosy.

The profits generated by this new economic activity are sometimes diverted into the pockets of a few unscrupulous managers, and the host country remains under-equipped.

Also, and this is by no means the least of the problems, the workers are extremely poorly paid and are genuinely exploited, with excessive working hours, dangerous or unhealthy working conditions, etc.

Fortunately, this is not the general rule. Many countries are conscious of their responsibility and ensure that the activity generated by offshoring benefits the public at large.

Also, undertakings that relocate are not necessarily indifferent to the fate of the local workers they recruit. The idea of "firms' responsibility to society" is not always mere lip-service, and employment practices are moving forward.[3]

Nevertheless, in many cases workers' employment conditions leave a lot to be desired. How can we ensure that ILO minimum standards, particularly those in the Social Charter, are met?

While the WTO makes a huge effort to ensure that the rules of competition are obeyed, there is no sign that the dignity and fundamental rights of workers are being protected and guaranteed effectively.

Once again, it is not really the lack of regulation that is the problem: in addition to ILO standards, workers the world over can rely on the rights proclaimed by the UN (Universal Declaration of Human Rights; New York Protocol). But how can we ensure that they know what their rights are, and, even more importantly, that there are independent and impartial courts that will uphold respect for those rights? In the absence of free and effective trade unions, NGOs sometimes try to support employees and help them to defend their rights. These are welcome initiatives, but still few and far between.

There is no doubt that the ILO has a role to play here.[4]

The fact is that the social and human problems generated by the process of offshoring have not yet really been tackled. Although the WTO keeps a watchful eye on compliance with the trade and industry competition rules, nothing like this happens in the social field. If globalization is something positive for the countries where new activities are set up, it is totally unacceptable that the conditions in which the workers are employed are neither guaranteed by regulations that are effective in practice, nor are they monitored. Rights are worthless if they are not applied effectively, and this requires checks to be carried out and the possibility of legal action.

It should be pointed out here that there is another opening for social development: the appearance of new forms of collective bargaining at international

---

[3] *Le Monde Economique*, 10 May 2005.

[4] World Commission on the Social Dimension of Globalization: *A fair globalization: creating opportunities for all*, 2004.

level. One example is the agreement between a number of global trade union federations on the growing and marketing of bananas.

Another form of social self-discipline is the codes of conduct introduced by multinational firms. And are we not also seeing the emergence of the idea of "corporate governance", which should enable workers – through their pension funds – to demand that account be taken not just of financial, but also of social imperatives?

Human imagination is boundless; all that remains is to put these various possibilities into practice, but that is quite another matter.

The problems faced by countries which lose activities are very different.

4. PROBLEMS OF THE COUNTRY OF ORIGIN

French law is often described as excessively protective, and Community law as the product of unbridled liberalism. This is a complete caricature of reality. In reality, French law is very largely based on Community law when it comes to collective redundancies.[5] Community law has introduced mandatory guarantees for workers affected by collective economic redundancies in a number of directives (Directive 75/129/EEC of 17 February 1975; Directive 92/54/EEC of 24 June 1992; Directive 98/59/EC of 20 July 1998) and in the Community Charter of the Fundamental Social Rights of Workers of 9 December 1998.

The measures applied fall into two categories.

First, both the Community and domestic legislation has fully developed the procedures for informing and consulting workers. Although sometimes condemned as excessive and anti-economic, these procedures are actually a fundamental guarantee for workers.

First of all, they require firms to open up their files and to disclose the reasons and justification for any restructuring plans involving site closures and job losses. Those who will be affected by these measures have the right to know why and how the plan was decided. A worker actually has a fundamental democratic right to know why he is going to lose his job. However, the staff representatives then have the right to discuss the measures planned, and to suggest changes or alternatives. Not only do they have to have the time and resources to prepare an informed opinion, but also the aim set out in Article 2(1) of Directive 98/59/EC is that a collective agreement should be concluded.

Secondly, the Community directive requires efforts to be made to redeploy or retrain workers laid off. In France, people tend to forget that the social partners – not just the workers' representatives, but the employers too – made this a requirement as early as 1974, in a rider to the national interoccupational agreement of 10 February 1969. The rider required employers planning collective lay-offs to draw up a redundancy plan setting out all the measures to be taken to avoid or at least limit the number of redundancies, and to facilitate the redeployment of staff whose redundancy could not be prevented.

---

[5] In relation to offshoring.

Successive laws (Laws of 2 August 1989, 27 January 1993, 17 January 2002 and 18 January 2005) have incorporated and expanded the requirements of the initial 1974 agreement. The redeployment obligation has never been watered down, and has become an absolute must for employers. In reality, it has gradually become clear that redundancy should be the last resort, acceptable only when all other options have been exhausted.

This is also why restructuring operations designed to increase profits or to boost the company's share price have never been acceptable in case law. Keeping a company economically prosperous, which generates jobs and activity in the sector concerned, is a healthy and necessary goal. Increasing profit for profit's sake, at the expense of employment, is not acceptable.

The solution that has prevailed is neither to make redundancy an easy option, nor to ban it. It is a middle way, reconciling (or attempting to reconcile) economic imperatives with the workers' right *a priori* to keep their jobs provided that there is no personal reason to terminate their employment. If, as a result of financial problems, technological change or the specific prospect that the firm will become uncompetitive, the economic situation is such that measures have to be taken to cut or transform jobs or to modify employment contracts, and if no internal or external redeployment is possible, then redundancies on economic grounds are justified.

It is vital in a democracy that economic redundancies are curbed and controlled either in this or some other way. Community legislation leaves it up to the EU member States to choose how, but imposes on them all the same objectives of safeguarding jobs and revitalizing local labour markets damaged by restructuring or offshoring.

There is one separate aspect of offshoring that I should mention.

Alongside the setting up of workshops, factories and companies in the emerging countries, illegal immigration (outside the EU rules for the admission of foreign labour) towards the EU Member States is constantly growing.

This is one of the paradoxical aspects of the situation that jobs are being cut in France and transferred to emerging countries, while the nationals of those countries are trying to come to France to find jobs. This phenomenon, which can be explained, if not justified, by Europe's declining demography, has certain worrying aspects. It can trigger xenophobia or even racism, and it challenges France's version of secularism and generates cultural tensions. In any event, it shows us a different side to globalization, involving huge movements of people and goods in more than one direction. This again demonstrates the importance of labour law, for without it these displaced populations, without a valid residence permit, are themselves at risk of being exploited in jobs without any guarantees regarding pay, working hours or working conditions.

5. CONCLUSION

What conclusion can we draw from these few basic observations? Quite simply that there is no miracle solution. It is not unrestrained liberalism, allowing workers to be laid off without justification or controls, nor is it a ban on economic redundancies, recommended by certain politicians, that will bring prosperity and industrial harmony. We have to accept that the primary need to safeguard jobs by keeping businesses economically healthy means that we have to accept redundancies on economic grounds.

However, we also have to concede that respect for human rights means that workers cannot be deprived of their jobs, their only resource and guarantee of independence, simply for profit or convenience.

Labour law and economics are condemned to coexist, and therefore to talk to each other and reach compromises together.

THE SOCIAL DIMENSION OF GLOBALIZATION AND CHANGES IN LAW[1]

BY MIREILLE DELMAS-MARTY

1. INTRODUCTION

In taking up the challenge of a "fair globalization",[2] the social dimension of employment is undoubtedly one of the most difficult issues. Starting from either economic analysis on globalization and employment,[3] or from an anthropological analysis of the perverse effects of a system which continues to count people as costs and never as assets,[4] the issue is one of finding out how to counter the adverse effects of increasing international economic integration. The OECD working group on employment, proposing structural adjustment measures, has no qualms about propagating improbable pairings such as "creative destruction" and "protected mobility" or even strange neologisms such as "flexi-curity".[5]

These expressions cannot but underscore the ambivalence of an interdependence which not only offers an opportunity, through the opening up of borders and the proliferation of communications technologies that go with it, but also poses a risk as a result of the financial and social instabilities that it entails. Moving beyond this contradiction and changing an imposed interdependence into a plan constructed as a common destiny requires a legal framework based on the principles of international solidarity and responsibility recalled by the UN Secretary-General in the Millennium Declaration,[6] whose necessity has been highlighted by the World Commission on the Social Dimension of Globalization.[7] Such a framework nevertheless has to be based on a clearly defined political plan.

---

[1] Paper based on a more general conclusion to the work *Le pluralisme ordonné*, to be published, Seuil, 2006.

[2] World Commission on the Social Dimension of Globalization: *A fair globalization*, ILO, 2004.

[3] On outsourcing, see M. Lübker: "International outsourcing, its trends and impact: a literature survey"; and also D. Cohen: "Mondialisation et emploi", in the present volume.

[4] A. Supiot, *Homo Juridicus, essai sur la fonction anthropologique du droit*, Seuil, 2005, p. 266.

[5] *Les coûts d'ajustement liés aux échanges sur les marchés du travail des pays de l'OCDE*, DELSA, April 2005, pp. 30-31. In this volume, see also M.-A. Moreau, "L'internationalisation de l'emploi et les délocalisations en Europe: perspectives juridiques".

[6] Report of the UN Secretary-General, UN General Assembly, 2003, doc A/58/323.

[7] ibid, in particular p. 118 et seq.

A plan linking peace with social justice and the economy was sketched out by the creation of the International Labour Organization in 1919. It was reaffirmed, in June 1945, by the San Francisco Charter, supplemented by the Universal Declaration of Human Rights (UDHR) of 1948 (peace through collective security, and fundamental rights that are universal because they are indivisible) and provided with a new architecture (the General Assembly, Security Council, Economic and Social Council, Trusteeship Council, Secretariat and International Court of Justice),[8] which is officially still in force.

Everything nevertheless seems to show that this plan failed to withstand the major political upheavals which followed: decolonization, cold war, collapse of the Soviet empire, globalization, and the development of international terrorism. Increasing from 51 countries to close on 200, the UN faced an ideological split from the start of the cold war onwards: between the UDHR and the two Pacts of 1966, universalism was weakened by the fundamental rights split; economic globalization then exploded the factors of internationalization,[9] to the point at which the "globalization of law", which focuses domestic legal orders around human rights and tries to "civilize" globalization, and the "law of globalization", which produces specific market-related rules and seems to be paving the way for a return to the natural state,[10] are in opposition to such an extent that relativism seems more threatened by globalization than by universalism, especially as, after the attacks of 11 September, the concept of "war against terrorism", in the full and non-metaphorical sense of the term, has helped to blur the borders between the inside and the outside, between crime and war, between unilateral and multilateral action.

The paradox is that, over a century, the plan has become both richer and more volatile: richer, with the adoption of instruments having legal force in fields as diverse as commercial law, labour law, or more broadly human rights; but more volatile, since these legal instruments have been broken up into scattered objects subject to the national (and sometimes regional) strategies of States or the transnational strategies of enterprises. The result now looks more like total world disorder than the world order heralded by the UDHR (Article 28). From the legal point of view, globalization is not therefore associated with a world law which is already established, and whose components could be described, but with the transformation of the field of law through the growing diversification of a law organized in a plural but rarely pluralist way.

---

[8] See *Questions internationales, L'Onu à l'épreuve*, La documentation française, No 11, January 2005.

[9] M. Delmas-Marty: *Vers un droit commun de l'humanité*, Textuel, 1996, 2nd edition, 2005, *Trois défis pour un droit mondial*, Seuil, 1998 ; "La mondialisation du droit: chances et risques", D.1999. Chr. 43; A.J. Arnaud, *La mondialisation du droit*, LGDJ, 1999, 2nd edition, 2004; B. Auby, *La globalisation, le droit et l'Etat*, Montchrestion, 2003; M. M. Salah, Les contradictions du droit mondialisé, PUF, 2002; La mondialisation du droit, edited by E. Locquin and C. Kessedjian, Litec, 2000; *Le droit saisi par la mondialisation*, edited by C. A. Morand, Bruylant, 2001.

[10] J. Chevallier, in *Le droit saisi par la mondialisation*, op. cit., p. 36 et seq.; F. Ost, "Mondialisation, globalisation, universalisation, s'arracher encore et toujours à l'état de nature", ibid., p. 5 et seq.

From *Disorganized developments* (I) to *Balancing systems* (II), and then the *Models* of a world order in formation (III), a review is proposed here to try to measure the extent of the changes in the legal field brought about by the social dimension of globalization.

2. DISORGANIZED DEVELOPMENTS

With the proliferation, diversification and dispersion of sources,[11] the monopoly of the State in all its forms is being called into question: the central state is being hit by the decentralization of sources, the public-sector State by their privatization and lastly, and in particular, the nation State, expressing the sovereignty of a community of interlinked interests and identical aspirations, is being threatened by the internationalization of law. It is not just that "the State is no longer the only captain on board",[12] but that the concepts of normative order, space and time are starting to elude it, raising the question of whether there is still a captain on board and, if so, who.

Speaking of developments encourages us in practice to observe *processes of interaction* in the normative order, *organizational levels* in space and *speeds of change* in time, rather than their outcomes. Each of these three strands characterizes a potential dynamic, a paving of the way; their dissociation nevertheless brings about apparently disorganized developments: in the normative order, multiple, horizontal and vertical interactions, bringing about integration as well as disintegration, weakens hierarchical relationships; whereas, in the normative space, the superimposition of levels, of the national, regional and world areas, is reflected by expansions as well as contractions; lastly, changes in the speeds of normative time may pave the way for progressive synchronization or may lead to desynchronization, as is precisely the case for employment, trade and human rights.

Processes of interaction: integration/disintegration

Integrating norms coming from outside starts by horizontal interactions, the hierarchy-free *interlinkages* which characterize soft law, so prevalent in the field of employment either in the public (ILO recommendations) or private sector (enterprise codes of conduct).

Other examples are also to be found, not just from the point of view of inter-regional exchanges (between the European Court of Human Rights (ECHR) and the CJEC) but also at a world level: the WTO is not isolated from this and the question of the integration of some rules of labour law (like the environment) has now been raised. Over and above the explicit referral to the ILO by the

---

[11] M. Delmas-Marty: "Surgissement de sources", in *Pour un droit commun*, Seuil, 1994, p. 53 et seq.; "Dispersion des sources", in *Les forces imaginantes du droit, Le relatif et l'universel*, Seuil, 2004; C. Thibierge, "Sources du droit, sources de droit: cartographie des sources", to be published in *Mélanges Jestaz*.

[12] J. Chevallier: L'Etat post-moderne, 2nd edition, LGDJ, 2004, p. 205; A.J. Arnaud : "De la globalisation au post-modernisme en droit", in *Modernité et mondialisation*, 2nd edition, LGDJ, 2004, pp. 265-300.

Singapore Ministerial Declaration of 1996, the most recent discussions of the reform of the WTO tend to show that the question of the integration of fundamental rights is likely to be raised in an increasingly open way in the WTO. Their recognition as universal standards could lead the Dispute Settlement Body to impose a social clause and a human rights clause on member countries,[13] making it possible to envisage, in the long term, interactions between the WTO and the UN Human Rights Committee, or the WTO and ILO.[14]

The notion of internormativity could thus become more specific, if it is envisaged to impose trade sanctions on countries which fail to respect labour norms,[15] or as new interpretation systems are suggested: the parties to a dispute before the WTO could raise an exception of incompetence and obtain a referral to an ad hoc organization placed under the auspices of the competent organization (ILO for labour law, UNESCO for culture, etc.).[16] This is nevertheless only a prospect. If there is no hierarchy, the process remains incomplete and the horizontal interactions at best enable, through mutual information, an openness, which may facilitate, but not guarantee, the exchange of one construction for another.

To ensure coherence, and bring order to pluralism, these interactions will have to be "verticalized", the neologism implying a return to a hierarchy, made more flexible, however, by the recognition of a national margin of appreciation, along the lines of that accepted by the ECHR. By enabling a rapprochement of systems around common higher principles, sufficiently flexible to preserve national margins, this second type of interaction, by *harmonization*, is by definition pluralist as the national margin means that not all differences are suppressed. Similarly, it is undoubtedly necessary to accept a degree of imprecision of the social rights set out in the EU Charter, like the principles of the ILO, since this makes it possible to provide for these margins which are undoubtedly necessary to preserve specific national features. In the long term, flexible vertical interactions could also be based on the recognition (through these instruments to protect human rights) of imperative rules (*jus cogens*),[17] or the use of concepts such as the common good of humanity.

Lastly, the third kind of interaction, by *unification*, does not allow any margin and presupposes the merger of systems, or more modestly of legal concepts, in favour of a single norm imposed in the name of a strict hierarchy.

---

[13] E.U. Petersmann: "Comments and points for discussion" in *Trade negotiations and dispute settlement: what balance between political governance and judicialisation?* Conference on the WTO at 10 – 3rd Session, Stresa, 12 March 2005. Compare the preceding comments about China.

[14] World Commission on the Social Dimension of Globalization: op.cit..

[15] ibid, p. 105.

[16] A. Supiot: "Préface", in Critique du droit du travail, 2nd edition, 2003; *Homo Juridicus, essai sur la fonction anthropologique du droit*, Seuil, 2005, p. 315.

[17] See the International Commission of Jurists' advisory opinion of 9 July 2004 on the legal consequences of the construction of a wall in occupied Palestinian territory, accepting the admissibility of humanitarian law and personal rights, including labour law, even in a period of conflict and in occupied territory; see also Opinion of the IACHR of 17 September 2003, legal status of migrants without papers, Series A, No 18.

To prevent this from being reflected by the hegemonic extension of a single system, unification should involve a genuine hybridization between different systems. Progress could be made in this direction in fields such as trade union law where hybridization, framed by the principles of the ILO, could go together with an autonomization of supranational standards.

Interlinkages, harmonization, unification – the typology sketched out obviously does not rule out slippages from one process to another. In practice, the three types of normative interaction combine together to provide variable and evolving outcomes which may become stable at different levels.

Organizational levels: expansion/contraction

Between the national order overwhelmed by growing interdependences and a future world order that is still in formation, the regional international level could facilitate a progressive expansion,[18] but in practice expansion is as disorganized as integration. Through a premature, badly prepared or badly controlled expansion, regional organizations could in practice bring about a reverse movement of contraction, of which the current crisis in Europe has provided a foretaste.

To be acceptable, expansion first presupposes an institutional and normative autonomization with respect to the member States, but also calls for a neutralization of relationships of strength and a strengthening of cohesion factors which alone are able to pave the way for genuine roadmaps of convergence whose routes are not always discussed in a timely way. Even when linked together by processes of interaction, normative constructions are not readily transformed into organizations which are autonomous and stable enough to form a legal order. This order continues to be identified with the State, and legal organization is largely at national level: even in Europe the CPHRFF is not an autonomous order and Community law will be converted into a genuine legal order only with the incorporation of the Charter of Fundamental Rights which will make it possible in particular for social rights to be upheld more directly as regards both enterprises and States. In the case of the ILO, the status of "constitutionally-based institutional order"[19] has yet to be consolidated.

In the meantime, it is not at all by accident that the term "area" is increasingly being used to designate an evolving construct, with an imprecise content and unstable frontiers:[20] the *European legal area* to designate cooperation and harmonization rules common to all the EU member States; the *Schengen area* or *Euro area* for rules limited to some member States; then the *area of freedom, security and justice* bringing together instruments combining cooperation and

---

[18] "Regional integration as a stepping stone", in *A fair globalization*, op. cit., p. 78 et seq.

[19] V. Marleau: "Réflexions sur l'idée d'un droit international coutumier du travail"; J.C. Javillier: "Libres propos sur la part du droit dans l'action de l'OIT", in *Les normes internationales du travail, un patrimoine pour l'avenir, Mélanges Nicolas Valticos*, ILO, 2004, p. 400 and p. 659 et seq.

[20] G. Timsit describes, a system of belonging or inclusion of norms in a non-hierarchical construction, in "L'ordre juridique comme métaphore", *Droits*, No 33, 2001; *Thèmes et systèmes de droit*, PUF, 1986.

harmonization in the legal field. Even at a planetary level, expressions are appearing such as the *Kyoto area*, to designate the system building on the Rio Convention on climate change, or the *WTO area* for world trade (and maybe the *ILO area* in the near future?).

However, the "normative areas" generally negotiated between States do not, or only very incompletely, involve the creation of executive, legislative and jurisdictional institutions which would stabilize the whole. Hence the term variable geometry (or even variable geography depending on the accession of this or that State) which reflects less a mathematical analogy than the complexity of the problem, and in particular the changeability, and therefore instability, which goes with it.

The importance of organizational levels is therefore being recognized, as they control a progressive normative and institutional stabilization, and promote, as in Community law, the possible transformation of an area into a legal order. The problem is that the transformation does not take place in a linear way, from the local to the national level and then to the international, regional and ultimately world level – especially as legal constructions in most cases separate human rights from the market and differentiate between, or even oppose, a number of models of economic integration.[21]

Lastly, regional organizations may well be a forerunner of globalization, providing a kind of "test bench", but may also take an opposing view and try to change direction or simply speed (like an accelerator or, in the opposite case, a brake). As the rhythms diversify, changes of speed create further disorder.

Speeds of change: synchronization/desynchronization

Differentiating speeds ("polychrony") in a single area such as the Schengen area, the Kyoto area or the WTO area may well seem to generate a diversity that ensures both pluralism and order. Its implementation has to be framed and managed by objective criteria (enabling clause) and its effects determined either in advance (Kyoto timetable), or progressively through a gearing effect (a kind of automatic drive imposing a constant progression), or retrospectively by a locking effect marking the notion of irreversibility (integration of the Schengen system into the Community acquis).[22] If there is no legal framework, the variable-speed area designed as a front runner that everyone can join when they wish and when they are able (opting-in clause) may well become an "à la carte" area where everyone can exempt themselves from certain obligations (opting out). Rather than anticipating the process of integration, different timescales foster the reverse process of braking or even disintegration.

The risk is increased, from one construction to another, by problems of asynchrony, for instance between trade and human rights or more strictly

---

[21] J. Ténier: *Intégrations régionales et mondialisation, Complémentarité ou contradiction*, La documentation française, 2003; J. Dutheil de la Rochère : Mondialisation et régionalisation, in La mondialisation du droit, editors; E. Locquin and C. Kessedjian, Litec, 2000, pp. 435 – 453.

[22] D. Simon: "La dynamique de l'intégration économique", in *Le système juridique communautaire*, op. cit., No 19.

between the liberalization of trade, the harmonization of employment policies and their repercussions in the social field. A comparison between the progressive balancing in Europe and the growing divide at a world level suggests that synchronization requires new linkages between levels and between actors: in this respect, the ILO's tripartite composition is undoubtedly an asset which, if well used, should enable progressive synchronization without thereby excluding the notion of polychrony, i.e. the possibility of development at variable speeds provided that variability indicators are identified and their application monitored. For these articulations to be flexible enough in practice, they require legal systems which make it possible, by balancing and re-balancing, to order the plural in one way or another.

3. BALANCING SYSTEMS

"Balancing" describes the fluctuations and suggests a new conception of legal systems – a flexible conception[23] facilitating adjustments and re-adjustments between the domestic and international (regional or world) levels. It is not enough, however, to coin the term "flexi-curity" for flexibility to be combined with security likely to ensure fairer globalization.[24] On the contrary, flexibility is felt to be a threat which calls for an overhaul of methods: *regulatory concepts, adjustment techniques*, then *evaluation and control methods*, are the conditions for a balancing that do not reduce globalization to the law of the fittest.

Regulatory concepts

To adjust the national to the regional or world level, positive law has had to invent new systems to leave some play (like the "slack" for which the lead climber might be asked on a mountain face) between supranational norms and their national integration. We know that the hierarchical principle of the primacy of international law collides with national sovereignty. It was included in the European CT only in a discrete form and without being recognized as a principle: "the Constitution and the law adopted by the institutions of the Union shall have primacy over the law of the member States" (Article I-6).

However, the "principles" of subsidiarity and proportionality, already in force, were placed well to the fore in the first part of the CT (Article I-11, Fundamental Principles) on Union competences: "The Union shall act only if and insofar as the objectives of the proposed action cannot be sufficiently achieved by the member States". As regards shared competences alone, subsidiarity is coupled with proportionality: "the content and form of Union action shall not exceed what is necessary to achieve the objectives of the Constitution".

Subsidiarity, however, as shown by works on the origin of the term,[25] is not limited to a purely formal distribution of competences. To take up the term used

---

[23] On the scale of "normative density" between hard law and soft law, see C. Thibierge: "Le droit souple, réflexions sur les textures du droit", *RTDCiv.* 2003, pp. 599-628.

[24] See M..-A. Moreau, op. cit.

[25] P. Carozzza: "Subsidiarity as a Structural Principle of International Human Rights Act", *The American Journal of International Law*, January 2003.

by Denys Simon, it is a "regulatory concept",[26] seen both as a justification for Union action and as a limit on that action. In other words, subsidiarity functions as a mechanism of variation leading to greater integration if member States do not achieve the Union's objectives, or to lesser integration if they do. As it involves ongoing checking of the actions envisaged by a European legislative instrument against the EU's assigned objectives, it has a more political than legal function.[27]

This "logic" of subsidiarity also seems to be at issue in the social field. As regards trade union freedom, the stress is on the guiding notion that "rules must avoid suffocation of grass-roots initiatives".[28] Where employment is more directly involved, it can be supplemented by the mechanism of "flexi-curity" whose aim is to link, rather than to oppose, the flexibility of labour markets and the security of employment. Again, elements making it possible to ensure both need to be found. From this point of view, Marie-Ange Moreau proposes to differentiate several types of flexibility (external, internal, organizational, etc.) thereby making it possible to reconcile "water and fire".[29]

While regulatory concepts are necessary, as they introduce the flexibility needed for any match between national and international norms, it has to be acknowledged that they are not enough as too much flexibility entails a risk of arbitrariness. Hence the usefulness of adjustment techniques.

Adjustment techniques

A surprising term, perhaps. Accustomed as we are to perceiving the creation of norms according to a principle of hierarchy, our view is that adjustment and regulation are little more than a single operation by the national transposer to integrate an international norm. However, only techniques such as the national margin of appreciation and variability indicators enable a pluralist regulation of all the processes.

Unlike the margin of interpretation of a court, through which the hierarchical principle can be made more flexible without calling into question the continuity between the higher norm and the lower norm, the national margin of appreciation enables, as has been stressed, a partial integration, seen as a simple rapprochement of national norms, a harmonization without unification. This is, in the European treaties still in force, the difference between a regulation and a directive (which the CT refers to as a European law "binding in its entirety" and a framework law "binding, as to the result to be achieved, upon each member State to which it is addressed, but shall leave to the national authorities the choice

---

[26] D. Simon: *Le système juridique communautaire*, PUF, No 78; J. Clam and G. Martin, *Les transformations de la régulation juridique*, LGDJ, 1998.

[27] However, the "scrutiny of the application of the principles of subsidiarity and proportionality" that the CT sets out for National Parliaments includes both a political review procedure by the legislative authorities and an appeal to the CJEU for breaches of the principle of subsidiarity. Ratification of the CT seems thus to call for an adjustment to determine the extent of the margins left to Member States.

[28] V. Marleau, op, cit., p. 393 and 408.

[29] M.- A. Moreau, op. cit.

of form and methods"). Even though national margin is not explicitly used as a term, it underpins the distinction and would have helped to prevent the confusion between directives and regulations.

The notion of margin, invented by the ECHR to limit its own competence, has nevertheless been taken up in other international contexts such as the WTO[30] and could undoubtedly be applied within the ILO. A change of approach would nevertheless be required. Explicit or implicit, legislative (in the broad sense) or jurisprudential, the national margin seems in practice to rule out the disjunction inherent in binary reasoning. It replaces the notion of conformity according to which any difference, however small, is judged not to comply, by a notion of compatibility which allows for differences between countries. It therefore presupposes a reasoning based on non-standard logic (fuzzy logic or, more broadly, gradation logic), there being degrees of integration leading to partial integration.[31] However, not all differences are acceptable. The notion of margin thus has a limit beyond which it is not possible to go. Hence the need to set a compatibility threshold which may nevertheless vary in space and in time. If this variability is not to be arbitrary, the adjustment must comply with explicit variability indicators.[32]

To date, only the ECHR has tried to make these indicators explicit. Over and above very general formulae such as "the scope of the margin of appreciation will vary according to the circumstances, the subject matter and its background" which merely affirm variability, the Court has sketched out two types of indicator. Through the notion of "common ground" it refers to the degree of comparability of legal practices from one country to another: "the existence or non-existence of common ground between the laws of the Contracting States may be a relevant factor".[33] Taking the objectives listed by the CPHRFF to legitimize restrictive measures,[34] it refers to the degree of social consensus on values: the margin is therefore more restricted when the purpose is to protect the authority of the judicial authority (consensual value) and less restricted when other objectives are involved such as the protection of morals or of religion (less consensual values).

By transposition, the variability indicators could undoubtedly be extended to other fields such as employment. Thus, the elements identified by M.-A. Moreau could undoubtedly provide a framework for the application of flexicurity. It should be borne in mind, however, that variation is not admissible in all fields. In the same way as inderogable rights in the human rights field, there is, in the employment field, a "hard core in all countries": whether it involves sever-

---

[30] C. Ruiz Fabri and P. Monnier: On sanitary and phytosanitary measures, WTO Appellate Body, 26 November 2003 (United States v Japan), *JDI*. 3. 2004, p. 1025.

[31] See M. Delmas-Marty and M. L. Izorches: "Marge nationale d'appréciation et internationalisation du droit", RIDC 2000, pp. 753 et seq.

[32] *Le flou du droit*, PUF, 1986, 2nd edition, 2004, coll. Quadrige; *La marge nationale...*, op. cit.

[33] Judgment *Rasmussen v Denmark*, 28 November 1984.

[34] Judgment *Sunday Times v UK*, 26 April 1979.

ance pay, protection against dismissal or the traceability of dismissals, this "hard core" marks the limits of admissible variability.

The very complexity of these adjustment techniques shows that they cannot be fully controlled by the issuer of the norm. As we have stressed, when researching fuzzy logic,[35] the transition from a binary logic to gradation logic, involving a decision-making process based on compatibility thresholds, entails a transfer of power to the recipient of the norm. Hence the importance of evaluation and control methods.

Evaluation and control methods

As determined by variability indicators, adjustment techniques could go together with regulatory concepts by regulating normative intensity in the same way as a rheostat adapts light intensity as a function of the ambient light, adapting it as continuously as possible to the observable data.

The complexity of such a system raises a risk of denaturation either through excessive integration when the international legislator, going beyond his/her competence, fails to respect the principle of subsidiarity (a criticism often heard in Europe); or, in contrast, through inadequate integration when the national authorities undertake, under the pretext of transposing the norm into domestic law, a genuine re-nationalization.

Peer evaluation is a first response, as it makes it possible to draw up, as can be seen in the field of the fight against transnational corruption or against money laundering,[36] variability indicators which may facilitate control by national courts. In the case of the ILO, its tripartite nature undoubtedly enriches, as a result of a sharper critical spirit,[37] the concept of peer evaluation. This is not enough, however, as the development of international mechanisms, ranging from arbitration (ICSID) to dispute settlement (WTO) and on to jurisdictional controls (ECHR, ICHR, CJEU, CFI, etc.) shows that it possible, and undoubtedly necessary,[38] to provide for a more exacting control of subsidiarity in both directions (adjustment of the national to the international level and vice versa, respect at international level of national margins) as well as of flexi-curity.

Lastly, to function as a genuine generator of diversity, in both space (difference from one country to another) and in time (threshold of evolving compatibility), the control authorities will have to integrate extra-judicial indicators. The ECHR has started to do so, for instance, in relation to criminal proceedings for offences of homosexuality between adults:[39] although this is a moral question, and despite the absence of common legal ground, societies are moving, in the

---

[35] JF Coste and M. Delmas-Marty: "Les droits de l'homme: logiques non standard", *Le genre Humain*, Seuil, 1998, pp. 135-154.

[36] *Le relatif et l'universel*, op. cit.

[37] J. C. Javillier: op. cit., p. 663.

[38] See F. Maupain: "Persuasion et contrainte aux fins de la mise en œuvre des normes et objectifs de l'OIT", in *Mélanges Valticos*, op. cit., p. 687 et seq.

[39] Judgments *Dudgeon v UK*, 22 October 1981, *Norris v Ireland*, 26 October 1988, and *Modinos v Malta*, 22 April 1993.

view of the Court, towards greater tolerance and this convergence makes it possible to reduce the national margin almost to the point of excluding it. In the employment field, the issue of these extra-judicial indicators (social and economic) is also in the foreground.

These heterogeneous variability indicators may well reduce the objectivity of an assessment,[40] without thereby ensuring correlations with other changes. Be they from the point of view of expansion (enlargement) or synchronization (acceleration and braking), the models of a new legal order have yet to be constructed.

4. MODELS OF ORDER

To take up the challenge of a fair globalization, it is necessary to avoid both the disorder of the world (absolute relativism) and the order that would be imposed by the strongest in the name of a total universalism of the hegemonic type. i.e. to take up the challenge, already relative and universal,[41] of a law which manages to order complexity without suppressing it, learning to transform it into an "ordered pluralism".

Legal globalization nevertheless guarantees neither justice nor pluralism. The *plurality of models* available for imagining a future world legal order makes it more than ever necessary to *go beyond* them.

Plurality of models

In the domestic legal order, the representations most widely used at present are those of the paradigms, made popular by François Ost and Michel van de Kerchove,[42] of the pyramid and the network: the pyramid is ordered by a vertical hierarchical relationship (sub/ordination); whereas the network is conditioned by a set of interactions which may or may not entail hierarchies. The "dialectical" theory developed by these authors leads them to conclude that "contemporary law continues to oscillate between the potential universality of networks and the highly localized anchorage of pyramids", an oscillation which reflects, in their opinion, "the diffident and initial ethics of complex societies at the time of networks". In practice the two paradigms also express the transition from a simple (closed and stable) structure to a complex (open, unstable and polymorphous) structure.

When transposed to the phenomena of the internationalization of law, i.e. the expansion of the national to the international, regional or world area, representations of legal order are further diversified.

Expansion according to the pyramid model leads to an order of the *hegemonic* type which continues to be seen as a simple structure ordered around

---

[40] A. Lajoie: *Jugements de valeur*, PUF, coll. Les voies du droit, 1997.

[41] See M. Delmas-Marty: *Les forces imaginantes du droit, Le relatif et l'universel*, op. cit.

[42] F. Ost and M. van de Kerchove: *De la pyramide au réseau? Pour une théorie dialectique du droit*, Facultés universitaires Saint-Louis, 2002.

the hierarchical principle – doubly simple because the legal order (in the sense of the process of creation of norms) is predetermined by the hierarchical principle and because its coherence is ensured by a correlation, in some ways "natural" in the hegemonic model, between normative integration, organizational levels and speeds of change.

However, expansion according to the network model may lead to two types of legal order depending on whether priority is given to horizontal interactions (inter/national or transnational which are organized between public or private actors) or they are combined with vertical interactions (by harmonization or by unification). The former is ordered by the play of horizontal interactions. Complex as its structure is interactive, this is an order whose movements are nevertheless spontaneously correlated,[43] i.e. a *self-regulated* order as is claimed by ultra-liberalism so as not to promote more hidden forms of hegemony.

A genuinely *pluralist* order calls, however, as we have seen, for an arrangement which I would call "hypercomplex" as it has to combine horizontal and vertical interactions and correlate this variable-geometry integration with other changes, at various levels and various speeds.

This highlights the limits of "legal" reasoning which may absorb a degree of complexity, sometimes successfully as is shown by the first 50 years of European integration, but without guaranteeing political legitimacy.[44] It is tempting for lawyers to enjoy this complexity and shut themselves away in it. However, citizens may reject a system which they discover at a late stage and about which they do not understand a great deal. This is perhaps what is happening today as legal Europe, of which we were so proud, has been caught up and in some cases sidelined by the political debate. Hence the need to go beyond the models to find a flexible articulation between the legal, social and economic fields.

Going beyond the models

The main choices continue to lie in the policy field as modelling of the legal order does not unlock the door of the dialectic between one model and another. Reason, as Bachelard said, "has to obey science". In practice, if science tends to describe what is, reason is at its service; however, law is "normative", it says what should be and thus calls on will or voluntarism. It is for this reason that, in the main founding texts, legal reasoning seems in some cases to depart from actual reality, as a way of protesting against it, for instance by proclaiming, contrary to any observable reality, that "all human beings are born free and equal in dignity and rights" (Article 1 of the Universal Declaration of Human Rights). Between the descriptive and the normative, there is therefore a gap which can be filled only by a jump into the unknown, a wager on the future.

---

[43] Fisher-Lescano A. and Teubner G., "The vain search for legal unity in the fragmentation of global law" in: *Michigan Journal of International* law 2004, p. 999-1045.

[44] Quermonne J.L. et al., L'Union Européenne en quête d'Institutions légitimes et efficaces, *La Documentation Française*, Paris, 1999.

Because it involves such a wager, globalization cannot be left to lawyers alone, and cannot be enclosed in law or relate solely to the market. Precisely because it calls upon will, globalization pre-supposes a return to the political. To avoid overly disorganized and unpredictable movements, it is not only necessary to control changes in the legal field by new balancing systems, but also to identify the transnational strategies of enterprises and trade unions. In other words, re-introducing the actors[45] on whom the policies through which a social dimension can be given to globalization will ultimately depend.

---

[45] World Commission on the Social Dimension of Globalisation, ILO, Geneva, 2004.

APPENDIX I: LIST OF PARTICIPANTS *

Peter Auer, Chief, Employment Analysis and Research Unit, Employment Strategy Department

Rajendra K. Bandi, Chairperson, Center for Software & IT Management, Indian Institute of Management, Bangalore

Geneviève Besse, Chargée de mission internationale, Direction de l'animation de la recherche, des études et des statistiques (DARES)

Haroon Bhorat, Director,Development Policy Research Unit (DPRU) University of Cape Town, South Africa

Daniel Cohen, Professeur, Économiste, ENS

Alexia Dauchy, Chargée de mission au Département Synthèses, DGEFP

Michael Dauderstädt, Head, International Policy Analysis Unit, Friedrich Ebert Stiftung, Bonn

François Eyraud, Chief, Conditions of Work and Employment Programme

Rashid Filali Meknassi, Professeur de droit, Université de Rabat

Klara Foti, Economist, Institute for the World Economy, Budapest

Annie Fouquet, Directrice de la DARES

Michel Fouquin, Directeur adjoint du CEPII

Jacques Freyssinet, Président du Conseil scientifique du Centre d'études pour l'emploi

Bernard Gazier, Professeur, Chercheur, Matisse, Université de Paris 1 Panthéon-Sorbonne

Damian Grimshaw, Professor, Director European Work and Employment Research Center, University of Manchester

Michel Guerre, Conseiller technique pour les Affaires européennes et internationales, DRT

Maryse Huet, Chargée de mission à la Mission interministérielle sur les mutations économiques (MIME)

Jean-Claude Javillier, Senior Adviser, International Institute for Labour Studies

Brian Langille, Professor, University of Toronto

Jean-Pierre Laviec, Director a.i., International Institute for Labour Studies

Frédéric Lerais, Chef de la mission analyse économique, DARES

Jean-Daniel Leroy, Director, ILO, Paris Office

Malte Lübker, Expert, Policy Integration Department, ILO

Adriana Marshall, Senior Labour Economist, Instituto de Desarollo económico y social, Buenos Aires

Dominique Méda, Cheffe de la Mission Animation de la recherche, DARES

---

* Functions at the time of the conference, April 2005

Marie-Ange Moreau, Professeur de droit, Juriste à l'Institut européen de Florence

Marie-Laure Morin, Conseiller à la Cour de Cassation

Anne Muxart, Ministère des finances (DGTPE, PCN)

Tom Palley, Chief-Economist US-China Economic and Security Commission, Washington

Jean-Marie Paugam, Institut français des Relations internationales (IFRI)

Emmanuel Reynaud, Chief, Social Security Policy and Development Branch

Gerry Rodgers, Director, Policy Integration Department

Richard Alexander Roehrl, Research Manager, European Foundation for the Improvement of Working and Living Conditions, Dublin

Valérie Rouxel-Laxton, Economist, EU Commission

Werner Sengenberger, Consultant of International Organizations, Former Director of the Employment and Training Department of the ILO, Geneva

Mazyar Taheri, Délégation aux Affaires européennes et internationales, DAEI

Michel Thierry, Inspecteur général des Affaires sociales, Délégué suppléant du Gouvernement français auprès du B.I.T.

Raymond Torres, Head Employment Analysis and Policy, OECD

Jean-François Trogrlic, Observateur au titre du Gouvernement français

Leonelli Tronti, Head, Short-Term Statistics on Employment and Labour Incomes, Central Directorate for Short-Term Business Statistics, Rome

Johanna Walgrave, Director, Social Dialogue, Labour Law and Labour Administration Department

Philippe Waquet, Conseiller Doyen Honoraire à la Cour de Cassation

APPENDIX II: INTERNATIONAL OUTSOURCING, EMPLOYMENT, AND INEQUALITY: SOME ISSUES

BY MALTE LÜBKER[1]

INTERNATIONAL OUTSOURCING: MEDIA HYPE OR A REAL THREAT FOR JOBS IN THE NORTH?

1. Introduction

The term 'outsourcing' has made headlines for several years now, and spectacular announcements of plans to relocate jobs to low-cost locations by corporations such as IBM have fuelled fears of job losses (Wall Street Journal, 12 March 2004). Furthermore, market research companies have presented some alarming headline statistics predicting massive future job offshoring and reinforced these fears (Forrester, 2002, 2004a and 2004b). Outsourcing has been hotly debated in the United States (especially during the 2004 presidential campaign), but also in Europe. A prime example for the prominence of the issue in the Old World are the extensive considerations that can be found in the recent reports produced by the French Senate's *Groupe de travail sur la délocalisation des industries de main-d'oeuvre* (Grignon, 2004) and the *Conseil d'analyse économique* (Fontagné and Lorenzi, 2005).[2]

The controversy on outsourcing must be put in the context of the wider debate on trade and global economic integration. Here, a prominent concern has been that many developing countries have been left behind and benefited little from globalization.[3] Others have argued that the rapid opening to trade and financial flows has made developing countries prone to crisis, and resulted in significant economic and social cost (see e.g. Lee, 1998). More recently, the intervention by Nobel laureate Paul A. Samuelson (2004) has questioned the standard conclusion of trade economists that industrialized countries gain from trade and specialization. He disputes the "popular polemical untruth" that welfare gains from trade necessarily exceed any losses. Instead, he argues that technical

---

[1] "I am grateful for feedback and comments by Peter Auer, Duncan Campbell, Rolph van der Hoeven and Gerry Rodgers. John Sendanyoye shared some very helpful ideas at an early stage. All errors and omissions are mine."

[2] These reports can also be consulted for a comprehensive coverage of the French literature on the topic.

[3] See the discussion in Chapter II.2 of the Report by the World Commission on the Social Dimension of Globalization (2004).

progress in China can induce a permanent loss in the per capita income of the United States – to the extent that it reverses any US gains from trade over autarky.

This paper discusses some of the issues raised in the debate on international outsourcing. It starts by defining the term and then maps the different attempts made in the literature to measure the extent and development of outsourcing. It further considers the explanations given for the rise in outsourcing and discusses how the literature views the employment effects, both in the countries that outsource and those that host outsourced activities. Special attention is given to the potentially adverse effects on wage inequality and social exclusion. Finally, it identifies three areas emerging from the literature that are of particular relevance to the ILO's mandate that would warrant the development of adequate policy responses.

2. Definitional issues: what is 'international outsourcing'?

Although there is an intuitive understanding of what outsourcing means, the precise definitions given to the term differ throughout the literature. Expressions such as 'offshoring', 'offshore sourcing', 'vertical specialization', 'fragmenta-tion', 'delocalization' and 'global production sharing' that are often used as synonyms, or to describe closely related phenomena. For example, Arndt states that "[o]ffshore sourcing occurs when some activities involved in the making of a product are performed abroad" (Arndt, 1997: 71). To Egger and Stehrer "[...] 'outsourcing' [...] means the international splitting of production processes either within or between firms to exploit new, technologically feasible gains from specialization" (Egger and Stehrer, 2003: 61), but Jones and Kierzkowski refer to the "splitting up of a previously integrated production process into two or more components" as "fragmentation" (Jones and Kierzkowski, 2001a: 18; see also Jones and Kierzkowski, 1990). Grossman and Helpman use the term "outsourcing" and emphasize that it "means finding a partner with which a firm can establish a bilateral relationship and having a partner undertake relationship-specific investments so that it becomes able to produce goods or services that fit the firm's particular needs" (Grossman and Helpman, 2002: 2).

In addition to the above definitions that describe a qualitative aspect of the outsourcing process, other authors have put forward definitions that lend themselves more readily to measurement: they normally use the foreign content in a final product as a basis. For example, Görg et al. (2004) define "international outsourcing as the value of imported [services and non-services] intermediates" (ibid.) and Amiti and Wei (2004) speak of international outsourcing when they mean "the procuring of service or material inputs by a firm from a source in a foreign country" (ibid.: 6). Feenstra and Hanson exclude energy inputs and hence "measure outsourcing as the share of imported intermediate inputs in the total purchase of non-energy materials" (Feenstra and Hanson, 1996: 240). There is, however, some uneasiness about this definition since for example the purchase of foreign steel by a car-maker would fall under it – even though most people would hardly consider this to be a case of 'outsourcing'. Feenstra and

Hanson therefore suggest an additional, narrow definition of outsourcing that only contains intermediate inputs from the same industry (e.g. brakes and gearboxes in the case of the car-maker). This suggestion has since been taken up by others such as Geishecker and Görg (2004: 6) or Hijzen et al. (2004: 5f.). Contrary to this, Anderton et al. (2002) have widened the definition by including the import of final goods, as long as they originate from low-wage countries. The idea is that companies sometimes outsource the entire production of a product, but continue to sell it under their own brand name in their home market. Others have criticized this operation as an "excessively wide" measure for outsourcing (Egger and Egger, 2001: 247).

3. Measurement issues: what is the extent of outsourcing, and how has it evolved over time?

Taking the different definitions of outsourcing, there are a number of possible approaches to measure its extent, and to track its evolution over time. These approaches sometimes face considerable data problems and often resort to 'proxy' measures, i.e. they do not measure outsourcing directly, but use those data that are available and reflect the concept under question the most closely. As a general rule, the preciseness of measurement will decrease as the coverage – both geographical and over time – is extended. Whereas data for a single point in time at the level of the individual firm can often contain significant detail, global time-series data will necessarily have to rely on crude proxies of international outsourcing. As several publications emphasize, "there are currently no reliable statistical indicators of the extent or nature of global outsourcing" (European Foundation for the Improvement of Living and Working Conditions, 2004: 10). For the international sourcing of services, van Welsum regrets that "there are no official data measuring the extent of the phenomenon or its economic impact" (van Welsum, 2004: 32). As the World Trade Organization (2005: 267) argues, one of the root causes for this is that outsourcing refers to management decisions made at the micro-level (i.e. to replace in-house production by the purchase of service inputs) that cannot be easily linked to trade statistics that are collected on the national and sectoral levels. Nonetheless, several statistical sources can illustrate recent trends in outsourcing. In what follows, they are organized according to the type of data used.

Data on outward-processing trade

A number of studies have illustrated trends in outsourcing by making use of bilateral trade data that capture the re-import of products that were shipped abroad for assembly or processing. Baldone et al. (2001) show that EU producers of textiles and apparel have increasingly relocated some stages of their production, mainly to Central and Eastern Europe. For example, re-imports of apparel to the Netherlands were equal to 42.2 per cent of domestic production in 1994-96 (up from 20.4 per cent in 1988-90), and they increased in Germany from 10.8 per cent in 1988-90 to 24.1 per cent in 1994-96 (ibid.: 85). French and Italian producers have engaged in production outsourcing to a far smaller degree (with ratios of 4.9 and 2.3 per cent in the final year, respectively). The results presented by Egger and Egger (2001) indicate that this particular kind of 'outsourcing' is less prevalent in other sectors. According to their data, outward processing equalled only 0.249 per cent of gross production of all EU industries in 1995-1997 (ibid.: 247f.).

A similar picture emerges for the United States. Feenstra et al. (2000: 89ff.) utilize US customs data for the Offshore Assembly Program (OAP) and find a marked increase of re-imports in the Apparel (SIC 23) and Footwear and Leather (SIC 31) industries, mainly from Mexico and Caribbean countries. By 1993, OAP imports accounted for 6.4 per cent of all incoming shipments in the former industry (up from 1.1 per cent in 1981) and 8.5 per cent in the latter (up from 1.0 per cent in 1981). By contrast, OAP imports fluctuated around their initial level over the period for the Machinery (at 1.0 per cent or below), Electrical Machinery (between 2.4 and 4.0 per cent) and Transportation Equipment industries (below 1.0 per cent in all years but 1987).

Input-output tables

Many researchers have relied on input-output tables to measure outsourcing. These tables generally break down the inputs received by each industry according to the industry of origin and their source (domestic or foreign) and state the value added by the industry itself – the sum of which is an industry's total output. This makes it possible to calculate the share of foreign inputs contained in the final product, and therefore the degree of outsourcing as defined by several of the above quoted authors. Given that inputs are listed by supplier industry, both the broad and the narrow definition of outsourcing, proposed by Feenstra and Hanson (1996), can be operationalized. The approach, however, is not without drawbacks. Hijzen et al. (2004) point out that outsourcing of the final production stage (as in the case of outward processing trade) will not be captured by input-output tables.

National statistical offices provide one source for input-output tables. Hijzen et al. (2004) had access to those from the United Kingdom and calculated the ratio of intermediate inputs over the value added in the industry (not gross output or total inputs, as done elsewhere). In the narrow version (that takes into account only inputs from the same industry), the share went up from 15.2 per cent in 1984 to 18.6 per cent in 1995, and it increased from 45.9 (1984) to 48.8 per cent (1995) under the broad definition (non-weighted averages across all industries). A more recent study for the United Kingdom by Amiti and Wei (2004: 33) shows that growth in outsourcing during the 1990s was mainly due to developments in non-tangible inputs. The authors distinguish between service inputs and manufactured inputs and find that in the years from 1998 to 2001 the latter was around its 1992 level, 28 per cent of total non-energy inputs, after having peaked at just over 30 per cent in the mid-1990s. In contrast, the share of imported service inputs has been on a steady rise between 1992 (3.5 per cent) and 2001 (5.5 per cent). For Germany, Geishecker and Görg (2004) find an even steeper increase in total outsourcing during the 1990s. The narrow measure of outsourcing, here expressed as a share of gross output, increased from just over 5 per cent in 1991 to more than 8 per cent in 2000, and the broad version from under 11 per cent to just over 15 per cent (ibid.: 18).[4]

Campa and Goldberg (1997) report a similar result from their four-country study of manufacturing industries. The input-output tables used by them do not differentiate between domestic and imported inputs; rather Campa and Goldberg combine them with data on import penetration to derive a similar measure. For the United States, the estimated share of imported inputs from manufacturing industries in total production rose from 4.1 per cent (1975) to 8.2 per cent (1995), and for the United Kingdom from 13.4 per cent (1974) to 21.7 per cent (1993). While the measure of outsourcing for these two countries falls somewhere between the narrow and the broad definition as described above, the data for Canada and Japan include all imported inputs (and hence apply the broad definition). The imported inputs share rose from 15.9 per cent (1974) to 20.2 per cent (1993) in Canada, but fell from an already low 8.2 per cent (1974) in Japan to only 4.1 per cent (1993). Among all the countries surveyed, Japan therefore stands out as the single country where the use of foreign inputs actually declined. Strauss-Kahn (2003) faces a similar data-problem in her study of France and proceeds like Campa and Goldberg (1997). Her within-industry measure of outsourcing rose from 4.9 per cent in 1977 to 7.3 per cent in 1993, while the broad measure increased from 9.2 per cent to 13.8 per cent over the period (ibid.: 25).

Standardized input-output tables produced by the OECD (1995) better facilitate cross-country comparison. They cover the G-7 nations plus Australia, Denmark and the Netherlands for the period from ca. 1970 to ca. 1990 in intervals of approximately five years. Even though the number of countries included is small, they still capture roughly 60 per cent of world trade. Geographical coverage was extended in a later – but not comparable – issue for the mid-1990s that includes a total of 18 OECD countries along with China and Brazil (OECD, 2002). Hummels et al. (2001) base their measure of 'vertical specialization' on the earlier dataset and calculate the "value of imported inputs embodied in goods that are exported" (ib-id.: 77). This ratio grew from an average 0.162 to 0.198 over the 20-year period covered (export-weighted). In nine out of ten countries the ratio increased, with Japan again being the single exception. Additional data from national sources show rising 'vertical specialization' for Ireland, Taiwan and the Republic of Korea, and a particularly sharp increase in Mexico (from 0.10 in 1979 to 0.32 in 1997) that reflects the growth of export processing in the country's *maquiladoras*. Yi (2003) provides an extension on the article by Hummels et al. (2001), exploring the impact of vertical specialization on the volume of world trade.

Trade statistics for intermediate inputs

Since outsourcing will generally generate trade in intermediate products, other researchers have attempted to map the flow of such products. While ready-

---

[4] Note that the different denominators of the ratios make it impossible to directly compare the extent of outsourcing across these three studies; they only allow relative trends to be assessed.

to-use statistical compilations such as the UNCTAD Handbook of Statistics (UNCTAD, 2004a) and others that are based on the UN's COMTRADE database have the advantage of comprehensive coverage across time and countries, the approach necessarily relies on "rather arbitrary classifications of goods into intermediate and final" (Hummels et al., 2001: 76). Yeats (2001) tries to find a way around this by concentrating on the machinery and transport equipment group (SITC 7) where parts and components can be identified with relative ease (under SITC Revision 2). He can demonstrate that the share of parts and components in all OECD exports from this group rose from 26 to 30 per cent between 1978 and 1995. Nonetheless, this is no direct evidence of increased outsourcing since the parts and components that are recorded in trade statistics might not have been used for further manufacturing, but for repair and maintenance purposes. However, sectoral studies reinforce the view that outsourcing is a likely driving force behind these changes. For example, Nunnenkamp (2004: 32f.) reports that the content of imported intermediates per car produced in Germany almost quadrupled in real terms between 1980 and 2002, while intermediates exports grew by 170 per cent.

As the United Kingdom example cited above reflects, outsourcing of service inputs still accounts for only a small portion of total outsourcing. But given its continuous growth, concentrating solely on statistics for intermediate manufactured, or other tangible goods inputs would mean missing an important, dynamic part of the overall picture. It is therefore useful to supplement such statistics with data on trade in services. Precisely this task was undertaken by Amiti and Wei (2004) who draw on the IMF's Balance of Payments (BoP) statistics for 'computer & information services' and 'other business services' – two categories that much of the recent public debate has concentrated on. While the trade statistics do not differentiate by the use of these imports, they are typically (and in contrast to service imports such as travel or education) demanded by firms – and not final consumers – and are therefore a good proxy for services outsourcing.

The data confirm that the import of 'computer & information services' and 'other business services' has been growing rapidly in many countries, sometimes doubling relative to GDP within a decade. For the United States, imports equaled 0.1 per cent of GDP in 1983, 0.2 per cent in 1993 and 0.4 per cent in 2003; for the United Kingdom the figures are higher at 0.9 (1983), 0.7 (1993) and 1.2 per cent (2003). Other industrialized countries such as Germany, France and the Russian Federation report higher figures (between 1.4 and 2.4 per cent of GDP for 2002), but some developing countries like Angola (35 per cent), the Republic of Congo (22 per cent) and Mozambique (17 per cent) have even higher import ratios. Some of the industrialized nations named above are also among the world's top exporters of services (see Box 2).

For business services, by far the larger of the two categories, the United States is in fact the biggest exporter, followed by the United Kingdom and Germany, well ahead of India ranking 6th and China ranking 14th. The United Kingdom and the United States are also the two countries with the greatest trade

Box 1: Trade in automotive Parts and accessories

While studies such as that of Yeats (2001) show that trade in intermediate products has risen slightly over the past two decades, the available data also show that the import of intermediaries is by no means a new phenomenon. This can be illustrated by using the automotive industry as an example. The Standard International Trade Classification (SITC) Group 784 contains the most important parts and accessories of motor vehicles (such as bodies, brakes, gearboxes and axles). Even though trade in dollar terms has grown rapidly since 1980, this expansion has been roughly in line with total trade in motor vehicles (SITC groups 722, 781, 782 and 783). The first graph shows that worlwide trade in parts and accessories (calculated as the sum of exports and imports divided by two) expressed as a percentage of trade in finished motor vehicles has fluctuated betwween 35 and 40 percent since 1980.

Trade in Automotive Parts (SITC 784) as Percentage of Total Motor Vehicles Trade (SITC 722, 781, 782 and 783), 1980-2002

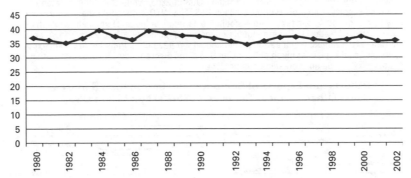

The data further show that three of the five largest exporters of motor vehicles were also net exporters of parts and accessories: Germany, Japan and France recorded substantial trade surpluses, while the United States and Canada had imports in excess of exports.

Trade in Automotive parts (SITC 784), 2002 in billion US$

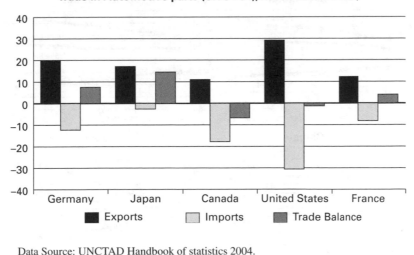

Data Source: UNCTAD Handbook of statistics 2004.

Box 2: Some Evidence on Trade in Services from the IMF's Balance of Payments Statistics

The IMF's Balance of Payment data allow taking a closer look at recent developments in the two service categories that Amiti and Wei (2004) concentrate on: 'computer & information services' and 'other business services'. Aggregating the two categories, the graphs below show the trading positions of four main industrialized trading partners alongside with those of China and India. While both the United Kingdom and the United States have maintained or increased their substantial trade surpluses from 1986 to 2003 (around 20 billion US$ per year), Germany has recorded a deficit over the entire period, and France saw its surplus diminish. The graphs also show the rapid rise of India and China as service exporters: Starting with relatively minor exports seven years ago, they each expanded their exports to just under 20 billion US$ – close to those of France. However, as the World Trade Organization (2005: 277ff.) cautions, these figures should be taken with a grain of salt, given the large discrepancies between reported exports and imports on a global level. In the case of bilateral trade between India and the United States, two of the largest trading partners, India reported exports to the United States worth 6.8 billion US$ in 2003, while the United States only recorded imports from India worth 0.9 billion US$. The WTO argues that these figures can only be reconciled "if one takes into account the earnings of Indian IT specialists which are [...] considered by the US Department of Commerce as residents" (WTO 2005: 280). According to a WTO estimate, such earnings that should not have been included in Indian export statistics could explain as much as 4.8 billion US$ of the discrepancy. Indian export statistics are thus likely to be an overestimate of actual exports.

Imports and Exports of Computer and Information Services and Other Business Services, 1986-2003 (in billion US$)

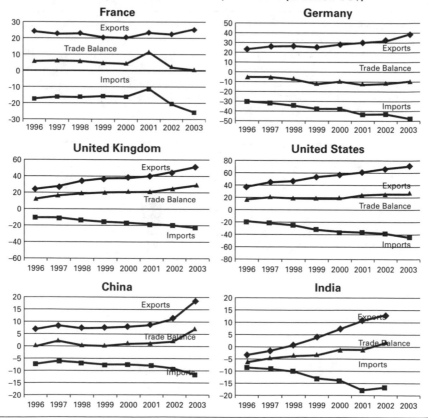

surplus in business and computing services, while Japan and Germany have the greatest deficits (ibid.). Using a wider definition (total exports of services, excluding government services) and WTO data, van Welsum (2004) produces broadly similar results. However, the inclusion of other services dilutes the market shares of China (2.5 per cent) and India (1.5 per cent).

Business surveys

The data on the rapid rise of cross-border services outsourcing must, however, be put into perspective. To do so, business surveys are a valuable complementary source. For example, the Centre for European Economic Research (2005) conducted a large-scale survey among 4,400 German companies and found that some 87 per cent of them had outsourced some or all of their IT-related activities. However, the lion's share of the contracts went to domestic suppliers: Only 0.1 per cent of the surveyed companies awarded contracts to overseas service providers, and 5.9 per cent to companies from other EU countries (ibid.).

Conclusion: outsourcing is an age-old phenomenon, but services have added dynamism

Overall, the results of recent research seem to indicate that there has been a rise in outsourcing, particularly since the early 1990s. The phenomenon is most widespread in labour-intensive industries such as consumer electronics, leather goods and apparel where production is relocated from the old OECD countries to low-cost destinations such as Mexico, the Caribbean and Eastern Europe. Imported parts and components are also an important factor in the motor vehicle and other manufacturing industries, which have relied on production sharing for several decades. Although trade in business services and computer and information services is still at a nascent stage, it is the most dynamic and fastest growing area. Developing countries like India and China have managed to gain a share in this market, but are still far behind the leading exporters of these services, the United States and the United Kingdom, that continue to enjoy substantial trade surpluses.

4. How are trends in outsourcing best explained?

A major driving force behind international outsourcing is international differences in factor prices (see e.g. Nunnenkamp, 2004; Kohler, 2002). Given that capital is generally more mobile than labour, price differences are usually greatest for labour. Outsourcing labour-intensive production stages to a low-wage country can hence be seen as a "vehicle for arbitraging" on these differences (Kohler, 2004). While there are potentially large arbitrage gains to be made, several barriers restrict the feasibility of international outsourcing. Among them are technological limits to decompose the production process, customs tariffs and transportation costs. Hence, as these barriers are overcome (or as factor price differences widen) the extent of outsourcing is expected to grow. Several researchers have thus sought to make this link in order to explain the rise in outsourcing.

Reductions of trade barriers

Venables (1999) develops a simple model to demonstrate that as trade costs fall, fragmentation of production becomes feasible. One interesting implication of his model is that when the final production stage is relocated to the country where a final product is consumed, overall trade in value terms might actually fall since exports of intermediates replace exports of finished products. Trade will only grow as a result of outsourcing when intermediates that where previously produced domestically are imported (ibid.). While Venables assumes that intermediary goods cross one border at most, Yi accounts for the fact that "[v]ertically specialized goods or goods in process cross multiple international borders while they are being produced" (Yi, 2003: 55). When they incur a tariff upon crossing every border, tariffs accumulate and can make production fragmentation unfeasible. However, a small decrease in the tariff rate can lower the overall cost below a critical threshold and generate a large effect. Yi uses this logic to explain the non-linear response of trade volumes to tariff reductions. He develops a model that explains more than 50 per cent of US trade growth since the early 1960s (by his account substantially more than standard trade models). In addition to a general fall in tariffs, regional free-trade agreements such as NAFTA have often facilitated the outsourcing of production stages (see Arndt, 2002). The reduction of trade barriers between West and East Europe after 1990 and the subsequent integration of Eastern European countries into the European Union is another example (see Egger and Egger, 2005).

Declining transportation costs

In contrast to this, a review of the available data on transportation cost by Hummels (1999) suggests that changes in freight costs have played a comparatively minor role. While his research confirms that the cost of air transport has fallen substantially over the past 50 years, he concludes that – contrary to conventional wisdom – the cost of ocean transport has actually risen. At the same time, changes in the rate structure have favoured long-distance shipments relative to shorter distances (ibid.: 21). The picture is of course entirely different if one looks at transmitting information as opposed to the cost of moving merchandise. While the cost of telecommunication was prohibitively high only a few decades ago, the price for a single voice circuit has become almost infinitesimally small during the 1990s (see Blake and Lande, 1999: Table 12). This rapid decline plays a major role in services outsourcing – a call centre in India to serve British customers would have been unthinkable until very recently.

Technological change

More generally, technological change is often cited as one of the enabling factors for outsourcing (see e.g. McKinsey Global Institute, 2003: 4). The ILO's World Employment Report 2001 analyses how advances in computing and network technology have led to 'spatial dynamics' in teleworking, call-centres, software production and information-processing work (ILO, 2001: 126ff.). The 2004 edition of the report continues the discussion on the subject and asserts that the ITC revolution has enabled an expansion of outsourcing to the services industries (ILO, 2004: 86). And in the words of the World Investment Report 2004, the possibility to store and transmit information digitally has led to the 'tradability' of services that were formerly considered non-tradable (UNCTAD 2004b: 148). The new developments in communications technologies have had an important impact even in manufacturing. Hummels et al. (2001: 94) suggest that "the sequential nature of vertical specialization" make "oversight and coordination of production" an important restraining factor that can be overcome more easily with the help of modern technology.

Box 3: Wage Differences as a Driving Force for Services Outsourcing

A fundamental driving force behind outsourcing is the difference in labour costs (see e.g. Dossani and Kenney 2004: 10ff.). While this has long been the case for manufacturing, the advances in information and communication technology have made outsourcing a viable option for services. Bardhan and Kroll (2003) have illustrated the potential for cost saving by contrasting average hourly wages in the United States (as published by the US Bureau of Labor Statistic) with the typical range in India (based on their own research). Their results show that Indian wages in medium-skill occupations like health record technologists or payroll clerks are typically 10 to 20 per cent of those in the United States. However, the wage differential is smaller for higher-skilled professions such as accountants or financial researchers where Indian workers get a higher percentage of their US counterparts.

Hourly Wages for Selected Occupations in the United States and India,

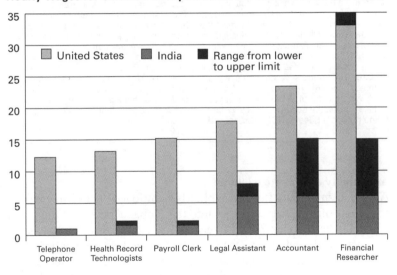

2002/2003 (in US$)

Source: Bardhan and Kroll (2003).

Box 4: The Rise of India as a Exporter of IT-related Services

While wage differentials between India and developed countries like the United States can account for the drive to outsource activities to India (see Box 3 above), they cannot explain why India has been immensely more successful in exporting IT-related services than other countries with similar – or even lower – wage levels. The key to the phenomenal growth in Indian service exports since the early 1990s is that the country was able to offer high-quality IT-related services, easing the skill-shortages that became particularly severe in the developed countries during the boom years of the late 1990s. Kumar and Joseph (2004) attribute this success in IT world markets to a series of strategic policy choices that build the country's export capacity. As far back as the 1970s, the Indian Government recognized the potential of the software sector, and subsequently the first degree courses in computer sciences were offered. The tertiary-level training capacities were further extended under the Computer Manpower Development Programme, launched in 1983. In addition to courses offered at public institutes, privately run centres established a range of courses since the early 1980s, many of which have since been accredited (see ibid.: 7ff.). The rapid growth in the number of graduates with degrees in computer science and related engineering and technology disciplines was arguably "crucial for software success" in India (Arora and Gambardella 2004: 8). However, as a result of the sector's rapid growth, some Indian companies now find it hard to recruit adequately trained professionals (see Vijayabaskar et al. 2001).

Public policy was not limited to investment and promotion of education. The Department of Electronics played an active role in fostering the industry, most notably by establishing networking infrastructure during the 1980s, and from 1990 onwards by setting up Software Technology Parks in cities such as Mumbai and Bangalore. The parks provided firms with the necessary infrastructure, especially high-speed communication links (see Kumar and Joseph 2004: 9ff; Kumar 2001: 5). This was supplemented by promotional measures such as tax and import duty exemptions, and an early relaxation of foreign ownership rules. Kumar and Joseph hence call the Indian success "a typical case of proactive state intervention wherein the Government laid the foundation and the industry took off with greater participation by the private sector" (Kumar and Joseph 2004: 1). Another crucial factor that helped the export-led growth in IT-related services was the emigration of Indian IT specialists who provided links between the emerging Indian software industry and the established companies abroad (see Arora and Gambarella 2004: 10f.). While the companies that provide outsourced software services – either on-site in the developed countries or from India – are mainly home-grown (see Kumar 2001: 31f.), India has also managed to attract many export-oriented FDI projects. A survey commissioned by UNCTAD found that the country had received a total of 118 greenfield and expansion projects in IT-related services during 2002-2003. With a share of 19 per cent in worldwide projects within this category, India was the FDI leading destination in numerical terms – ahead of the United Kingdom (12 per cent) and China (9 per cent) (see UNCTAD 2004b: 161ff.).

Availability of low-wage labour

A fundamental, but often not explicitly mentioned change that has brought many millions of low-wage workers into the global economy is the opening of China's and India's labour markets (see e.g. ILO, 2004: 86). This means that the effective wage differential between the industrialized economies and the lowest available wage rate has widened substantially; wages in some services professions are only a fraction of those paid in the United States (see Box 3). India has also positioned itself as a location with a skilled labour force, especially in IT-related services (see Box 4). Similarly, the transformation in Central and Eastern Europe has effectively added millions of workers, many of them highly skilled, to the globalized labour force – and this in close proxy to the industrialized economies of Western Europe. Richard Freeman (2005) argues that the opening of these countries, and their embracing of capitalism, has effectively doubled the global labour force from 1.47 billion to just below three billion workers.

Empirical studies have investigated the relevance of the aforementioned factors in a firm's decision to outsource production stages to a foreign country. For the manufacturing sector in Austria, Egger and Egger (2003: 633f.) report that outsourcing to Eastern Europe is essentially low-wage seeking and was boosted by the reduction of tariff barriers after 1990. A study of the EU apparel sector concludes that "labour costs, along with geographical and cultural proximity, are the most important reasons for the original choice of a given country as a processing partner" (Baldone et al., 2001: 102). The research has, however, an additional finding: once a choice has been made, outsourcing firms are unlikely to reverse it – even when, at a later stage, cheaper labour becomes available in another country. This finding becomes plausible when outsourcing is seen to involve substantial search-costs and relationship-specific investments as well as effort to establish trust between partners in an environment of often non-enforceable contracts (Grossman and Helpman, 2002).

5. The employment effects of outsourcing

Employment effects in developed countries

Dramatic estimates of outsourcing activities have stirred up a great deal of public debate about their employment impact. For example, Forrester Research predicts that by 2015, Europe will lose more than one million jobs as a result of 'offshoring' to overseas service providers (Forrester, 2004a). An even greater impact is predicted in the United States, with an estimate of 3.3 million jobs lost during the same period. The claim was first made by the consultancy in 2002, and then it was revised it slightly upwards two years later (Forrester, 2002, 2004b). Others believe that this figure is still 'conservative' and estimate that in the United States alone some 14 million jobs are 'at risk' as a result of outsourcing (Bardhan and Kroll, 2003). On the other hand, some studies argue that "fears about job losses, however reasonable, tend to overplay the likely impact of offshoring" (McKinsey Global Institute, 2003: 9). According to the latest estimates from McKinsey, offshore employment in services had reached 1.5 million jobs worldwide in 2003 and could grow to 4.1 million jobs by 2008 (Farrell et al., 2005a: 23f.). Still, this would equal only a small fraction of services employment in the developed countries (around 1.2 per cent).[5] Similarly, the World Employment Report 2001 concludes that "very few jobs in industrialized countries are contestable by developing countries" (ILO, 2001: 140). A study commissioned by the Information Technology Association of America even predicts that offshore sourcing will lead to a net gain of 317,000 jobs in the United States by 2008 (ITTA, 2004).

In part, the differences between the estimates arise because some studies refer to gross effects (or direct job losses through outsourcing), but others to net

---

[5] While this puts the dimension of outsourcing into perspective, it would be misleading to equate the number of jobs created through outsourcing in transitional and developing countries with the number of jobs lost in developed countries, as will be argued below.

effects (and therefore take into account possible indirect job gains). While the first approach can deliver information on how many workers are likely to be displaced by outsourcing, only the second can be informative about the overall effects on employment. It takes into account the fact that new jobs may also be created as a result of outsourcing: Firstly, there is a direct job creating effect since the fragmentation of production or service provision process entails need for co-ordination and supervision (see e.g. Burda and Dluhosch, 2001). Secondly, outsourcing might lead to efficiency gains for the firm that relocates some of its labour-intensive activities abroad and improve its overall competitiveness. In an influential paper, Arndt argues along these lines and concludes that by shedding "their less competitive operations" companies will be "more effective competitors in world markets for end products" (Arndt, 1997: 77). Therefore, "offshore sourcing enhances [employment] in industries which make use of it" (ibid.). An empirical study that uses plant-level data for the Irish manufacturing sector confirms that productivity gains can be realized in the case of intermediate inputs, but that the evidence is less clear-cut for outsourcing of services (Görg et al., 2004: 12).

However, the conclusion that outsourcing improves competitiveness need not necessarily hold. Since competitiveness is a relative concept, not all producers of a certain good can gain a competitive advantage at the same time – even if all of them outsource production stages or service inputs. The argument that outsourcing enhances employment hinges on a supply side effect: If cost savings lead to cheaper production, prices will fall and this shift in the supply curve should stimulate higher demand for the product (see e.g. Amiti and Wei 2004: 16). This can in turn cause higher output, a growth in the remaining activities and subsequent employment gains. On the other hand, the initial job losses in the outsourcing country can lead to losses in income, and to a shift in the demand curve. It is therefore possible that the new equilibrium is at a lower level.

A different approach is to understand the net employment effects of outsourcing through the framework of fragmentation (going back to Jones and Kierzkowski, 1990). Jones and Kierzkowski (2001a and 2001b) model what can happen when a formally integrated production process is broken down into two (or more) segments that can be traded internationally. One possibility is that a country that was able to produce the integrated product ceases to produce the labour-intensive segment (or, in the alternative terminology, *outsources* it), but remains competitive in world markets for the more capital-intensive segment and becomes an exporter for this segment. If the country is relatively capital-abundant, it will employ more labour in producing the fragment than it previously used to produce the integrated product (Jones and Kierzkowski, 2001b: 374). At the other extreme is the possibility that a country is initially "second best" in either of the segments of an integrated product, but has the most competitive *average* cost structure. However, once it becomes possible to fragment production, either segment will move to the country best at producing it. In this case, the country loses all production (and employment) as a consequence of fragmentation (ibid: 377ff.). Jones and Kierzkowski can thus explain opposite employment outcomes from within a single theoretical framework, and attribute them to a country's factor endowments.

It then becomes an empirical question whether job gains will be sufficient to offset job losses, and whether a positive net effect remains. Relatively few studies have addressed this issue. Among them is the recent paper by Amiti and Wei (2004) which examines the job effects of service outsourcing for the United States and the United Kingdom. They summarize their main finding as follows:

> When the U.S. economy was decomposed into 450 sectors, a faster growth in outsourcing at a sector level is associated with a small negative growth in jobs in that sector [...]. However, when the U.S. economy was decomposed into 96 sectors [...] there is no correlation between job growth and growth of outsourcing at the sector level. These results seem sensible. At sufficiently disaggregated levels, every outsourced job is a job lost. Hence, job growth and outsourcing may be negatively related. At the other extreme, for the economy as a whole, outsourcing is likely to change only the sectoral composition of the jobs, but not necessarily the aggregate level of employment. (ibid.: 17)

The results for the United Kingdom are similar and support the assumption that outsourcing services has no negative net effect on manufacturing employment, while no robust result was obtained for services employment (ibid.: 19f.). While these findings are highly informative in themselves, they contain no information about the effects of non-service outsourcing. Further, they only cover two countries with particularly flexible labour markets.

However, as Anderton et al. (2002) argue, labour market institutions are likely to make a difference in the way an economy adjusts to the effects of outsourcing, through changes in employment or in relative wages. Their study for Sweden, Italy, the United States and the United Kingdom contains no information on the absolute employment effects, but they show that outsourcing is associated with a relative decline in demand for less skilled labour as reflected in falling employment and wage-bill shares for low-skill labour (ibid.). The authors use imports from low-wage countries as a (very wide) proxy for outsourcing which they operationalize as imports from non-OECD countries (based on the OECD-membership before 1994; see ibid.: Fn. 10). Kucera and Milberg (2003: 604) use the same measure to examine how growing import penetration from these countries has affected absolute employment in the manufacturing sector (without however labelling it 'outsourcing'). Based on a factor content analysis they estimate that trade with non-OECD countries, from the late 1970s to the mid-1990s, cost a total of 3.5 million manufacturing jobs in ten old OECD member-countries. It is important to bear in mind that this should not be equated with the net effect of outsourcing, and that gains in service employment could potentially offset the job losses. Falk and Koebel (2002) take a different approach in their study of the German manufacturing sector. They conclude that the growing demand for imported intermediates and purchased services is a consequence of output growth, and does not substitute domestic labour inputs (ibid.: 582).

A potential source of error in most conventional studies is the assumption of inter-sectoral independence, i.e. they assume that jobs are lost in the sector that outsources. Egger and Egger (2005) argue that neglecting any interdependence of industries is "a major shortcoming, since the estimated wage and employment effects of international outsourcing may be downward biased, if inter-sectoral multiplier effects are ignored" (ibid.: 351). This critique also applies to some of their own, earlier research for Austrian manufacturing (Egger and Egger 2003).

Are jobs "exported" from one country to another?

On a global scale, outsourcing is likely to have positive effects on employment. In addition to the effects of output growth, the employment intensity of production might increase. If different factor scarcities drive outsourcing, relocation of production or services to a country with relative abundance of labour should change the factor mix used for production or service provision towards higher employment intensity, i.e. more jobs will be created in the 'South' than are lost in the 'North'. Agrawal et al. (2003) provide examples of why it makes sense, from a business standpoint, to reengineer service provision processes (or production methods) towards greater use of labour, while decreasing the use of capital. Cheaper labour also allows companies to carry greater "slack" to meet peak demand, hence increasing the quality of service delivery (see e.g. Dossani and Kenney, 2004: 13).

What follows from this, however, is also that the new jobs created in the 'South' will have a lower productivity than those that are lost in the 'North' (since more work hours are spent in producing the same output). Nonetheless, from the perspective of the southern country, this can still mean (and will generally mean) that labour is shifted to a higher-productivity use than before. But there is an additional effect: The availability of low-wage labour can make it feasible to carry out activities where the cost previously exceeded the value created (see ibid.; Agrawal et al. 2003; Bhagwati et al. 2004: 99). It is thus possible that a job created in the 'South' is not just a job relocated from the 'North', but a genuinely new job. As UNCTAD emphasizes in the World Investment Report 2004, outsourcing is not a "zero sum game" and "[j]obs created in [service] exporting locations through offshoring do not equal jobs lost in importing countries" (UNCTAD, 2004b: 176). It would thus be misleading to look at the employment effects in terms of jobs being "exported" from one country to another.

Employment effects in developing and transitional countries

It is difficult to say with any certainty how much employment is generated in the host countries as a result of outsourcing. This is true for manufacturing outsourcing (where one would, depending on the definition used, have to distinguish between the production of intermediate inputs and final products), but even for services outsourcing. For India, the National Association of Software and Services Companies (NASSCOM) estimates that IT-Enabled Services/Business

Process Outsourcing accounted for just over 250,000 jobs in fiscal 2003-04 (up from 106,000 in 2001-02). The software exporting sector employed another 270,000 people, compared to 170,000 two years earlier.[6] A survey by UNCTAD indicates that these job gains make India the greatest net beneficiary in the developing world (UNCTAD 2004b: 169ff.). Although this represents a substantial number of job opportunities, it is relatively minor in relation to India's rapidly growing labour force. Moreover, a detailed study shows that there are "high entry barriers based on caste, class and gender in the software [and IT-enabled] labour market in India" that work against already disadvantaged groups (Vijayabaskar et al., 2001: 46).

According to UNCTAD, the Philippines has also seen a rapid growth in service centres; the call centre industry alone gives employment to some 27,000 people. Malaysia and Singapore have also received investments in new software development centres or have been selected to host the regional headquarters of multinational enterprises. In Latin America and the Caribbean, Brazil, Chile, Costa Rica and Mexico have attracted investments in service centres by mayor international companies that have relocated back-office support or software development, among others. In Africa, investment has mainly been in call-centres. Here, South Africa has been the prime location and now employs close to 80,000 people to handle calls from overseas customers,[7] with countries like Ghana, Mauritius, Morocco, Senegal and Tunisia following. In Eastern Europe, the Czech Republic, Poland and Hungary have received major investments by multinationals in service centres; among them are DHL's new European IT centre in the Czech Republic and the relocation of Philips' European accounting services to Lódz (see UNCTAD, 2004b: 169ff.). It is, however, difficult to decide whether a company's decision to concentrate certain activities in one location to reap the benefits of economies of scale should qualify as 'international outsourcing' or 'offshoring' just because this location happens to be a transitional or emerging economy.

While the number of jobs created as a result of outsourcing or relocation of in-house service provision is likely to grow in the future, there are supply-side constraints that restrict future growth. Although the above cited figure on the "doubling of the global workforce" (Freeman 2005) suggests that labour supply is abundant, only a small fraction of the new entrants have college education in disciplines relevant to the skilled segment of services outsourcing – such as engineering, accounting and finance, life sciences and medicine. A recent study by the McKinsey Global Institute estimates that there are some 33 million young professionals with such degrees in 28 developing and transitional sample countries that include the main outsourcing destinations such as India, China, Russia and Brazil (see Farrell et al., 2005b). However, interviews with human

---

[6] See various fact sheets on www.nasscom.org.

[7] While substantial, this number must be put into perspective, and appears minor if compared to the roughly 540,000 agents that were employed by call centres in the United Kingdom (see Department of Trade and Industry, 2004: 26)

resource managers of multinational companies suggest that only 13 per cent of these would be suitable for actual employment, given obstacles such as insufficient language proficiency, cultural barriers and lower educational standards. Competition from domestic companies and lack of regional mobility further reduces the pool. As a result, McKinsey estimates that only "2.8 to 3.3 million [...] young professionals are available for hire by export-oriented service offshoring companies" (Farrell et al. 2005b: 50). However, the study also indicates that, with the possible exception of engineering, demand falls far short of supply in the short term (Farrell et al. 2005c: 22ff.). By 2008, total offshore service employment in eight high-skills job categories is expected to reach 1.24 million, up from an estimated 0.57 million in 2003 (Farrell et al. 2005a: 24ff.). Extrapolating to all job categories (including support staff), McKinsey arrives at the already cited total of 4.1 million outsourcing-related services jobs by 2008, up from 1.5 million in 2003 (ibid.). However welcome such a job creation would be, it is obvious that it does not by itself solve the un– and under-employment problem that developing and transitional countries face.

4. Effects on skill differentials and inequality

Skill bias, income inequality and social exclusion in developed countries
Looking at the employment impact of outsourcing exclusively in terms of the number of jobs lost or gained would mean missing an important part of the picture. After a careful survey of the available evidence, a publication by the European Union concludes that "the impact on employment in the EU may not be so much a quantitative one, in terms of absolute decline in the numbers of jobs, but a qualitative one" since the remaining jobs (and the newly created ones) were "likely to demand relatively high skill levels" (European Foundation for the Improvement of Living and Working Conditions, 2004: 12). Similarly, Bhagwati et al. (2004) argue for the United States that low-skills, low-wage jobs in call centres, for example, will be lost, while higher-skilled jobs in medical, legal and other services will be gained as a result of insourcing – with little overall net gains or losses (ibid.: 110). This skill-bias implies that the transition from one job to another can be difficult for individual workers. There can thus be substantial adjustment costs at the micro-level even when the overall number of jobs does not decline. The problem is exacerbated when job losses accumulate in one region (see Rowthorn, 2004: 11f. for an example). Given the distributional consequences and the danger that unskilled workers or other groups may be excluded from the labour market, this becomes an area of high social and political relevance (see Box 5 for a related aspect, the gender dimension of outsourcing).

The skill-bias of outsourcing is an area that has been subject to intense academic research, especially with respect to the countries that outsource (and to a lesser degree for those that provide service or goods inputs). Feenstra and Hanson (2001) develop a simple theoretical model where the production of a low-skill labour intensive input is outsourced. They can show under different specifications that this will depress the relative demand for low-skill labour within industries, and that relative wages for low-skilled workers will fall. They emphasize that the employment shift in favour of skilled workers occurs within industries, whereas standard models of trade can only explain shifts between industries (generally from low-skill to high-skill industries). Outsourcing thus has effects similar to those of skill-biased technological change (ibid.: 20), and adds to the labour market consequences of the latter. On the other hand, Kohler (2002) concludes from his general equilibrium model that the distributional consequences are not determined by the factor-intensities of the production stage that is outsourced, but by the factor intensities of the activities that remain in the domestic economy. Since these increase in value, it may well be that unskilled labour actually benefits.[8] Similarly, Jones and Kierzkowski (2001a) can not only model how the loss of a labour-intensive production segment will lead to a drop in unskilled wages, but also show that – under certain conditions – wages will actually rise. They stress that they do not wish "to dispute the wisdom of the observation that losses of labour-intensive activities to other countries in trade spells trouble for unskilled labour, but to suggest that this is not always the case" (ibid.: 29). Put together, the theoretical literature suggests that the mechanism is more complex than often assumed, and warrants empirical investigation.

There are a number of studies available that have addressed this task. Using data for the United States, Japan, Hong Kong and Mexico, Feenstra and Hanson (2001) show that outsourcing is indeed associated with a rising wage share for non-production (i.e., skilled) workers. This is consistent with their earlier finding that outsourcing explains roughly 15 per cent of the rise in relative wages of skilled workers, whereas technological change accounts for circa 35 per cent (Feenstra and Hanson, 1999). Other studies support the same conclusion. For example, Anderton et al. (2002) demonstrate in their previously cited study that outsourcing (which they measure as imports from low-wage countries) has led to falling employment and wage-bill shares of low-skilled workers in the United Kingdom, the United States, Italy and Sweden. In a study for the United Kingdom, Hijzen et al. (2004) find that "international outsourcing has had a strong negative impact on the demand for unskilled labour" (ibid.: 17). For Germany, Geishecker and Görg (2004) show that outsourcing reduced real wages for workers in the lowest of three skill categories by 1.8 per cent during the 1990s, while those of workers in the highest group increased by 3.3 per cent due to outsourcing.

In the case of France, Strauss-Kahn (2003) argues that the country's labour market institutions prevented large movements in relative wages and that outsourcing predominantly affected the employment prospects of unskilled workers. According to her findings, outsourcing "accounts for 11 per cent to 15 per cent of the within-industry shift away from unskilled workers toward skilled workers over the 1977-1985 period and for about 25 per cent over the 1985-1993 period" (ibid.: 23). Much of the remainder can, however, be attributed to technological change. A similar result is reported by Egger and Egger (2003) for

---

[8] A similar point was previously made by Arndt (1997).

Box 5: The Gender Dimension of Outsourcing

The mainstream economic literature remains largely silent about the gender implications of outsourcing. This is a somewhat crucial omission since some of the jobs that are most in danger are dominated by female employment. For manufacturing, this is the case in the textiles, apparel, leather and leather goods industries that have all seen a substantial re-location away from the industrialized countries. The rising import penetration for these goods therefore often led to a disproportionate fall in female employment in the old OECD countries. Kucera and Milberg (2000) can show that this was crucial to the gender-biased, negative employment effects caused by an expansion in trade with non-OECD countries. For the service sector, the re-location of call centres from the high-income countries to lower-wage destinations could again affect female employment disproportionately. Estimates for the United Kingdom show that about two thirds of all call centre-agents are female, and women would thus bear most of any potential job losses (see Department of Trade and Industry 2004: 61).

There is a similar gender dimension on the receiving end of outsourcing. Ngai (2004) reports for the Shenzhen Special Economic Zone in China that "more than 90 per cent of the labour force in the light manufacturing industries was young, female, and under 25 years of age" (ibid.: 30). While the establishment of factories producing for European and North American corporations provides female migrant workers with job opportunities absent in the rural areas, the jobs created often do not constitute 'decent work'. For example, a case study of a typical garment factory in Shenzhen by the NGO Chinese Working Women Network gives testimony of a lack of rights at work (including no protection against unfair dismissal). In contravention of Chinese law, working times were between 72 and 77 hours per week (Ngai 2004). Like in the case of China, the textiles and apparel sector is strongly dominated by female employment in most of the countries that produce for Western brands. Again, the general picture is that outsourcing has helped to create jobs for women that are superior to traditional alternatives in e.g. agriculture, but that gender-biased wage discrimination and poor working conditions often remain issues of concern (see Tran-Nguyen and Beviglia Zampetti 2004: 141ff.). As Barrientos et al. (2004) argue, female employment is generally concentrated at the informal end of global production chains, leaving women without adequate social protection and job security.

Services outsourcing has also created numerous job opportunities for women in developing countries such as India and the Philippines. While precise data seem to be scarce, some studies suggest that women are still significantly under-represented and that female employment is concentrated in the relatively low-skilled segments of the software industry and in ITC-enabled services (for India see Vijayabaskar et al. 2001: 41).

Austria, a country with one of the highest unionization rates in Europe. They find that manufacturing outsourcing to Eastern Europe had little effect on wage rates, and attribute this to union bargaining power and the centralized wage-setting process. Outsourcing did, however, have a significant skill bias in terms of employment prospects. They conclude that "[o]utsourcing to Eastern economies accounts for about one quarter of the change in relative employment in favour of high-skilled labour in the last decade" (ibid.: 639). In a more recent article, they concede that "these results are potentially as preliminary as those of others, since they were derived under the assumption of inter-sectoral independence" (Egger and Egger, 2005: 353). However, they can show that indirect spill-over effects from one industry to another have substantial impact on employment, and that neglecting them leads to an underestimation of the employment impact of outsourcing (ibid.).

The empirical evidence is thus broadly in line with the theoretical argument that outsourcing of low-skill intensive production stages away from the high-wage countries predominantly affects low-skilled workers. They will, depending on labour market institutions, either suffer a fall in relative wages or see their employment prospects diminish. Falling relative wages and zero earnings in case of unemployment both work in the same direction and increase inequality of (market) incomes. International outsourcing thus has effects similar to those of labour-saving technological change, and adds to the consequences of the latter (see e.g. Feenstra and Hanson, 1999 and 2001, Strauss-Kahn, 2003). Gottschalk and Smeeding (1997) argue that the shift in demand from low-skilled towards highly-skilled workers was in fact a significant factor behind the rise in earnings dispersion which they can detect for most industrialized countries in the 1980s. In turn, rising earnings dispersion was a major cause of growing inequality of disposable household incomes (ibid.).[9] More recent studies confirm that income inequality has grown in many OECD-countries during the 1980s and 1990s (Atkinson 2003; Cornia et al. 2004).

Although the isolated contribution of outsourcing to rising income inequality is probably still relatively small, the dynamism of the phenomenon indicates that it is a factor that cannot simply be neglected. If the extent of outsourcing is to rise further, the downward pressure on low-skill wages will grow. Greater earnings dispersion does, however, not translate into higher income inequality in a quasi-automatic manner. As Atkinson (2004) emphasizes, government policy has a significant impact on how changes in market incomes (i.e. prior to taxes and transfers) translate into changes in inequality of disposable incomes (i.e. after taxes and transfers). He investigates the redistributive impact of the government budget and finds remarkable differences between countries and across time. It is informative to look at the cases of Finland and the United Kingdom, two countries that saw significant rises in inequality of market incomes throughout the 1980s and early 1990s. In Finland, the Gini coefficient for market incomes grew by ten percentage points between 1981 and 1994 (in particular due to rising unemployment in the early 1990s). This sharp rise in inequality was, however, "offset by the government budget to the extent that inequality in disposable income did not increase" (ibid.: 229). In the United Kingdom, inequality in market incomes grew less rapidly than in Finland. However, the redistributive impact of the government budget fell dramatically between 1984 and 1990 and amplified income inequality. Different policy choices in Finland (rising replacement ratios in case of unemployment, and a growth in total transfers) and the United Kingdom (less transfers, but also less progressive direct taxes and more regressive indirect taxes) clearly had a major impact on the distribution of disposable incomes (see ibid.). There is thus a role for public policy in coping with adverse distributive consequences of outsourcing.

While cushioning the effects of rising earnings dispersion is one policy option, policy can also attempt to contain rising inequality of market incomes. Of particular relevance in this context are labour market institutions and policies. In addition to their allocative and dynamic efficiency functions, they also have

---

[9] However, it should not be overlooked that growth at the very top of the distribution, in part through capital income, is another significant factor (see Atkinson, 2003).

a role in promoting equity (van der Hoeven and Taylor 2000; van der Hoeven and Saget, 2004). Instruments that can enhance equity include minimum wage legislation, employment protection, collective bargaining arrangements and active labour market policies. With their explicit focus on enhancing labour market participation, active labour market policies have a particular relevance in the context of outsourcing. Even if their primary focus is on allocative and dynamic efficiency through matching labour demand and supply, they can at the same time enhance equity by reintegrating displaced workers and by upgrading skills of low-skilled workers to match them with jobs that have higher skills requirements (see Auer et al., 2005). In the light of mixed evaluation results, Auer et al. recommend that active labour market policies "should evolve towards a more permanent policy instrument for the management of change" (ibid.: 78). The need for such an instrument will be greatest in the countries most affected by globalization; it is thus not surprising that spending on active labour market policies in OECD countries increases with economic openness (ibid.: 4).

Skill bias and income inequality in developing and transitional countries

Simply put, the theoretical consequences are quite clear for the countries that *receive* outsourced activities: since they predominantly require low-skilled labour, workers in this group should benefit in the receiving countries at least. However, this need not be the case since activities that are considered to involve low skills might well be high-skilled from the perspective of a developing country (Feenstra and Hanson 1997). Again, the effect of outsourcing on wage dispersion remains open to empirical investigation. Unfortunately, the evidence collected to resolve the issue is still rather patchy. Feenstra and Hanson (1997) themselves offer some insights in the case of Mexico. Here, the outsourcing of production from the United States caused a sharp increase in the demand for skilled labour in the country's northern border regions. Their estimations show that FDI into the *maquila* sector, that is closely associated with the outsourcing activities, can "account for a large portion of the increase in the skilled labor share of total wages" and an associated shift in relative wages (ibid.: 391). In a similar exercise, Egger and Stehrer (2003) examine the distributional effects of rising intermediate goods exports of 14 manufacturing industries in the Czech Republic, Hungary and Poland during the 1990s. They find that, while the skill-premium in all three countries has risen over the period, outsourcing activities have helped to contain this rise. Thus, and in contrast to Mexico, outsourcing has worked in favour of unskilled labour there. A likely explanation for these diverging results is that the skill levels in Central and Eastern Europe are similar to those in the old EU countries, while there is a gap in terms of skill endowments between the United States and Mexico. The same would hold for outsourcing of IT services to India, where the increased demand for software engineers is likely to widen wage gaps. While strongly advocating the free trade in services on the merits of welfare gains, the WTO concedes that IT outsourcing "may not have a [...] favourable effect on income distribution" in India (WTO, 2005: 289).

Returns on capital and labour

In addition to shifts in the skill-premium, there is another channel through which outsourcing can affect inequality: general changes in the returns on labour (of all skill levels) relative to those on capital. Richard Freeman (2005) argues that the entry into the global workforce of workers from countries with relatively low capital stocks has led to a substantial decline in the global capital/labour ratio. This is likely to depress wages since it "shifts the balance of power in markets towards capital, as more workers compete for working with that capital" (ibid.). The power shift in favour of capital holds for trade in general, but also for the specific case of outsourcing. As discussed above, outsourcing enables companies to cut labour costs by a substantial margin while retaining identical levels of output, or even improving them. The McKinsey Global Institute (2003) estimates that the direct cost savings amount to 58 cents for every US$ 1 a company spends on outsourced services in India. In theory, these cost savings could be passed on to consumers, distributed to the company's remaining workforce (through increased wages), or kept as profits (and hence accrue to the owners of capital).

These distributional aspects are not discussed prominently in the literature, but there is no indication that Freeman's assessment is wrong and that that workers in the developed countries are in a position to negotiate wage increases. While benefits to consumers do not directly influence the relative returns on capital and labour (and are hence neutral), McKinsey argues that outsourcing-induced cost-savings "will lead to higher profitability [and] increased [stock market] valuations" (McKinsey Global Institute, 2003: 10). In the light of generally positive market reactions to the announcement of outsourcing plans, this assessment seems to be in line with the dominant perception among market participants. Given the intense competition among Indian service providers, it is not surprising that the additional income that accrues to Indian labour (by McKinsey's calculation ten cents for every US$ spent) and profits retained in India (another ten cents) are relatively small if compared to the gains that accrue to the US. In sum, it seems likely that the "arbitrage gains" realized through outsourcing first and foremost increase the earnings of enterprises in the industrialized countries, with corresponding benefits for shareholders.

5. DISCUSSION: WHAT ARE THE POLICY IMPLICATIONS OF OUTSOURCING?

The rising trend in international outsourcing has several implications for national and international policies that relate to the ILO's mandate. Three areas would seem of particular importance:

-   Firstly, outsourcing has an employment-generating effect in developing countries. If it can be ensured that the jobs created are 'decent jobs', outsourcing could offer women and men a chance to work their way out of poverty. From this angle, outsourcing is a facet of globalization that has the potential to make it more 'fair' between countries.[10] On the other hand, this will be of little comfort to those workers in the developed world who see their own jobs put at risk by outsourcing. However, a thorough examination of the literature leads to the conclusion that the fears of job-losses due to outsourcing are often greater than the actual threat. The literature indicates that international outsourcing might even have a positive net effect on the quality and quantity of employment in the industrialized countries. Hence, the simplistic notion of jobs being "exported" from one country to another is often misleading.

– However, and this is the second main implication, outsourcing has important consequences for the labour markets in the industrialized countries. Since outsourcing is likely to shift the demand towards highly skilled workers, policy makers need to find ways to mitigate the social and economic cost of job losses for low-skilled workers. This necessitates not only adequate social safety nets, but also makes skills upgrading even more urgent as a strategy for the industrialized countries. Key to making outsourcing a 'win-win game' is to re-employ those workers that are made redundant in a productive way and to ease their transition into a new job (see ILO, 2004: 79). Arguably, carefully designed active labour market policies have a role to play in achieving this objective (see Auer et al., 2005).

– Thirdly, outsourcing has potentially negative effects on inequality in both the South and the North. It has often led to a rising skill-premium and growing wage-differentials, or, when labour market regimes in the North prevent a fall in wages for low-skilled workers, it reduced the employment prospects of workers in this group. Moreover, it can weaken the position of workers versus the owners of capital, and change the relative returns on labour and capital. The development of policies that ensure social inclusion and distributional justice thus becomes a central issue if outsourcing is to be made politically and socially sustainable.

All of the above indicates that outsourcing is an aspect of globalization that requires active governance.[11] The policies needed create new sources of employment to ease the transition of workers between jobs, and to contain rising inequality, will differ between countries, but it is essential to recognize the challenge ahead. Actively managing change will be the best way to avoid a protectionist response, the initial instinct of many policy makers,[12] and to reap the potential benefits that outsourcing can bring for developed and developing countries alike.

---

[10] This is one of the main themes of the World Commission on the Social Dimension of Globalization report (2004).

[11] See the more detailed discussion by the World Commission on the Social Dimension of Globalization (2004: 54ff.).

[12] For an overview of existing and proposed anti-outsourcing legislation in the United States, see Klinger and Sykes (2004). The authors conclude that both the US constitution and the WTO's Government Procurement Agreement limit the ability of state and federal governments' attempts to restrict services outsourcing.

APPENDIX III: NOTES ON THE FRANCE/ILO DIALOGUE ON THE SOCIAL DIMENSION OF GLOBALIZATION

BY LEONELLO TRONTI

If we take a look at the impact of globalization from the Italian point of view, we see that the tendency of Italian goods and services to deteriorate in international competitiveness, as has strongly emerged in recent months and years, is by no means new: its first signals can be traced back to the mid-1970s. What makes the present situation different is that today Italy cannot resort to monetary deval-uations such as those that had long helped it to counteract its tendency to become less and less competitive. The Euro has reduced the trade balance constraint on growth; nevertheless, it has brought to the fore the need to confront and solve the structural problems that hinder Italian competitiveness.

In analysing these problems, it is quite easy to dispense with some of the ideological residuals on the social origins of this long-term tendency. It is, in fact, impossible to blame the bad results of these years (as in the past) on such socially sensitive areas as industrial conflicts, fast-growing labour cost, the lack of flexibility in labour relationships and the excessive presence of government-owned enterprises. After a long decade of very low-level conflicts, wage moder-ation (if not wage deflation), widespread diffusion of flexible labour contracts and relevant privatizations, the problems are still there, possibly greater than before.

We have, therefore, to look elsewhere. The debate on the unsolved problems that are impeding the development of the Italian economy has been, in the last decade, quite extensive. Wide convergence, however, has been found on some structural aspects of the Italian economic system, such as:

i)   the weight of small and medium-sized firms in the industrial structure is overwhelming, and the system too biased towards traditional production;

ii) the capacity of the system as a whole to invest in learning and innovation is insufficient;

iii) the presence of segments and areas sheltered from international (and often also national) competition is widespread, fuelling inflation and burdening the exposed sector;

iv) the survival of large inefficient segments protected by the poor functioning of the market;

v) the ownership structure of big enterprises is prevalently family-based, inefficient and often not transparent;

vi) the capital market is underdeveloped and inefficient;

vii) the public administration often appears inadequate to the tasks facing it.

Industrial policies (where implemented) have often not succeeded in being effective; but also many employers seem to have failed in successfully confronting the market: the lack of investment in innovation has to be attributed above all to the shortcomings of the private sector, that has conversely invested much in activities sheltered from international competition or in financial assets.

In recent years, however, production and employment globalization has increased its relevance for Italian firms and, within this process, there have been many examples of production system fragmentation as a consequence of international outsourcing and relocation. These new tendencies are not confined simply to multinational corporations, but have become an opportunity (or an obligation) also for small and medium-sized firms.

Italy is a latecomer in the process of international outsourcing, but is quickly making up ground. As the possibility of a gap between economic gains from international offshoring and national employment appears to be growing, the problem of designing effective policies to upgrade the production systems so to ensure the quantity and quality of employment is becoming increasingly evident. The question entails not only the choice of adequate public policies but, above all, that of the relationship between the public and private spheres upon which to build the future economic development of the country. This situation, however, is not a peculiar feature of the Italian economy as, with some differences, it may well apply to many if not all European countries.

In a national perspective, the problem rests with the prevention, early identification and management of labour redundancies – a subject on which there has been ample discussion and wide proposal and experimentation of solutions. In an international perspective, however, a relevant part of the problem could be tackled by an extension to the global dimension of the European Union concept of social dumping, and of the rules and practices devised to fight it. The European experience in this field should serve as a basis for the creation of an international understanding of the problem of *socially unfair competition*, and provide guidelines both to countries and international organizations on the ways to contain it.

In addition, new directions could be found in designing the instruments to discourage socially unfair competition, both at the national and at the company level. Useful results could come from the development of social rating services, provided by public or even by private agencies covered by national or international mandates. These bodies should engage in the activities necessary to investigate both the working and living conditions of workers in the different parts of the globe, and the international production chain of multinational enterprises and groups, so to evaluate and rate both countries and companies from the point of view of socially unfair economic competition.

A relevant part of the necessary information could come from the ILO as well as from the WTO. Also many of the actions to be undertaken to fix the rules of a socially fair economic competition, and sanction companies and/or countries responsible for breaking those rules could find their natural seats in the ILO, the WTO and their increased collaboration. But national and EU regulations also can foster the creation of private social rating services by requiring European firms to be "socially certified" by these services.

"Socially unfair" companies could be subject to fines, and the income could be used both to help nationally displaced workers and to finance international social rating bodies.

APPENDIX IV: INTERNATIONALIZATION OF EMPLOYMENT: NOTES ON LATIN AMERICAN COUNTRIES

BY ADRIANA MARSHALL

In these notes, I discuss scattered evidence on the employment outcomes of trade liberalization and foreign direct investment (FDI), with reference to Latin American countries, paying special attention to the effects of outsourcing under traditional and new forms.

1. INTERNATIONAL TRADE

It is common knowledge that in many Latin American countries the long period of highly-protected import substitution industrialization ended during the 1980s and particularly in the 1990s. In these decades, the drastic economic reforms included liberalization of international trade to diverse degrees and at different speeds. In addition, there was an increasing emphasis on export diversification, namely on the need to expand manufactured exports.

The GDP share of international trade in the Latin American and Caribbean region as a whole increased from 25 to 36 per cent between 1985 and 2001, this being mainly the result of the increase in the GDP share of imports (from 10 to 19 per cent), whereas the share of exports rose only from 15 to 18 per cent. Countries like Brazil and Mexico (where it went from 10 to 30 per cent) showed above average relative increases in import shares. In Mexico and Chile the GDP share of exports also increased considerably, from 15 to 27 per cent, and from 28 to 35 per cent, respectively. The share of manufacturing exports in total merchandise exports rose, for the region as a whole, from 25 to 48 per cent in the same period, with above average relative increases in Chile, Colombia, Bolivia and Mexico, among others (World Bank data). These increases reflect in part, and in certain countries, the growing incidence of *maquiladora* industries; the share of *maquiladora* exports in total exports increased considerably in Mexico – from 19 per cent in 1985 to 47 per cent in 2003 – and in several Central American (Buitelaar et al., 1999; www.inegi.gob.mx).

The combination of trade liberalization and domestic currency appreciation proved to be the worst in terms of economic and labour market effects. In Argentina, manufacturing experienced a profound restructuring process that affected industries producing for the internal market (closing down of firms unable to compete, rapidly increasing productivity in those that survived), that was extremely adverse in terms of employment effects (employment decreased at an annual rate of almost – 4 per cent between 1992 and 2000, before the crisis and devaluation of 2002). Adverse effects were noted also with reference to Mexico and Brazil, where manufacturing employment increased slightly. The employment share of manufacturing decreased markedly in, among others, Argentina, Chile and Uruguay, while in Brazil there was practically no change and in Mexico it rose, mainly due to the positive export performance of *maquiladoras*.

While the negative employment effects of trade liberalization with domestic currency appreciation seem to have been widely documented and recognized, it is not clear whether trade liberalization per se, carried out in the context of sound industrial policies would have had the same impacts. On the other hand, there is serious disagreement as to the effects of trade liberalization on the degree of wage inequality, opposing views presenting evidence in favour of each position. The effects of trade liberalization via rising import levels differ from those derived from increasing manufactured exports, and in those countries that succeeded in expanding exports this might have generated additional employment, (partially) offsetting the negative impacts of unregulated imports.

2. FOREIGN DIRECT INVESTMENT

The employment effects of FDI are varied, depending on the type of and reason for the investment. The net effects in terms of employment creation (not counting multiplicative impacts) depend on whether investment is via either acquisition of existing firms (and, in this case, on whether it is followed by employment cuts or not), or creation of new businesses (and, in this case, on whether it displaces existing domestic business or not).

FDI may also be classified according to the reason that transnational firms have for investing in particular countries (CEPAL, 2003). Foreign firms may search for: i. natural resources; ii. national or regional markets; and iii. greater efficiency in order to expand third markets (there is a fourth alternative, search for technological assets, not applicable to FDI in Latin America). The objective behind FDI bears on the employment effects. Whereas investment either via acquisitions or installation of new firms pursuing the first two strategies (search for natural resources, and for domestic or regional markets) may be less dependent on the level of labour costs in the host country, the "search for efficiency to expand the third markets" is very often determined by low labour costs and other incentives (tax exemptions, proximity, natural resources, skills, exchange rate, etc.) that reduce costs, and in this sense it would be the most likely to provide low quality employment and to require greater effort. Employment conditions might vary according to each country's global labour market situation, and to the regulatory regime existing in each country, e.g. according to whether foreign firms are exempted or not from applying the general labour regulations, being governed by special regimes for export processing zones (EPZs).

According to CEPAL (2003), mining in Argentina and Chile, as well as tourism in Mexico and the Caribbean basin, are examples of FDI seeking natural resources. The search for internal or regional markets explains FDI in the automobile industry in MERCOSUR countries; in food, beverages and tobacco in Argentina, Brazil and Mexico; and in banking, telecommunications, retail trade, gas and electricity in many countries, including Argentina, Chile and Mexico. Finally, the objective of expanding third markets by way of improved efficiency is behind FDI in the automobile industry in Mexico, and in the electronic and garment industries in Mexico and the Caribbean basin, as well as in administrative services in Costa Rica.

In fact, FDI has a long tradition in Latin America. Apart from the agricultural and mining enclaves, from the 1960s FDI in the manufacturing sector of the most industrialized Latin American countries generally meant creation of local branches of multinational firms. In this period, during which the growth model was based on import substitution for the domestic market and a high level of tariff protection, the main incentive for investment in manufacturing was to cater for, at the time expanding, internal markets. There might have been some displacement of local firms, but generally installation of foreign firms implied net employment creation, with multiplicative effects in others sectors. On the whole, there was not much difference between foreign and domestic manufacturing firms in wages and employment conditions, once economic, skill, and other factors are controlled.[1] Moreover, foreign firms, more advanced technologically, often had better wages and employment conditions than domestic firms. They signed collective agreements with industrial or enterprise trade unions.

The economic reforms of the late 1980s and the 1990s included measures not only to liberalize international trade but also to privatize public utilities. FDI (including capital from other Latin American countries) played a role in the privatization of public enterprises, most of which became foreign-owned firms, enjoying monopoly conditions. In addition, in several countries, there were many acquisitions (in manufacturing, retail trade, banking, insurance, etc.). The GDP share of FDI in the Latin American and Caribbean region as a whole increased fivefold between 1985 and 2001 (from 1 per cent in 1985, to almost 5 per cent in 2001; gross FDI; World Bank data). Foreign manufacturing firms operated in the context of trade liberalization, and many restructured (as domestic firms did), or moved plants or production of parts across countries. In the new context of increased unemployment and, sometimes, of new labour regulations, foreign as domestic firms re-negotiated wages, employment and working conditions, with trade unions, seeking to reduce labour costs and improve productivity. The need for cutting labour costs and for increasing external competitiveness was more imperative in those countries where economic reforms had led to domestic currency appreciation as in Argentina, and Mexico before 1995. Employment conditions tended to be downgraded in both foreign and domestic

---

[1] FDI in agriculture and mining enclaves might have had distinctive characteristics.

firms (through collective bargaining or not), and both increasingly externalized part of their production and administrative components. Also privatized firms, now in foreign hands, deeply restructured employment and work organization, often externalizing many activities. In addition, many countries established free zones to attract FDI, some of them with ad hoc labour regulations.

3. FDI SEEKING TO REDUCE COSTS FOR EXPANDING THIRD MARKETS: OUTSOURCING AND FREE ZONES[2]

The advantages and disadvantages of developing EPZs to promote economic growth and their effects on labour received considerable attention in the literature. Some consider that EPZs contribute to economic diversification, provide export income, and create jobs with better wages and working conditions than in other sectors, whereas others argue that they lead to specialization in a limited number of goods, require mainly imported inputs, have few linkages with the rest of the economy, and provide poor working conditions.

In Latin America, many EPZs are already well established, having started, as the manufacturing *maquiladoras* in Mexico, in the 1960s. In the 1980s and 1990s more and more countries were keen on creating EPZs, enacting legislation to this effect, as in Ecuador, Peru, and countries in Central America. EPZ employment, concentrated in electronics and the garment industry, rose spectacularly, mainly during the 1990s. In the period 1983-1994, Mexican *maquiladoras* created 40,000 new jobs annually, but the figures increased to 120,000 per year in 1995-2000 (Alarcón and Zepeda, 2004). In El Salvador and Honduras *maquila* employment rose from about 2,000 in 1986 to 50,000/60,000 ten years later. In spite of fast employment growth and important local impacts, EPZs seldom absorbed a large segment of the total labour force. From their inception, women, generally young and single, have accounted for the majority of the labour force employed in Latin American EPZs.

Undoubtedly, the net employment effect of foreign *maquiladoras* is substantial, particularly where, as in Mexico, this is in sharp contrast with the disappointing employment performance of non *maquiladora* manufacturing (Alarcón and Zepeda, 2004). However, while the devaluation of the Mexican peso in the early 1990s had strengthened the *maquiladoras*, its later appreciation and the impact of NAFTA slowed down export and employment growth (Alarcón and Zepeda, 2004). After 2000 employment in *maquiladoras* first ceased to expand, and then over 200,000 workers lost their jobs. This (as discussed in Bendesky et al., 2003) casts doubts on the continuity of employment absorption by a sector now facing the competition of lower-wage countries that attract FDI at the expense of Mexico, and vulnerable to recessions in the US, main destination of *maquiladora* exports.

With reference to the Caribbean basin, Buitelaar et al. (1999) argue that the high import content and small added value of local *maquilas* limit their possible

---

[2] This section draws partially on Marshall (1999) and the literature cited therein on EPZs.

contribution to overall growth; that the majority of the workforce of *maquilas* lack skills, and this despite the fact that foreign firms make more use than local firms of advanced technology and modern work organization and management methods. They contrast the experience of these countries with that of Mexico, where, allegedly, the *maquilas* had shifted from a mainly unskilled workforce to incorporating more skilled labour. However, Bendesky et al.. (2003) criticize this "optimistic" view of Mexican *maquiladoras* (e.g. in Gerber and Carrillo, 2003), claiming, on the basis of new and more complete information, that unskilled workers still make up the majority of *maquiladora* employment.

Wage rates and working conditions in EPZs are aligned with levels in the country where they are located, and are evidently lower than in the countries of origin of the foreign investment; this is only natural as one of the key factors for the very existence of EPZs is their lower-cost production in general and lower labour costs in particular. But compared with wages in non-EPZ manufacturing or with average wages in the same country where the EPZ is located, and once the differential skill composition of the labour force is controlled for, wages are not necessarily lower in EPZs. There seems to be considerable variation across countries. In any case, one reason for higher earnings in EPZs is the prevalence of piece-rate and incentive payment that generally means greater work effort in terms of hours of work and labour intensity.

An issue on which there is little disagreement is the weakness of trade unions and collective bargaining in EPZs, even in those countries where trade unions had been making progress. Causes of union weakness include restrictive legal requirements to permit union formation, employer hostility to trade unions; low union density elsewhere in the same country; and high turnover (among a predominantly female and young labour force). However, recently more positive developments in this area (e.g. in Mexico) were noted.

4. NEW DEVELOPMENTS: OUTSOURCING IN THE SERVICE SECTOR

In addition to manufacturing free zones of older origin, outsourcing of services is a newer and fast growing activity. Outsourcing of services has been expanding in the context of technical progress in telecommunications. As FDI in manufacturing free zones, FDI in services seeks lower costs, but demands more skilled labour, with knowledge of English, electronics and computers. In Costa Rica, since 2001, the availability of this type of labour and of adequate technological infrastructure in communications attracted FDI that developed call centres, business centres, data centres and production of software, shared services, back offices, all under the legal form of free zones (CEPAL, 2003). The availability of a relatively skilled, bilingual workforce at low cost seems to have been one important incentive attracting call centres and other services to Argentina and Costa Rica. As with manufacturing EPZs, wages and contractual conditions in services are set in relation to those prevailing in each country.

Call centres are perhaps the most conspicuous of these new developments, and recently received substantial attention. Still, there is practically no systematic collection of employment information with reference to call centres and similar new developments. Sparse information shows that for example in Argentina employment in call centres has been growing rapidly since the 2002 devaluation. Del Bono (2004) reports that in Argentina employment in call centres, many of which have offshore activities, increased from some 5,000 in 2002 to about 20,000 at present. Call centres demand high work intensity, and productivity-based supplements account for a substantial part of total wages (Del Bono, 2004).

5. FINAL COMMENTS

New FDI generates additional employment unless it displaces domestic firms with a larger or equivalent employment volume, or unless acquisitions of existing firms are followed by personnel reductions. Working conditions and wages are determined by general conditions in the host country, undoubtedly worse than those in the country of origin of the FDI. All of the host countries have high levels of open and/or hidden unemployment, and this is reflected in the level of average wages, and in wages rates paid by foreign firms including those in free zones. Undoubtedly, in situations of large unemployment, FDI tends to be beneficial in terms of job and income generation, but free zones and similar forms should not be considered to be more than transitional components of development policy, as they are very vulnerable to the economic cycle in the countries of export destination, and to the new opportunities for investing in still lower-cost labour in other regions.

Against the expected benefits of FDI in EPZs (growth of manufactured exports, incorporation of technological progress, and provision of training), stands the usual penalty of, among others, becoming trapped in import-dependent, low-added-value production with limited impact on other sectors (CEPAL, 2003). Comparable pros and cons may apply to FDI in free-zone services. Those countries that deliberately choose the type of FDI they want to have in the context of a previously defined development and industrial policy (e.g. Costa Rica, CEPAL, 2003) have the best prospects. This will be reflected in the types of employment offered and the potential for upgrading the labour force.

The level of cash transfers to the unemployed (through unemployment benefits, or anti-poverty and employment programmes) and of minimum wages contribute to determine the wage at which workers are willing to be employed in general and in free zones specifically. Increases in the amount of such cash benefits and of minimum wages will contribute to improve the labour situation in the free zones and elsewhere, but, unless more and more countries pursue the same policies, may deter new investments or even lead to disinvestment, the raison d'être for FDI in free zones being lower costs generally including labour costs. Nonetheless, in addition to labour costs, decisions to invest in free zones take into consideration other important factors (tax incentives, relative exchange rates, location and proximity to third markets, skill availability), and the margin for increasing labour protection depends on how strategic for the foreign firm is each specific investment location. Naturally, the most obviously beneficial measure would be that those countries with special labour regimes for free zones (with no employment stability, easy dismissal, etc.) eliminate them. The potential effects of "certification" (establishing and monitoring a code of conduct to be followed by multinationals) on the quality of employment in free zones has also been discussed in the literature on Latin American free zones (e.g. Frundt, 2004) but conclusions are not clear as yet.

Apart from investigating the degree of introduction of advanced technologies and work organization methods and their diffusion to other sectors in the host country, and the impacts on exports and on economic growth, research is needed on the employment effects of all types of FDI that have only occasionally been investigated. How conditions in foreign firms (including free-zone firms) compare with similar sectors in the same country, and the extent up to which they are stipulated by ad hoc labour regulations, requires more systematic investigation with reference to Latin America. Research on the employment impacts of FDI in general, and in free zones or EPZs in particular, should look specifically at least into: volume of net employment creation and share of total employment; structure of skills demanded; comparative employment conditions in terms of quality dimensions including work effort; comparative wages; compliance of standards; and training offered.

BIBLIOGRAPHY*

Addison, J.T.; McKinley, L. and Blackburn, L. (1997) "A Puzzling Aspect of the Effect of Advance Notice on Unemployment", *Industrial and Labor Relations Review*, Vol. 50, No 2, pp. 268-288.

Aglietta, M. and Rebérioux, A. (2004) *Dérives du capitalisme financier*, Albin Michel, 391 pages.

Agrawal et al. (2003) "Offshoring and beyond. Cheap labour is the beginning, not the end", in *The McKinsey Quarterly*, No. 4 (Special Edition: Global Directions), pp. 25-35.

Alarcón, D. and Zepeda, E. (2004) "Economic reform or social development? The challenges of a period of reform in Latin America: Case study of Mexico", in G.Indart, ed.: *Economic Reforms, Growth and Inequality in Latin America*, Ashgate.

Ambrosi, C.; Baleste, M. and Tacel, M. (1967) *Histoire et géographie économiques des grandes puissances à l'époque contemporaine*, Delagrave.

Amiti, M. and Wei, S-J. (2004) *Fear of Service Outsourcing: Is It Justified?* IMF Working Paper 04/186, International Monetary Fund, Washington, DC.

Andersen and Regini. (1996) *Global Law without a State?* Oxford.

Anderton, B.; Brenton, P. and Oscarson, E. (2002) *Outsourcing and Inequality*. CEPS Working Document 187, Brussels: Centre for European Policy Studies.

Andreff W. (1995) *Les multinationales globales*, La découverte, 212 pages.

Antonmattei, P.H. (2000) "Plan social: il y a urgence à réformer!", in *Droit social*, No 6, pp. 597-599.

Arnal, E., Ok, W. and Torres, R. (2001) *Knowledge, Work Organization and Economic Growth*, Labour Market and Social Policy Working Papers, No 50, June.

Arndt, S.W. (1997) 'Globalization and the Open Economy', in *North American Journal of Economics and Finance*, Vol. 8, No. 1, pp. 71-79.

—. (2002) *Production Sharing and Regional Integration*, Claremont Colleges Working Paper 2002-10, Claremont, CA: Claremont Colleges.

Arora and Gambardella (2004) *The globalization of the software industry: perspectives and opportunities for developed and developing countries*, NBER WP 10538.

Askenazy, P. (2001) "La croissance moderne", *Economic*.

Atkinson, A.B. (2003) "Income Inequality in OECD Countries: Data and Explanations". *CESifo Economic Studies*, Vol. 49, pp. 479-513.

---

* As help to readers, we have left references in articles that proovided footnotes but clustered other references in common bibliography.

—. (2004) "Increased Income Inequality in OECD Countries and the Redistributive Impact of the Government Budget", in G.A. Cornia (ed.), *Inequality, Growth, and Poverty in an Era of Liberalization and Globalization*, Oxford: Oxford University Press, pp. 221-248.

Atkinson, T.; Glaude, M. and Olier, L. (2001) "Inégalités économiques", CAE report No 33, in *La Documentation Française*.

Aubert J.P. and Beaujolin-Bellet R. (2004) "Les acteurs de l'entreprise face aux restructurations: une délicate mutation", in *Travail et emploi*, n° 100, October, pp. 99-112.

Auer, P. (2001): *Labour market policy for socially responsible workforce adjustment*, Employment paper 2001/14, ILO, Geneva.

—. (ed) (1991) "Workforce adjustment patterns in four countries: experiences in the steel and automobile industry in France, Germany, Sweden and the U.K.", in *Discussion paper FS 1914*, WZB Berlin.

—. and Speckesser, S. (1998) "Labour Market and organizational change: Future working structures for an ageing work force", in *Journal of Management and Governance*, 1: 177–206.

—. mit, E. and Leschke J. (2005) *Active labour market policies around the world. Coping with the consequences of globalization*, ILO, Geneva.

Baldone, S.; Sdogati, F. and Tajoli, L. (2001) "Patterns and Determinants of International Fragmentation of Production: Evidence from Outward Processing Trade between the EU and Central Eastern European Countries", in *Review of World Economics* (*Weltwirtschaftliches Archiv*), Vol. 137, No. 1, pp. 81-104.

Banks K. (2004) "Globalization and labour standards, a second look at the evidence", in *Queen's Law Journal*, 29, p. 533.

Barba Navaretti G. and Venables A. (2004) *Home country effects of foreign direct investment for multinational firms in the world economy*, Princeton University.

Bardhan, A. and Kroll C. (2003) *The New Wave of Outsourcing*,. Fisher Centre for Real Estate & Urban Economics Paper 1103, Berkeley: University of California.

Barrientos, S.; Kabeer, N. and Hossain N. (2004) *The gender dimensions of the globalization of production*, Integration Working Paper No. 17, ILO, Geneva.

Benaroya (2005) "Le point sur les délocalisations", Supplement to the CAE report.

Bendesky, L. et al. (2003) *La industria maquiladora de exportación en México: Mitos y realidades*, Mexico, (mimeo).

Bethoux E. (2004) *European trade unions and the challenges and ambiguities of corporate governance responsibility: a focus on company level initiatives*, Paper given to the colloquium on "Organized labour – an agent of EU democracy", Dublin, 30 October, Irish Research Council for Humanities and Social Sciences, University of Dublin.

—. "Les comités d'entreprise en quête de légitimité", in *Travail et emploi*, n° 98, 2004, pp. 21-35.

Bhagwati, J. (1994) "A View from the Academia", in: *U.S. Department Of Labor, Bureau of International Labour Affairs: International Labor Standards and Global Economic Integration: Proceedings of a Symposium*, Washington, DC.

—. Panagariya, A. and Srinivasan, T.N. (2004) "The Muddles over Outsourcing", *Journal of Economic Perspectives*, Vol. 18, No 4, pp. 93-114.

Blake, L. and Lande, J. (1999) *Trends in the U.S. International Telecommunications Industry*, Federal Communications Commission, Washington, DC.

Blanchard, O. and Tirole, J. (2003) *Contours of Employment Protection Reform*, Massachusetts Institute of Technology, Department of Economics, Working Paper Series No 03-35, Cambridge, MA.

Blecker, R.A. (2004) *The Economic Consequences of Dollar Appreciation for US Manufacturing Profits and Investment: A Time Series Analysis*, Paper presented at the Post Keynesian Conference, University of Missouri, Kansas City, June 26-29.

Bloom, H. et al. (1999) "Testing a Re-employment Incentive for Displaced Workers: The Earnings Supplement Project", *Social Research and Demonstration Corporation (Société de recherche sociale appliquée)*, Ottowa.

Bonnaz; Courtot and Nivat (1994) *Le contenu en emplois des échanges industriels de la France avec les pays en développement*, Economie et Statistique.

Borga, M. and Zeile, W.: *International Fragmentation of Production and the Intra-firm Trade of U.S. Multinational Companies*.

Bourguignon, F. (1998) *Fiscalité et redistribution*, CAE Report No 11, La Documentation Française.

Bourque R. *Les accords-cadres internationaux et les fédérations syndicales internationales*, international seminar on "Le syndicalisme et les relations professionnelles", IRES, CRIMT, Montreal, in publication.

Brainard, L. and Litan R. (2004) *'Offshoring' Service Jobs: Bane or Boon – and What to Do?* Policy Brief No 132, Brookings Institution, Washington, DC.

Bresciani, L.P. (2001) "Labour and Innovation in the Brazilian Truck Industry: the case of MBB Sao Bernardo and WV-C Resende", *Actes du Gerpisa*, No 30, pp. 25-45, October.

Bronfenbrenner, K. (2000) *Uneasy Terrain: The Impact of Capital Mobility on Workers, Wages, and Union Organizing*, Report prepared for the US Trade Deficit Review Commission, Washington, D.C., September.

—. (2000) *Uneasy Terrain: The Impact of Capital Mobility on Workers, Wages and Union Organizing*, Report Submitted to the US Trade Deficit Review Commission. New York State School of Industrial and Labour Relations, Cornell University, Ithaca, NY, 6 September.

—. and Luce S. (2004) *The Changing Nature of Corporate Global Restructuring: The Impact of Production Shifts on Jobs in the US, China, and Around the Globe*, Report prepared for the US-China Economic and Security Review Commission, Washington DC, October.

Bronstein, A.S. (1997) "La réforme de la législation du travail en Amérique Latine: régime de garanties et exigence de flexibilité", *Revue Internationale du Travail*, Vol 136, No1, pp. 5-27.

Bruggeman, F. et al. (2002) *Plans sociaux et reclassements: quand l'innovation est promue par les représentants des salariés*, Report for DARES, Ministry of Employment and Solidarity, Paris.

Buitelaar, R.M.; Padilla, R.and Urrutia, R. (1999) "Industria maquiladora y cambio técnico", in *Revista de la CEPAL* 67.

Bulmer, M.I.A. (1981) "Mining Redundancy: A Case Study of the Working of the R.P.A. in the Durham Coalfield", *Industrial Relations*, Vol. 2, No 4, pp. 3-21, winter.

Bureau of Labor Statistics (2005) *Extended Mass Layoffs in the Fourth Quarter of 2004 and Annual Averages for 2004*, US Department of Labor, Washington DC, 16 February.

Burrows, M. (2002) *Risk Management. Guidance for Employers Conducting a Reduction in Force*. (www.bnabooks.com/ababna/annual/2002/burrows.doc).

Burda, M. and Dluhosch, B. (2001): *Fragmentation, Globalization and Labour Markets*, Research Paper 2001/05, Nottingham, Leverhulme Centre.

Campa, J. and Goldberg, L.S. (1997) 'The Evolving External Orientation of Manufacturing: A Profile of Four Countries', in *Federal Reserve Bank of New York Economic Policy Review*, Vol. 3, No. 2, pp. 53-81.

Campinos-Dubernet, M. (2003) "Des restructurations discrètes: reconstruire l'emploi face à la mondialisation", in *Travail et emploi*, No 95, pp. 41-58, July.

Carabelli, U. and Tronti, L. (eds.) (1999) "Managing Labour Redundancies in Europe: Instruments and Prospects", in *Labour*, special edition, Vol 13, No. 1, pp. 3-39.

Centre for European Economic Research (ZEW) (2005) *ZEW-Umfrage unter 4.400 Unternmehmen – Deutsche Unternehmen setzten beim Outsourcig von IT-Dienstleistungen auf heimische Partner*. Press Release dated 07.03. Mannheim: Centre for European Economic Research/Zentrum für Europäische Wirtschaftsforschung.

CEPAL (2004) *La Inversión Extranjera en América Latina y el Caribe*, 2003, Santiago, CEPAL.

Cline, W. (1997) *Trade and Income Distribution*, Washington, D.C.: Institute for International Economics.

Cloarec N. (1998) "Le retour à l'emploi après une convention de conversion", *Premières informations Premières synthèses*, DARES, No 39.4, September.

Cornia, G. A.; Addison, A. and Kiiski S. (2004) 'Income Distribution Changes and Their Impact in the Post-Second World War Period', in G.A. Cornia (ed.), *Inequality, Growth, and Poverty in an Era of Liberalization and Globalization*. Oxford: Oxford University Press, pp. 26-54.

Cortes and Jean (1997) "Quel est l'impact du commerce extérieur sur la productivité de l'emploi?" CEPII Working Paper 97-08.

Courtioux P. (2001) *Marché du travail, politiques de l'emploi et sélection: une analyse évolutionniste des préretraites*, Thesis, University of Paris 1.

Chassard, Y. et al. (2002a) *Licenciements collectifs pour motifs économiques: comment font nos partenaires?* Study for Bernard Bruhnes Consultants.

—. (2002b) "Licenciements collectifs pour motifs économiques: comment font nos partenaires?" in *Premières synthèses*, DARES, No 35.3, August.

Daugareilh I. (2001) "Le rôle des acteurs sociaux face à la mondialisation de l'économie", in *Revue de l'ULB*, p. 111 et seq.

—. (2005) "La négociation collective internationale", in *Diritto e Lavoro*, April, in publication.

De Coninck F. (2004) "Du post-taylorisme à l'effritement des organizations", in *Travail et emploi*, n°100, October, pp. 139-149.

Del Bono, A. (2004) *Nuevas formas de trabajo emergentes. La deslocalización (offshore) de los servicios de atención telefónica a clientes. Argentina, el nuevo paraíso de los call centers*, presented at CLACSO Seminar on Modelo Económico, Trabajo y Actores Sociales, Rio de Janeiro (mimeo).

Department of Trade and Industry (2004) *The UK Contact Centre Industry: A Study*. London: UK Department of Trade and Industry.

Desseigne, G. (1997) *Les plans sociaux*, PUF.

Développement durable [Sustainable Development] Renault (2004) *Données sociales de l'établissement Dacia*, 12 April (www.developpement–durable.renault.com/h/h10dac.htm).

Dossani, R. and Kenney M. (2004): *The Next Wave of Globalization? Exploring the Relocation of Service Provision to India*. Working Paper No. 156. Berkeley, CA: Berkeley Roundtable on the International Economy.

Dubois, P. et al (eds). (1990) *Innovation et emploi à l'Est et à l'Ouest. Les entreprises hongroises et françaises face à la modernisation*, L'Harmattan.

Egger, H. and Egger, P. (2005) "Labor market effects of outsourcing under industrial interdependence", in *International Review of Economics and Finance*, Vol. 14, pp. 349-363.

—. (2003) "Outsourcing and skill-specific employment in a small economy: Austria after the fall of the Iron Curtain", in *Oxford Economic Papers*, Vol. 55, pp. 625-643.

—. (2001) 'Cross-border sourcing and outward processing in EU manufacturing', in *North American Journal of Economics and Finance*, Vol. 12, pp. 243-256.

Egger, P. and Stehrer, R. (2003) 'International Outsourcing and the Skill-Specific Wage Bill in Eastern Europe', in *The World Economy*, Vol. 26, No. 1, pp. 61-72.

European Foundation for the Improvement of Living and Working Conditions (2004) *Outsourcing of ICT and related services in the EU*. Luxembourg: Office for Official Publications of the European Communities.

—. (2004) *Employment in Europe 2004*, Employment and Social Affairs Directorate.

European Commission (1998) "Income benefits for early exit from the labour market in eight European countries. A comparative study", European Economy. Reports and Studies.

Evans–Klock, C. et al. (1998) "Worker Displacement: Public Policy and Labour-Management Initiatives in Selected OECD Countries", ILO Employment and Training Papers, Geneva.

Falk, M. and Koebel, B.M. (2002) 'Outsourcing, Imports and Labour Demand', in *Scandinavian Journal of Economics*, Vol. 104, No. 4, pp. 567-586.

Farrell, D. et al. (2005a) *The Emerging Global Labor Market: Part I — The Demand for Offshore Talent in Services*, San Francisco, McKinsey Global Institute.

—. (2005b) *The Emerging Global Labor Market: Part II — The Supply of Offshore Talent in Services*, San Francisco, McKinsey Global Institute.

—. (2005c) *The Emerging Global Labor Market: Part III — How Supply and Demand for Offshore Talent Mee*, San Francisco, McKinsey Global Institute.

Fazekas, et al. (1990) "Crise d'entreprise et crise d'emploi dans deux bassins industriels. Etude comparative: Ozd (Hongrie) et Le Creusot (France)", in Dubois, P., Koltay, J., Mako, C. and Richet X (eds)., *Innovation et emploi à l'Est et à l'Ouest. Les entreprises hongroises et françaises face à la modernisation*, L'Harmattan, pp. 197-231.

Feenstra, R.C. and Hanson G.H. (1996) 'Globalization, Outsourcing, and Wage Inequality', in *The American Economic Review*, Vol. 86, No. 2, pp. 240-245.

—. (2001) *Global Production Sharing and Rising Inequality: A Survey of Trade and Wages*. NBER Working Paper No. 8372. Cambridge, MA: National Bureau of Economic Research.

—. (1999) 'The Impact of Outsourcing and High-Technology Capital on Wages: Estimates for the United States, 1979-1990', in *The Quarterly Journal of Economics*, Vol. 114, No. 3, pp. 907-940.

—. (1998) "Integration of Trade and disintegration of production in the global economy." *In Journal of Economic Perspectives*, 12-4; 31-50.

—. (1997) 'Foreign direct investment and relative wages: Evidence from Mexico's maquiladoras', in *Journal of International Economics*, Vol. 42, pp. 371-393.

—. and Swenson D.L. (2000) 'Offshore Assembly from the United States: Production Characteristics of the 9802 Program', in: Robert C. Feenstra (ed.), in *The Impact of Trade on Wages*, Chicago and London, University of Chicago Press, pp. 85-122.

Fontagné, L. and Lorenzi, J-H. (2005) *Désindustrialisation, délocalisations*. Paris: Conseil d'analyse économique.

Forrester (2002) *3.3 Million US Service Jobs To Go Offshore*. Cambridge, MA: Forrester.

—. (2004a) *Two-Speed Europe: Why 1 Million Jobs will move Offshore*. Cambridge, MA: Forrester.

—. (2004b) *Two-Speed Europe: why 1 million jobs will move offshore*.

—. *Near-Term Growth of Offshoring Accelerating*. Cambridge, MA: Forrester.

Fouquet, A. and Lemaître F. (eds) (1997) *Démystifier la mondialisation de l'économie*, Les éditions d'organisation.

Frankel, J.A. and Romer, D. (1999) "Does Trade Cause Growth?", *American Economic Review*, Vol. 89, No 3, pp. 379-399.

Freeman, R. (2005) "What Really Ails Europe (and America): The Doubling of the Global Workforce", in *The Globalist*, dated June 3, (available at www.theglobalist.com).

—. (1995) 'Are Your Wages Set in Beijing', in: *Journal of Economic Perspectives*, Vol. 9, No. 3, pp. 15-32, 2004b.

Freeman, R.B. (2004) "Doubling the Global Work Force: The Challenge of Integrating China, India and the Former Soviet Bloc into the World Economy", lecture given at the University of Utah, Salt Lake City, October.

Freyssinet J. and Seifert H. "Pacts for employment and competitiveness in Europe", *Transfer*, 2001, Vol. 7, No 4, pp. 616-628.

Frundt, H. J. (2004) "Unions wrestle with corporate codes of conduct", in *Working USA*, Spring.

Fulton, L. (2001) "Marks and Spencer's closure plans and trade-union responses", in *Transfer*, Vol 7, No 3, pp. 525-529.

Gazier, B. (2005a) *Vers un nouveau modèle social*, Flammarion.

—. (2005b) *Marchés Transitionnels du Travail et restructurations: vers une gestion collective des transitions*, contribution to the IRES 2004 seminar on "Restructurations", to appear in *Revue de l'IRES*, 14 f.

—. (ed) (1999) *Employability. Concepts and Policies*, IAS, Berlin.

—. and Schmid G. (2002) *The dynamics of full employment: social integration through transitional labour markets*, Cheltenham, Edward Elgar.

—. and . (2001) *Transitional Labour Markets and their Impact on Industrial Relations. Report to the high level group on industrial relations and change*. European Commission, Employment and Social Affairs DG, August.

Geishecker, I. and Görg, H. (2004) *Winners and Losers: Fragmentation, Trade and Wages Revisited*, Discussion Paper 385 (updated version as of March 2004). Berlin: German Institute for Economic Research.

General Accountability Office (2004) "Current Government Data Provide Limited Insight into Offshoring of Services," International Trade Division, GAO, Washington DC, September.

Gerber, J. and Carrillo, J. (2003) "Competitividad al debate: la experiencia de las maquiladoras mexicanas", in *Revista Latinoamericana de Estudios del Trabajo*, 8(16).

Ghellab, Y. and Kelly, P. (2001) "Employment and competitiveness as challenges for collective bargaining: a global perspective", *Transfer*, Vol. 7 No 4, pp. 716-731.

Ghose, A. (2003) *Jobs and incomes in a globalizing world*, International Labour Office, Geneva.

Gimel (2005) *Repères quantitatifs sur les délocalisations industrielles à partir des relations extérieures avec les pays émergents ou à bas salaries*, Supplement to the CAE report.

Görg, H.; Henley, A. and Strobl, E. (2004) *Outsourcing, foreign ownership, exporting and productivity: An empirical investigation with plant level data*, Research Paper 2004/08, Nottingham, Leverhulme Centre.

Gottschalk, P. and Smeeding T.M. (1997) "Cross-National Comparisons of Earnings and Income Inequality", in *Journal of Economic Literature*, Vol. 35, No. 2, pp. 633-687.

Greffe, X. (1992) *Sociétés postindustrielles et redéveloppement*, Hachette.

Grignon, F. (2004) *Rapport d'information fait au nom de la commission des Affaires économiques et du Plan par le groupe de travail sur la délocalisation des industries de main-d'oeuvre par M. Francis Grignon*. Sénat session ordinaire de 2003-2004, No. 374. Paris: Sénat.

Grossman, G.M. and Helpman E. (2002) *Outsourcing in a Global Economy*, NBER Working Paper No. 8728. Cambridge, MA, National Bureau of Economic Research.

Guéry, G. (1999) *Restructuration d'entreprises en Europe. Dimension sociale*, De Boeck.

Guillemard, A.M. (2003) *L'âge de l'emploi*, Armand Colin.

Hansen, G.B. (2002) *A guide to worker displacement: some tools for reducing the impact on workers, communities and enterprises*, ILO, Geneva.

Hansen, G.H. (2001) *Should Countries Promote Foreign Direct Investment?* UNCTAD, G-24 Discussion Paper Series, No. 9, Geneva.

—. et al. (2001) *Vertical production networks in multinational firms*, NEBR Working Papers, n° 9723.

Hanson, G.; Mataloni, R, and Slaughter, M. (2001) *Expansion Strategies of U.S. Multinational Firms*, NBER Working Paper No 8433.

—.; —. and—. (2003) *Vertical Production Networks in Multinational Firms*, NBER Working Paper No 9723.

Hepple B. (1995) "The future of labour law", in *Independent Law Journal*, 24 (4), pp. 320-322.

—. (2002) *Labour law, inequality and global trade*, Conference paper, Cambridge, November, unpublished.

—. (ed.) (2005) *Labour law and global trade*, Hart Publishing, for publication in April.

Hijzen, A.; Görg, E and Hine, R.C. (2004) *International Outsourcing and the Skill Structure of Labour Demand in the UK*. Research Paper 2004/24. Nottingham: Leverhulme Centre.

Hummels, D. (1999) *Have International Transportation Costs Declined?* Chicago: University of Chicago, (mimeo).

—.; Ishii J., and Kei-Mu Yi (2001) "The nature and growth of vertical specialization in world trade", in *Journal of International Economics*, Vol. 54, pp. 75-96.

ILO. (International Labour Organisation) *Report of the World Commission on the Social Dimension of Globalization*, 168 pages, available at www.ilo.org.

—. (2004a) *A fair globalization: The role of the ILO*, Geneva.

—. (2004b) *Eighth Synthesis Report on Working Conditions in Cambodia's Garment Sector*, Geneva.

—. (2004c) *World Employment Report 2004-05: Employment, productivity and poverty reduction*. Geneva.

—. (2001a) *International labour standards: a global approach*, Geneva, 736 pages.

—. (2001b) *World Employment Report 2001: Life at work in the information economy*. Geneva.

IMF. (International Monetary Fund) (2004) *Balance of Payments Statistics Yearbook 2004*. Washington, DC.

ITTA (2004) '*ITAA/Global Insight Study Finds Global Sourcing of Software and IT Services Bolsters Domestic Employment and Wages Across the Entire US Economy*', *Press Release March 30.*. Arlington, VA.

Jones, R.W. and Kierzkowski H. (1990) "The Role of Services Production and International Trade: A Theoretical Framework", in R.W. Jones and A. Krueger (eds.): *The Political Economy of International Trade. Essays in Honor of Robert E. Baldwin*. Oxford, Blackwell, pp. 31-48.

—. (2001a) "A Framework for Fragmentation" in: Sven W. Arndt and Henryk Kierzkowski (eds.), *Fragmentation. New Production Patterns in the World Economy*. Oxford, Oxford University Press, pp. 17-34.

—. (2001b) "Globalization and the Consequences of International Fragmentation", in G. Calvo, R. Dornbusch and M. Obsfeld (eds.): *Money, Capital Mobility, and Trade. Essays in Honor of Robert Mundell*. Cambridge, MA, MIT Press, pp. 365-383.

Jean. (2001) *Effects of globalisation on employment in the industrialised countries: a survey of the existing literature*, OECD.

Jacobson, L.; LaLonde, R.J. and Sullivan, D. (2003) *Should We Teach Old Dogs New Tricks? The Impact of Community College Retraining on Older Displaced Workers*, Working Paper 2003 – 25, Federal Reserve Bank of Chicago.

Jani-Le Bris, H. (1988) *L'insertion sociale des pré-retraités. Rapport de synthèse européen*, ECSC-EEC-EAEC, Brussels.

Jepsen, M. and Klammer U. (ed) (2004) "Flexi-curity: conceptual issues and political implementation in Europe", in *Transfer*, special edition, Vol 10, No 2.

Kerbourc'h, J.Y. et al.. (ed) (2001) *Le salarié, le juge et l'emploi*, Ministry of Employment and Solidarity, Cahier Travail et Emploi.

Kirkegaard. *Outsourcing – Stains on the white collar?*

—. (2005) *Outsourcing and offshoring: Pushing the European Model over the hill, rather than off the cliff!* Institute for International Economics WP 05-1.

Kirsch, J. and Knuth, M. (2001) "Restructurations économiques et protection des transitions: approches contrastées en France et en Allemagne", in Morin M.L. (ed), *Protection des transitions et retour à l'emploi, un aperçu comparatif*, Travail et emploi No 87, special edition, pp. 29-45.

Kletzer, L.G. (2001) *Job Loss from Imports: Measuring the Costs*, Institute for International Economics, Washington, DC.

—. and Rosen, H. (2005) *Easing the Adjustment Burden on US Workers*, Institute for International Economics, Washington, DC.

Klinger; Shannon and Lynn Sykes. (2004) *Exporting the Law: A Legal Analysis of State and Federal Outsourcing Legislation*. Arlington, VA, National Foundation for American Policy.

Kohler, W. (2002) *The Distributional Effects of International Fragmentation*. Department of Economics Working Paper No. 0201. Linz: Johannes Kepler University Linz.

—. (2004) "International Outsourcing and Factor Prices with Multistage Production", *The Economic Journal*, Vol. 114, pp. C166-C185.

Kohli, M. et al. (eds) (1991) *Time for retirement. Comparative Studies of Early Exit from the Labor Force*, Cambridge U. Press.

Koumakhov, R. and Najman, B. (2001) *Labor Hoarding in Russia: Where Does It Come From?* William Davidson Working Paper No 394, October.

Krugman, P. (1995) "Growing World Trade: Causes and Consequences," in *Brookings Papers on Economic Activity*, Washington, DC, Brookings Institution.

Kucera, D. and Milberg, W. (2003) 'Deindustrialization and Changes in Manufacturing Trade: Factor Content Calculations for 1978-1995', *Review of World Economics (Weltwirtschaftliches Archiv)*, Vol. 139, No. 4, pp. 601-624.

—. (2000) "Gender Segregation and Gender Bias in Manufacturing Trade Expansion: Revisiting the "Wood Asymmetry"", *World Development*, Vol. 28. No. 7, pp. 1191-1210.

Kumar, N. (2001) *Indian Software Industry Development: International and National Perspective*. RIS Discussion Paper No. 19/2001. New Delhi: Research and Information System for the Non-aligned and other Developing Countries.

—. and Joseph, K. J. (2004) *National Innovation Systems and India's IT Capability: Are there any lessons for ASEAN newcomers?* RIS Discussion Paper No. 72/2004, New Delhi, Research and Information System for the Non-aligned and other Developing Countries.

Lafay G.; Herzog C.; Freundenberg M. and Unal-Kesenci D. (1999) *Nations et mondialisation*, Economica, 385 pages.

Lee, E. (1996) "La mondialisation et l'emploi: des craintes justifiées?", in *Revue Internationale du Travail*, Vol 135, No 5, pp. 531-543.

—. (1998) *The Asian Financial Crisis. The Challenge for Social Policy*. Geneva, ILO.

Legrand, B.; de Taillac, L. and Terracol A. (2003) "L'intervention de l'Etat dans l'accompagnement des plans sociaux", in *Regards sur l'actualité*, No 290, pp. 39-52.

Lorenzi J.H. and Fontagné L. (2004) *Désindustrialisations, délocalisations: conseil d'analyse économique*, La Documentation Française, 397 pages.

Madsen P.K. (2004) "The Danish model of flexi-curity: experiences and lessons", in *Transfer* 2/2004.

—. (1999) *Denmark: flexibility, security and labour market success*, ILO, Geneva.

Mallet, L. et al. (1997) "A quoi servent les plans sociaux?", in *Travail et Emploi*, No 72.

Mann. (2003) *Globalization of IT services and white collar jobs: the next wave of productivity growth*, Institute for International Economics.

Marin. (2004) *A nation of poets and thinkers – less so with eastern enlargement? Austria and Germany*, CEPR Discussion Paper 4358.

Markusen J.R. (1995) "The boundaries of multinational entreprises and the theory of international trade", *Journal of economic perspective*, n° 9, 2, pp. 169-189.

Marshall, A. (1999) *Quality dimensions of women's employment*, unpublished report prepared for ILO, Development Policies Dept. (mimeo).

—. (1982) *Principles of Economics*, Philadelphia, Porcupine Press.

Martin Artiles, A. (ed.) (2001) "Collective agreements on competitiveness and employment", in *Transfer*, special edition, Vol 7, No 4.

Mataloni, R. and Yorgason, D. (2002) 'Operations by US multinational Firms, preliminary results from the 1999 benchmark survey', in *Survey of Current Business*, March.

Maurin, E., Thesmar D. and Theonig, M. (2003) "Mondialisation des échanges et emploi: le rôle des exportations", in *Economie et Statistiques*, 363-364-365, pp.33-44.

Mazade, O. (2004) "Passé professionnel et reconversions: le reclassement des mineurs du Nord-Pas-de-Calais", in *Formation – Emploi*, No 85, pp. 41-55.

McCarthy, J. (2004) "Near-Term Growth of Offshoring Accelerating: Resizing US Services Jobs Going Offshore," Forrester Research, Inc., Cambridge, MA, May 14.

McKersie, R.B. and Sengenberger, W. (1983) *Job losses in major industries, manpower strategy and responses*, OECD.

McKinsey Global Institute. (2004) *Can Germany win from offshoring?*

—. (2003) *Offshoring: Is It a Win-Win Game?* San Francisco: McKinsey.

Michalet C.A. (2002) *Qu'est ce que la mondialisation?*, La découverte, 210 pages.

—. (2000) "Les métamorphoses de la mondialisation: une approche économique", in E. Loquin and C. Kessedjian (eds): *La mondialisation du droit*, Litec, pp. 2-42.

Moreau, M.A. (2005a, forthcoming) "Peut-on déceler une dynamique spécifique de régulation de l'entreprise mondialisée dans l'Union européenne?", in *Toward Social Regulation of the global firm?*, CRIMT collective work, Montreal.

—. (2005b, forthcoming) "Fundamental social rights in Europe", in B. De Witte and G. De Burca (eds): *Social Rights in Europe*, Oxford University Press.

—. (1997) "A propos de l' "affaire Renault", in *Droit social*, No 5, May, pp. 493-503.

—. and Trudeau, G. (2000) "Les normes du droit du travail confrontées à l'évolution de l'économie: de nouveaux enjeux pour l'espace régional", in *Journal de droit international*, n° 4, pp. 915-948.

—. and—. (1998) "Le droit du travail face à la mondialisation de l'économie", in *Relations industrielles*, vol. 53, n° 1, pp. 55-87.

Morin, M.L. (ed) (2001) "Protection des transitions et retour à l'emploi, un aperçu comparatif", in *Travail et emploi*, No 87, special edition.

—. and Vicens, C. (2001) "Licenciement économique, flexibilité des entreprises et sécurité des travailleurs: les enseignements d'une comparaison européenne", in *Revue Internationale du Travail*, Vol 140, No 1, pp. 51-75.

Mucchielli J.L. (1998) *Multinationales et mondialisation*, Points Seuil, 375 pages.

Mückenberger, U. (2005) "Delocalisation and voice: a case of transnational employee status in Europe", Workshop on Globalization and Labour Law, European University Institute, Florence.

Murray G. and Trudeau G. (2004) "La régulation sociale de l'entreprise mondialisée: Introduction" in *Relations Industrielles*, vol. 59-1, pp. 3-26.

—.; Belanger, J.; Giles, A. and Lapointe, P.A. (2004) *L'organization de la production et du travail, vers un nouveau modèle?*, Presses de l'Université Laval, Canada, 261 pages.

Ngai, P. (2004) 'Women workers and precarious employment in Shenzhen Special Economic Zone, China', *Gender and Development*, Vol. 12, No. 2, pp. 29-36.

Network of Independent Experts on Fundamental Rights. (coordinator O. de Schutter) (2004) *Report on the situation of fundamental rights in the European Union*, 2003, Office for Official Publications of the European Communities.

Nunnenkamp, P. (2004) "Der Automobilstandort Deutschland unter Wettbewerbsdruck", *info Schnelldienst*, Vol. 57, No. 7, pp. 28-36.

OECD. (Organization for Economic Co-operation and Development) (2005) *Employment Outlook*, Paris.

—. (2004) *Employment Outlook*, Paris.

—. (various editions) *Employment Outlook*, Paris.

—. (2002) *OECD Input-Output Tables*. Paris.

—. (1999) *Implementing the OECD Job Strategy. Assessing Performance and Policy.*

—. (1995) *OECD Input-Output Tables*. Paris.

Oman, C. (2000) *Policy Competition for Foreign Direct Paris Investment: A Study of Competition among Governments to Attract FDI*, OECD, Paris.

Osaki M. (1999) *Negotiating flexibility: the role of the social partners and state*, ILO, Geneva.

Ost F. and van de Kerchove M. (2000) "De la pyramide au réseau: vers un nouveau mode de production du droit?", in *Revue interdisciplinaire d'études juridiques*, p. 44.

Outin, J.L.; Silvera R. and Perrier-Cornet F. (1988) *Que sont devenus les non-repris de Creusot-Loire?*, Supplement to the Bulletin Régional d'Information Travail et Emploi, Dijon, May.

Palley, T.I. (2004) *External Contradictions and the Chinese Development Model: Why China Must Abandon Export-led Growth or Risk a Global Economic Crisis*, paper presented at a conference on "China-US Relations in the Asia-Pacific Context," co-sponsored by the Graduate School of International Studies, Denver University and the School of International Studies, Peking University, held in Beijing, China, October 21-23, and Journal of Contemporary China.

—. (2003) "Export-led Growth: Is There Any Evidence of Crowding-Out?", in Arestis et al. (eds.): *Globalization, Regionalism, and Economic Activity*, Cheltenham, Edward Elgar.

—. (2002) *A New Development Paradigm: Domestic Demand-Led Growth*, Foreign Policy in Focus, September, http://www.fpif.org/. Also in: *After Neo-liberalism: Economic Policies That Work for the Poor*, in Jacobs, Weaver and Baker (eds.): *New Rules for Global Finance*, Washington, DC, 2002.

—. (1999) *Manufacturing Matters: The Impact on Productivity Growth, Wages, and Income Distribution*, AFL-CIO Economic Policy Working Paper, E035, AFL-CIO, Washington DC, October.

Papola, Trilok Sing (1994) "International Labour Standards and Developing Countries", In: Sengenberger and Campbell (eds.), in *International Labour Standards and Economic Interdependence*, IILS, Geneva.

Pottier C. (2003) *Les multinationales et la mise en concurrence des salariés*, L'harmattan, 243 pages.

Raveyre, M. (2001) "Implication territoriale des groupes et gestion du travail et de l'emploi. Vers des intermédiations en réseaux", in *La revue de l'IRES*, No 35, pp. 35-59.

Rehfeldt, U. (2001) "European Work Councils and International Restructuring: A Perspective for European Collective Bargaining?", in *Actes du GERPISA*, No 30, pp 109-114.

Robin-Olivier S. (1999) *La référence aux droits sociaux fondamentaux dans le Traité d'Amsterdam*, Droit social, pp. 609-621.

Rodière P. (2002) "Droit social de l'Union européenne", in *LGDJ*, 2nd edition, E.

Rodrik, D. (1998) "Why Do More Open Economies Have Bigger Governments?" in *Journal of Political Economy*, Vol. 106, No 51, pp. 997-1032.

Rosen, H. (2002) "Trade-Related Labour Market Adjustment Policies and Programs, with Special Reference to Textile and Apparel Workers", may be consulted at: www.newamerica.net/Download_Docs/pdfs/Pub_File_1426_1.pdf,

Rowthorn, R. (2004) *The Impact on Advanced Economies of North-South Trade in manufacturing and Services*. Cambridge: University of Cambridge, (mimeo).

Sachs, J. (1996) *Globalization and employment*. Public Lectures, International Institute for Labour Studies, Geneva, March 18.

Sachs-Durand (ed.) (2004) *La place des salaries dans les restructurations en Europe communautaire*, P.U. Strasbourg, 337 pages.

Sachwald, F. (2004) "Délocalisations: une "destruction créatrice"?", *Sociétal*, No 44, pp 6–11.

Samuelson, P.A. (2004) 'Where Ricardo and Mills Rebut and Confirm Arguments of Mainstream Economists Supporting Globalization', *Journal of Economic Perspectives*, Vol. 18, No. 3, pp. 135-146.

Schwartz, G. (2003) "Employment restructuring in Russian industrial enterprises: confronting a "paradox"", in: *Work, Employment and Society*, Vol 17, No 1, pp 49-72.

Sciarra S. (2004) "The evolution of labour law in the European Union, 1992-2003", summary report, European Commission, Brussels, in publication.

Scott, R. (2005) US-China Trade, 1989-2003: *Impact on Jobs and Industries, Nationally and State-by-State*, Report prepared for the US-China Economic and Security Review Commission, Washington DC, January.

Sen, A. (2000) "Work and Rights", in *International Labour Review*, Vol.193, No. 2, ILO, Geneva.

Sengenberger, W. (ed) (1989) "La restructuration industrielle en Europe: quelques experiences", in *Travail et Société*, special edition, April, pp. 111-219.

—. (2002) *Globalization and Social Progress: The Role and Impact of International Labour Standards*, Friedrich-Ebert-Foundation, Bonn.

Sisson, K. (2001) "Pacts for employment and competitiveness – an opportunity to reflect on the role and practice of collective bargaining", in *Transfer*, Vol. 7 No 4, winter, pp. 600-615.

Stolper, W.F., and Samuelson P.A (1941) "Protection and Real Wages", *Review of Economic Studies*, 9, pp.58 – 73, November.

Storrie, D.W. (1992) "Advance Notice and Post-Displacement Joblessness", Papers and proceedings of the fourth conference of The European Association of Labour Economists, University of Warwick, Warwick.

Strauss-Kahn, V. (2003) *The Role of Globalization in the Within-Industry Shift Away from Unskilled Workers in France*. NBER Working Paper No. 9716. Cambridge, MA: National Bureau of Economic Research.

Supiot, A. (1999) *Au delà de l'emploi*, Flammarion.

—. (2002) *Critique du droit du travail* (Introduction), Quadrige series, PUF.

—. et al. (2001) *Beyond Employment* […], Oxford, Oxford University Press.

Syndex (2003) "Restructurations", in *Regards. Les cahiers de Syndex,* No 2, special edition.

Tejada, R.L. and Swaim, P. (2004) "Trade adjustment costs in OECD Labour Markets: How Big is the Problem and How Should Policy Makers Respond to It?" in *Draft EAP contribution to the TASAP*, OECD, 42 f + annexes.

Teubner G. (2002) *De la pyramide au réseau: pour une théorie dialectique du droit*, P.U. Saint Louis, Brussels.

Teyssier, F. and Vicens, C. (2001) "La trajectoire des licenciés économiques: un nouvel équilibre de droits? Résultats d'une approche comparative européenne", in M.L. Morin (ed), "Protection des transitions et retour à l'emploi, un aperçu comparatif", in *Travail et emploi*, No 87, special edition, pp. 9-28.

Thoenig, M. and Verdier, T. (2003) "Une théorie de l'innovation défensive biasée vers le travail qualifié ", with Thierry Verdier, in Economie et Statistiques, 363-364-365, pp.19-32.

Tran-Nguyen, Anh-Nga and Zampetti, A.B. (eds.) (2004) *Trade and Gender: Opportunities and Challenges for Developing Countries*. New York and Geneva, UNCTAD.

Trebilcock A. (2001) "The ILO Declaration on Fundamental Principles and Rights at Work [...]" in *International Labour Standards*, ILO, Geneva, pp. 17-25; for more information see also www.ilo.org.

Tronti, L. and Carabelli U. (eds) (1999) "Managing Labour Redundancies in Europe: Instruments and Prospects", in *Labour*, special edition, Vol 13, No 1.

UNCTAD (2004a) *UNCTAD Handbook of Statistics*. New York and Geneva, United Nations.

—. (2004b) *World Investment Report 2004. The Shift Towards Services*. New York and Geneva, United Nations.

Upchurch, M. and Danford, A. (2001) "Industrial restructuring, "globalization" and the trade union response: A study of MSF in the south west of England", *New Technology, Work and Employment*, Vol 16, No 2, pp. 100-117.

Valticos, N. (1969) "Fifty years of standard-setting activities by the International Labour Organization", in *International Labour Review*, Vol.100, No. 3, September.

van der Hoeven, R. and Saget, C. (2004) 'Labour Market Institutions and Income Inequality: What are the New Insights after the Washington Consensus?', in: Giovanni Andrea Cornia (ed.), *Inequality, Growth, and Poverty in an Era of Liberalization and Globalization*. Oxford: Oxford University Press, pp. 197-220.

—. and Taylor, L. (2000) "Introduction: Structural Adjustment, Labour Markets and Employment: Some Considerations for Sensible People", *Journal of Development Studies*, Vol. 36, No. 4, pp. 57-65.

van Welsum, D. (2004) *In Search of 'Offshoring': Evidence from U.S. Imports of Services*. London: Birkbeck College (mimeo).

Venables, A.J. (1999) 'Fragmentation and multinational production', in *European Economic Review*, Vol. 43, pp. 935-945.

Vijayabaskar, M.; Rothboeck, S. and Gayathri, V. (2001) "Labour in the New Economy: The Case of the Indian Software Industry", in *Indian Journal of Labour Economics*, Vol. 44, No. 1, pp. 39-54.

Villeval, M.C. (1993) "Gestion des sureffectifs et politiques de formation de reconversion en Europe", in *Formation – Emploi*, No 43, pp. 25-39.

Visser J. (2001): "Industrial relations and social dialogue", in P. Auer: *Changing labour market in Europe: the role of institutions and policies*, ILO, Geneva.

Waddington J. (2004) paper delivered to CRIMT conference on "Le renouveau de l'action syndicale", Montreal, November 2004, unpublished.

Waquet P. et al.(eds) (2003) "Les lieux du travail", special edition of *La semaine sociale*, September-October, Lamy.

Wierink, M. (2004) "Pays-Bas: Réforme de la préretraite et crise des relations professionnelles", in *Chronique internationale de l'IRES*, No 90, pp. 20-30, September.

Wilthagen T. and Rogowski (2002) "Legal regulation of transnational labour markets", in B. Gazier and G. Schmid (eds): *The dynamics of full employment: social integration through transitional labour markets*, Edward Elgar, Cheltenham, pp. 233-273.

—. and Tros, F. (2004) "The concept of flexi-curity: a new approach to regulating employment and labour market", in *Transfer* 2/2004.

—.;—. and van Lieshout H. (2003) "Towards 'flexi-curity', balancing flexibility and security in EU Members States", 13th World Congress of the International Industrial Relations Association, Berlin.

Winter-Ebmer, R. (2001) *Evaluating an Innovative Redundancy-Retraining Project: The Austrian Steel Foundation*, Discussion paper No 277, IZA, March.

Wolff, E. (2004) *Changes in Household Wealth in the 1980s and the 1990s in the US*, Working Paper No 407, The Levy Economics Institute and NYU, May.

Wood, A. (1995) "How Trade Hurt Unskilled Workers", in *Journal of Economic Perspectives*, Vol. 9, No. 3, pp. 57-80.

World Bank. (2002) *Globalization, Growth and poverty*, Oxford University Press.

—. (2000) *Engendering Development*, Washington, DC.

World Commission on the Social Dimension of Globalization. (2004) *A Fair Globalization: Creating Opportunities for All*, ILO, Geneva.

World Trade Organization. (2004) *Trends in world trade in 2003 and prospects for 2004*, Geneva.

—. (2005) *World Trade Report 2005. Exploring the links between trade, standards and the WTO*, Geneva.

Yeats, A.J. (2001) "Just How Big is Global Production Sharing?", in: S.W. Arndt and H. Kierzkowski (eds.): *Fragmentation. New Production Patterns in the World Economy*. Oxford: Oxford University Press, pp. 108-143.

Yi, Kei-Mu (2003) "Can Vertical Specialization Explain the Growth of World Trade?" *The Journal of Political Economy*, Vol. 111, No. 1, pp. 52-102.

Zachert U. (2004, unpublished) "Flexicurité à l'entrée et à la sortie de l'emploi", Leiden conference on Labour law in Europe: steps toward 2010, 30 September.

In 2000 the French Ministry of Labour and the Director General of the ILO, initiated a series of conferences on the subject of "the future of work". Their aim was not only to provoke a high-quality international dialogue on changes in work and employment and their impact on social protection and worker security mostly in the industrialized countries, but also to stimulate exchanges between the academic and political communities and the social partners.

The present volume on "Offshoring and the Internationalisation of Employment: a challenge for a fair globalisation" is the third in a series of conference volumes, which also serve as a follow up to the report of the World Commission on the Social Dimension of Globalisation "A fair globalization" (ILO, 2004). The proceedings of the first two conferences were published in 2002 and offer a rich source of information for those interested in changes in the world of work.

The themes addressed by the first two meetings were:

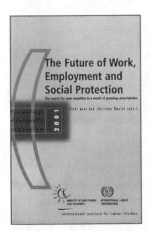

The first meeting took place in Annecy in 2001 and discussed the need for the development of policies to provide security to workers in the face of growing uncertainties, which were caused by the forces of globalisation, as well as technological and organisational change. In consequence the first conference discussed the large subject of the transformation of work and employment and its causes, the impact of these changes on work and society, the possible political response to the new challenges and the methods, the actors and levels of political action.

The International Institute for Labour studies published the proceedings of the first France/ILO conference as:
Peter Auer and Christine Daniel (eds.) The future of work, employment and social protection: the search for new securities in a world of growing uncertainties, IILS, ILO, 2002.

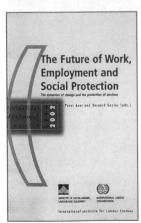

While the first meeting touched upon the necessity to see changes in a dynamic framework, the second meeting, organized in Lyon in 2002, focussed on the dynamic aspects of change. It stressed labour market dynamics and discussed trajectories, life cycle approaches and the evolution of regulations as well as the need for integrated policies. Concepts of how to protect transitions in the labour market were discussed, as well as the links between adjustment flexibility and workers security. The concepts of life-long security, with varying periods of work and non-work and the protection of risks at crucial moments during the life cycle was at the core of this volume. The balancing between family and working life was seen as a particularly important part of modern dynamic labour markets. The book ended with a series of articles looking for the adequate regulation based on the life cycle of individuals.

The second volume of the proceedings was published under the title:
Peter Auer and Bernard Gazier (eds.) The future of work, employment and social protection: the dynamics of change and the protection of workers, IILS, ILO 2002.